Outstanding Dissertations in
LINGUISTICS

edited by
LAURENCE HORN
YALE UNIVERSITY

NOUN PHRASE LICENSING

JEFFREY T. RUNNER

LONDON AND NEW YORK

First published 1998 by Garland Publishing, Inc.

2 Park Square, Milton Park, Abingdon, Oxon OX14 4RN
711 Third Avenue, New York, NY 10017, USA

Routledge is an imprint of the Taylor & Francis Group, an informa business

First issued in paperback 2016

Copyright © 1998 Jeffrey T. Runner

All rights reserved. No part of this book may be reprinted or reproduced or utilised in any form or by any electronic, mechanical, or other means, now known or hereafter invented, including photocopying and recording, or in any information storage or retrieval system, without permission in writing from the publishers.

Notice:
Product or corporate names may be trademarks or registered trademarks, and are used only for identification and explanation without intent to infringe.

Library of Congress Cataloging-in-Publication Data

Runner, Jeffrey T., 1963–
    Noun phrase licensing / Jeffrey T. Runner.
        p.   cm. — (Outstanding dissertations in linguistics)
    Revision of the author's thesis (Ph.D.—University of Massachusetts, 1995).
    Includes bibliographical references and index.
    ISBN 0-8153-3134-7 (alk. paper)
    1. Grammar, Comparative and general—Noun phrase.
2. Grammar, Comparative and general—Direct object. 3. Generative grammar. 4. Semantics. 5. English language—Grammar, Generative I. Title. II. Series.
P271.R86 1998
415—dc21
                                                98-21435

ISBN 978-0-8153-3134-6 (hbk)
ISBN 978-1-138-99453-9 (pbk)

To Opie, Butch, Calvin, and especially Javier, with love.

Contents

Foreword xi

Preface xv

Introduction xvii

Acknowledgments xix

1 Preliminaries 3
   1.1 Introduction 3
   1.2 AGRs and AGRo 3
   1.3 Checking Theory and Verb Movement 6
   1.4 The Basic Proposal 8
   1.5 Copying and A-Movement 10

2 Initial Motivation: "LF" Asymmetric C-Command 13
   2.1 Introduction 13
   2.2 LF Object Position(s) 15
   2.3 Prepositional Objects and Asymmetric C-Command 21
   2.4 Precedence vs. C-Command: More Data 39
   2.5 Conclusion 47

Contents

3 Constituency: the Surface Position of the Verb and the Object 49
   3.1 Introduction 49
   3.2 The Surface Position of Verbs and Objects 50
   3.3 Conclusion 59

4 VP-Shell or No VP-Shell: the Case of Adverb Placement 61
   4.1 Introduction 61
   4.2 Adverb Placement 62
   4.3 Alternatives 65
   4.4 V' Reanalysis and Light Predicate Raising 69
   4.5 Conclusion 86

5 ECM as Raising to Object AGR 87
   5.1 Introduction 87
   5.2 Exceptional Case Marking, a.k.a. Raising to Object 88
   5.3 The Surface Position of the ECM Subject 96
   5.4 Conclusion 123

6 The Double Object Construction 125
   6.1 Introduction 125
   6.2 The Objects at LF 127
   6.3 The Surface Configuration 131
   6.4 The Underlying Structure 136
   6.5 Considerations and Revisions 149
   6.6 Some Consequences and Further Motivations 153
   6.7 Remaining Issues 168
   6.8 Conclusions 174

7 LF Noun Phrase Positions 175
   7.1 Introduction 175
   7.2 The Surface Position of Indefinite Objects 176
   7.3 The LF Position(s) of Noun Phrases 180
   7.4 The Mapping Hypothesis 187
   7.5 How to Get There 189
   7.6 Constraints on Deletion 197
   7.7 Conclusion 208

Contents

8 Extensions and Conclusions 209
 8.1 Introduction 209
 8.2 *There* Insertion 210
 8.3 Stylistic Inversion 216
 8.4 Conclusions 221

Bibliography 224

Notes 230

Index 237

Foreword

Most of the research reported here was done in 1993 and 1994. Since then some important literature has been published or circulated that bears directly on the issues discussed here. I would like to mention just a few things that were either being written at the same time as my research or became available to me only after my research had been completed.

The most influential piece of work that has been published since I wrote this dissertation would have to be Chomsky's (1995) "Categories and Transformations," which is Chapter 4 of his *The Minimalist Program* book. This paper picks up where Chomsky's (1993) "A Minimalist Program for Linguistic Theory," republished as Chapter 3 of the same book, leaves off. The present work is couched in terms of this earlier minimalist program. One of the claims of Chapter 4 is discussed in its final section: that AGR plays no role in syntax. Since my basic hypothesis is that English object NPs appear overtly in Spec,AGRo, and not in VP, as is currently assumed, Chomsky's claim is worth looking into.

While AGRo is argued to play no role in Chomsky's Chapter 4 syntactic theory, there is a new semi-functional head v introduced as, among other things, the head responsible for accusative Case checking. And languages which show overt object shift are argued to exploit the specifier position of this head. In many ways, this head is parallel to AGRo. The arguments presented here try to show that object NPs appear to the left of some constituent that contains the rest of the VP-type material: PPs, adverbial phrases, and the like. As it turns out the specifier position of v is a position that is external to a constituent (VP), containing the remainder of the VP-type material. If it turns out to be advantageous from a theoretical point of view to dispense with AGRo, then it seems reasonable to attempt to recast my arguments as being in favor of the claim that object NPs in English appear overtly in Spec,vP.

A question that arises with the claim that object NPs appear in Spec,vP is, Where does V appear? A second consequence of Chomsky's claim that AGR plays no role in syntax is that the functional head T is the only head assumed to be VP-external. What this implies is that the difference in verb position in English vs. French is accounted for by assuming that V moves to T in French, and stays *in situ* in English. My analysis, however, requires that even in English V escapes vP, since it appears overtly to the left of the object NP, argued to be in Spec,vP. If English V moves out of vP, where does it move to?

Chomsky (1995) argues that AGR played no LF role and could be dispensed with in the syntax, and therefore on "minimalist" assumptions must be dispensed with. If this is indeed the correct analysis one might look for other VP-external heads, besides T, that are relevant to the LF interpretation. One possibility that suggests itself is a functional head associated with aspect. This head, called ASP, has already been proposed to play a role in a number of analyses over the past several years. To name a few that I am familiar with: Hagit Borer's (1994) "The Projection of Arguments" and Montserrat Sanz's (1995) *Telicity, Objects and the Mapping onto Predicate Types*. If it could be argued that there is some functional head, aside from T, external to VP, this would be a candidate for what I call F, the head position to which the English V moves overtly.

Another tack to take would be to disagree with Chomsky's claim that AGR plays no role in the LF representation. In earlier work, this is precisely the claim that I have made (my (1993) "Quantificational Objects and Agr-o, (1994) "A Specific Role for AGR," and (1995) "Reconstruction and Mapping") and the claim that David Adger defended in his (1993) thesis, *Functional Heads and Interpretation*. If AGR could be justified as relevant to LF interpretation, then dispensing with it would be unnecessary and the arguments of the present work would remain unaffected.

Other recent research that is relevant to the issues discussed here include the following: Koizumi's (1995) *Phrase Structure in Minimalist Syntax*, Lasnik's (1995) "Last Resort and Attract F," and Rohrbacher's

(1994) *The Germanic VO Languages and the Full Paradigm*, which all discuss the possibility that the verb moves overtly out of VP in English (the first two claim it does, while the last claims it does not); Hornstein's (1995) *Logical Form: from GB to Minimalism* and Collins & Thráinsson's (1996) "VP-Internal Structure and Object Shift in Icelandic," which both discuss the double object construction; Speas' (1994) "Null Arguments in a Theory of Economy of Projections," which inspired part of my analysis of specifier licensing in Chapter 7; and Lasnik's (1995) "Case and Expletives Revisited: on Greed and Other Human Failings," which discusses *there* sentences in English. There are no doubt a number of other important papers that have circulated recently that I have failed to mention here. The issues discussed here are "hot" topics currently and it is safe to say that there is still much research to be done before they are resolved.

I would like to take this opportunity to acknowledge the help of a few people over the past few years: Greg Carlson, Elissa Newport, and Mike Tanenhaus, who have made my stay here at the University of Rochester extremely intellectually stimulating and challenging; Roberta Colon, the department's Administrative Assistant, who has helped me out in too many ways to be able to mention; Rebecca Wipfler, the editor at Garland; and Joy Hanna, who proofread and helped edit the manuscript. Thanks to all.

Rochester, March 1998

Preface

Before turning to the thesis itself a few biographical remarks are in order. The title of the thesis, *Noun Phrase Licensing and Interpretation*, is somewhat misleading. This thesis is about noun phrase licensing, only touching on interpretation and its interaction with NP licensing in one chapter (chapter 7). I really began my research on this thesis in 1988, studying impersonal constructions and agreement in Spanish for my UC Santa Cruz B.A. thesis (see Runner 1989, *Left Conjunct Agreement in Spanish*, and later work in collaboration with Judith Aissen, Aissen & Runner 1989). The question of impersonal constructions, and particularly existential *there* sentences in English, revived itself in work I did in 1991 in Amherst and 1992 in Barcelona (see Runner 1992, "Expletives, 'Replacement' and Economy."). At that time, however, I began to discover the interesting relation between the syntax of existential sentences and the interpretation of the noun phrases in them; like many a syntactician before me, I undertook it to figure out what exactly the connection was between the syntax and the interpretation of a noun phrase.

Inspired by the work of Molly Diesing and Angelika Kratzer I familiarized myself with what linguists were saying about NP interpretation. De Hoop's (1992) thesis, which claimed there was a connection between Case and interpretation, combined with Diesing's mapping hypothesis and Chomsky's minimalist program, led me to synthesize an account which seemed to bring together a number of different connections between the syntax and interpretation of NPs (see Runner 1993, "Quantificational Objects and Agr-o.").

The coup was the discovery that my friend David Adger was working on the same topic in Edinburgh. Many a night was spent arguing about NP positions, AGR, NP interpretation, etc. Adger's (1994) thesis, *Functional Heads and Interpretation*, goes a long way towards saying what I would have liked to have said here: that there is some direct connection between Spec,AGR and interpretation. This seems right, looking cross-linguistically, though the question of why AGR still remains mysterious.

At first I had planned to answer that question in this thesis. I began its research, urged by my thesis advisor, Hagit Borer, by trying to nail down the syntax of AGR phrases, in particular AGRo. What ended up happening, however, was that the syntax of AGR quickly overtook my interest in the interpretation of AGR. So the result is a thesis which spends seven of its eight chapters almost entirely on the syntax of AGR phrases, and one chapter that discusses the relation between the two. As it became clearer that my focus was on the syntax, I pulled back from some of my earlier views which tried to link AGR to the discourse directly (see Runner 1994, "A Specific Role for AGR," and 1995, "Reconstruction and Mapping,") and chose to go the almost "standard" root of assuming Diesing's (1992) mapping hypothesis, "or something like it" (with a footnote to Adger 1994), is what negotiates the relation between the NP syntax and the NP interpretation.

What I take as my goal, then, is to accept that the interpretation of an NP is related to its position at LF, and to focus on the syntax of the distribution of these NPs at that and the overt level of syntax (PF). So, though the title appears misleading, this thesis is really part of the result of a number of years of research on the topic the title suggests. And now, on to the show.

Introduction

The central claim of this thesis is that direct objects in English move overtly to a Case position external to VP. This proposal differs from the standard GB (e.g. Chomsky 1981) approach in which the verb assigns Case to the direct object within VP. This proposal also differs from the current Minimalist (Chomsky 1993) approach in which the direct object is in VP in the overt syntax, only moving to a VP-external Case position at LF.

The first four chapters outline this basic hypothesis, concentrating on standard direct objects in English. The evidence is of various sorts: at LF, objects asymmetrically c-command VP and other VP-internal material; overtly the main verb and the direct object are external to a constituent containing the remainder of the VP material, analyzed as VP itself; adverb placement distinguishes between functional and lexical projections providing further support for the present proposal over a VP-shell account (Larson 1988).

The subsequent two chapters examine other types of "object" construction: ECM and the double object construction. The sorts of evidence adduced for the preceding claims show the ECM subject as well as both objects of the double object construction to appear overtly in VP-external AGRo specifiers, further supporting a Case-checking account invoking functional specifiers.

The final two chapters explore the differences between LF and PF NP positions. There various LF "lowering" phenomena are explained by exploiting the copy and delete strategy for movement (Chomsky 1993).

This account leads to an examination of copying and deleting and a proposal for the mechanics of such an account. *There* insertion and stylistic inversion are provided a new account by putting together the parts of the analysis proposed here.

An interesting conclusion reached in this thesis is that there is no A-movement at LF in English. In fact, if copying is interpreted as proposed here (following Marantz 1994), there can be no A-movement at LF universally. The differences between pre-SPLIT and LF "movement", then, follow from the different strategies exploited at these levels, only the former exhibiting "reconstruction" effects due to using the copy and delete strategy.

Acknowledgments

There are so many people who have helped me get to where I am, many in fact unwittingly. I hope at least to mention some of those I can think of and apologize to those I will certainly forget. Thanks to all.

To begin I must thank my committee, who were wonderful throughout this at times difficult process. Hagit Borer, my advisor and friend, has been a mentor for years now, beginning with my interest in clitics straight through the dissertation years and my current interest in NP positions. Kyle Johnson, though he only came to UMass in my fifth year, turned out to be immensely helpful and someone I can turn to when I need a friend. Angelika Kratzer taught me much of what I know about semantics, though she should not be held responsible for it! Her careful comments on earlier drafts of this thesis really helped me clarify its direction. Roger Higgins has been a source of facts and helpful criticisms throughout my graduate career at UMass. Chisato Kitagawa was a wonderful "external" member of my committee. He showed real interest in my work and made a number of useful comments and suggestions along the way.

After my committee, though, I should step back a bit and make sure to point out why I am even doing linguistics. This is because of the time I spent at UC Santa Cruz and the great environment provided in that department. First and foremost I have to thank Judith Aissen, who taught me my first linguistics classes and from whom I learned to start thinking like a syntactician. She became my undergraduate thesis advisor as well as someone I worked with doing my first field work and it would be impossible to point out how much I gained from our interactions. Also extremely influential to my development as a linguist and a teacher are Sandy Chung, Jim McCloskey, Junko Itô, Jorge Hankamer, Bill Ladusaw and Bill Shipley.

Back at UMass are some of the reasons I stuck with linguistics. The faculty there have been great as teachers and role models and I thank them; besides my committee, thanks to: John McCarthy, Peggy Speas, Lisa Selkirk, Emmon Bach, Barbara Partee, Ellen Woolford, Tom Roeper, Lyn Frazier and Jon Kingston. My classmates were there all along for me and I wish them all the best, as well: Tohru Noguchi, Amy Schafer, Kimberley Broderick, Jóhannes Jonsson, Man-Soon Kwon and Hsi-Chia Chao. Other friends at UMass who were particularly helpful either personally or linguistically include: Hotze Rullmann, Juli Carter, Satoshi Tomioka, Bernhard Rohrbacher, Kai von Fintel, Veena Dwivedi, Réjean Canac Marquis, Jingqi Fu, Noriko Kawasaki, Paul Portner, Tom Maxfield, Greg LaMontagne, Rose-Marie Dèchaine, Linda Lombardi, Molly Diesing, Laura Walsh Dickey, Su Urbanczyk, Sue Tunstall, Janina Radó, Elena Benedicto, Mercé Gonzalez, Mike Dickey, Laura Benua, Bill Philip, José Benki, Zvi Gilbert, Heather Gilmer, Bart Hollebrandse, Winnie Lechner, David Holton, Eugenia Casielles, Deanna Moore, John Alderete, Pat Deevy, Amalia Gnanadesikan, Rachel Thorburn, Ulricke Demske-Neumann, Anke Feldhaus, Bernhard Schwartz and Maribel Romero. An extra special thanks goes to Jill Beckman, who has helped me out in all sorts of ways.

I had the privilege of spending six months at the Universitat Autònoma de Barcelona and I thank some of the people there for helping to provide a rich environment in which to work and play: Carme Picallo, Jaume Solà, Albert Branchadell, and especially Josep Quer.

I have made many friends over the years at conferences and other linguistics events and I can only begin to name them all. I'd especially like to thank Joachim Sabel, Martin Haiden and Brian Lindsey. One other friend who has influenced me in more ways than I can mention is David Adger.

Two people at the University of Rochester who have been great friends as well as great role models are Itziar Laka and Phil LeSourd. Other people there who I want to thank for their help and friendship are: Koji Hoshi, Chris Barker, Karen Petronio, Greg Carlson and Peter Lasersohn.

Acknowledgments

Where would I be without the help and friendship of the folks who really run the linguistics departments? Thanks to: Kathy Adamczyk and Lynne Ballard at UMass, and Roberta Colon at the University of Rochester.

Then there are those friends who have stuck by me over the years listening to me babble about AGR and other "interesting" linguistic terms. Without these friends insanity certainly would have set in sooner: Vinnie Falciano, Bill Landis, Tim Garlick, Susan and Steve Robinson, Darrin Shaffer, Michael Fraser, Manmatha, J O'Neill, Carmel Weifert, Patty Frontiera, Lauren MacNeill and Sarah Clark. Besides the friends there are the places we hung out, which I owe some gratitude. In Santa Cruz: the Blue Lagoon; in Northampton: the Brewery, Packard's, Pearl St (Wednesdays), and the Northstar (Tuesdays); in Rochester: the Avenue Pub, the Bachelor Forum and the Bug Jar.

And finally and most importantly, always behind me and supporting me (and knowing when not to ask about my dissertation) are my family: Mom and Dad (Pat and Joe Runner), my brother Ron, Kim, my sister Sarah, Grammy and Grampa (Dottie and Charlie Dawson), Sally, Bob, Diane, Bobby, Johnny, John, Ann and Zoe. And besides Cillie and Britt, Butch has been a constant presence who normally doesn't get the thanks she deserves. Thank you all!

Noun Phrase Licensing

CHAPTER 1
Preliminaries

1.1 INTRODUCTION

The central claim of this thesis is that direct objects in English move overtly to a Case position external to VP. This proposal differs from the standard GB (e.g. Chomsky 1981) approach in which the verb assigns Case to the direct object within VP. This proposal also differs from the current Minimalist (Chomsky 1993, henceforth MPLT) approach in which the direct object is in VP in the overt syntax only moving to a VP-external Case position at LF.

In what follows I briefly outline the background assumptions which my proposal builds on. Then I turn to outlining the proposal itself.

1.2 AGRs AND AGRo

I take as a springboard Chomsky's (1991) proposal that structural Case assignment is a unified process involving a local relation between a specifier and a head, called Spec-Head agreement. This relation is already standardly assumed for nominative Case-assignment; what is novel about Chomsky's proposal is that accusative Case-assignment should proceed in a parallel fashion. Nominative Case is assumed to be assigned by a combination of (finite) tense and (subject) agreement in the INFL node. The new proposal is that accusative Case should be assigned by a combination of V and (object) agreement.

To put it more concretely, Chomsky, developing ideas of Pollock (1989), Kayne (1989) and Koopman (1984), proposes that the inflectional portion of the syntactic tree consists of a number of separate syntactic projections differentiated by their function in the syntax. Pollock had proposed that these functional projections include at least AGRs(ubject), T(ense) and Neg(ation). Chomsky argues for one more: AGRo(bject). His development of Case theory is outlined in what follows.

It has been assumed that T bears the relevant Case feature responsible for nominative Case assignment. Chomsky argues that T, in combination with AGRs, assigns nominative Case to the NP in the specifier of AGRsP:

1. Nominative Case Assignment

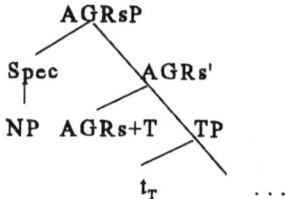

The innovation in Chomsky (1991) is that an analogous operation is responsible for accusative Case-assignment. Assuming the verb to be the element bearing the Case feature, the verb in combination with AGRo, a functional projection dominating VP, assigns Case to the NP in the specifier of AGRoP:

2. Accusative Case Assignment

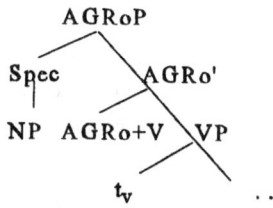

Chomsky (1991, 1993) is very careful to point out that the 's' and 'o' we speak of when we speak of AGRs and AGRo, respectively, are entirely mnemonic devices used by us to help differentiate parts of the tree. There is no difference between AGRs and AGRo. What differences appear come from the differences between the heads that adjoin to them. For example, the fact that AGRs is responsible for nominative Case assignment is due to the fact that T is the head that endows AGR with the nominative Case feature. Analogously, AGRo is an accusative Case-assigner because that happens to be the Case feature it gets from the V head which adjoins to it. The motto: AGR is AGR is AGR. Chomsky's view of AGR is that it is simply a mediator between NP and a syntactic head. I will continue to use the mnemonics AGRs and AGRo, and later argue for a second AGRo as well as AGRp(reposition) phrases; the reader should keep in mind that no inherent difference is assumed to exist between AGRs, AGRo and AGRp.

That said, a comment about terminology is due. Another change in Case theory introduced in Chomsky (1991) and glossed over in the above discussion is in the nature of Case "assignment" itself. Rather than a head "assigning" Case to an NP, the process is seen as something more symmetric: AGR (thanks to T or V being adjoined to it) has a Case feature; NP is assumed to be inserted into the structure fully inflected and thus also bears a Case feature. What AGR does is "check" to make sure that the feature it bears and the feature the NP bears "agree". Thus, this is called Case "checking". Analogously, NP has number, person (and gender, etc.) features, called its Φ features. The inflection-bearing element in T, perhaps aux or V, is also assumed to be inserted into the syntax fully inflected. Thus, the other side of checking is that AGR "checks" to make sure that the NP in its specifier and the T+aux/V "agree" in these Φ features. We can assume that Case, person, number (and gender, etc.) features are all the relevant features to be checked. What AGR does is mediate the relation between an NP bearing certain features and a head bearing certain features. AGR checks these features.

In what follows, then, I will often refer to what was Case-assignment as feature-checking, Φ feature-checking, Case-checking, etc., only distinguishing these when necessary. When I am speaking loosely I will perhaps refer to it as Case-assignment as well.

1.3 CHECKING THEORY AND VERB MOVEMENT

Chomsky (1991) followed Pollock (1989) in another respect, one that crucially differentiates his account from the one defended in this thesis. Pollock, following Emonds (1978), argued that main verbs in English do not move at all at S-structure, while main verbs in a language like French move overtly to T (T was the highest functional projection in Pollock's system). This account was forced by the assumption that certain adverbs were left-adjoined to VP. These adverbs appear between the main verb and the object NP in French, while they appear to the left of the main verb and the object NP in English. Thus, the claim was that in French the main verb had moved out of VP passing the adverb leaving the object behind. In English no verb movement occurred so the adverb preceded both the verb and object:

3. a. NP verb [$_{VP}$ ADV [$_{VP}$ t$_V$ NP]] [French]

   b. NP [$_{VP}$ ADV [$_{VP}$ verb NP]] [English]

What is important to note, I believe, is that the claim that the verb does not move out of VP in English is forced by the assumption that the adverbs in question are left-adjoined to VP. Clearly, the English main verb does not move as far as the French one. What may still be open is the position of the adverb itself. This open question will be exploited below in chapters 3 and 4.

Chomsky's acceptance of the Emonds-Pollock account of (lack of) verb movement in English combined with his new view of accusative Case-checking exploits another domain in the theory, this time LF movement. According to checking theory, object NPs move to Spec,AGRo to check accusative Case. According to assumptions about verb movement, the verb is in VP at S-structure. If Case-checking were to apply at S-structure the object would move out of VP overtly leaving the V behind, deriving the unattested order OBJ-V instead of V-OBJ. Thus, movement of the V to AGR, movement of the object to Spec,AGRo and Case-checking between the two, is all assumed to occur in the covert syntax of LF.

Preliminaries

LF A-movement for Case had been proposed in the past for *there* sentences (Chomsky 1986b) but now such covert movement would be the norm. LF, which had once been the level at which operations like QR and covert wh-movement occurred, would now be the level at which NPs are checked for Case. In many ways this was a surprising proposal because the empirical evidence did not seem very strong for the claim.

A couple of conceptual questions arise with respect to this proposal as well. It had often been assumed that abstract Case was something relevant to phonetically overt NPs (not e.g. PRO or A trace) and that the Case Filter applied at S-structure driving overt NP movement (Rouveret & Vergnaud 1980). By assuming Case to be checked at LF, first one wonders why LF would play a role in what was assumed to be an S-structure filter, and second, one wonders why subjects move to Spec,AGRs in the overt syntax if Case-checking does not occur until LF. If Case is used as a motivator for movement, why do some NPs need to move overtly and others covertly?

In MPLT Chomsky exploits the features of checking theory in an attempt at dealing with these sorts of issues. The basic claim is that the features of the heads in the syntax come in two strengths: strong and weak. A strong feature must be checked before PF. A weak feature can wait until LF. The idea is that a strong feature is uninterpretable at PF so that if it does not get checked (and then disappear) it will cause the derivation to crash at PF. A weak feature can be present at PF so it can wait to be checked until LF. In fact this "waiting" is something that in MPLT has been elevated to a principle: procrastinate. That is, taken broadly, if an operation can wait to apply at LF it will. This effectively blocks weak feature checking until LF if possible. Strong feature checking must happen before PF so procrastinating would end up causing a crash at PF.

For concreteness I will outline the account of subject and object movement assumed (a good overview of MPLT can be found in Marantz 1994). T and V each have features for V and N. I will concentrate on N features because they have to do with Case. In English, T is assumed to have strong N features. Since strong features must be checked before PF, otherwise leading to PF crashing, the subject NP will have to move to Spec,AGRs overtly. There T adjoins to AGRs and nominative Case is checked. V, on the other hand, has weak N features. These features need not, and because of procrastinate must not, be checked until LF. This means that the object NP is not forced to move overtly to Spec,AGRo. At LF, V moves to AGRo, NP moves to Spec,AGRo, and Case is checked.

1.4 THE BASIC PROPOSAL

Chomsky's feature strength approach was motivated in part by the facts surrounding English objects. An explanation was needed for why English apparently allowed LF A-movement for Case checking of objects and not subjects. Now, if it turned out that the empirical generalization was mistaken, and English does not in fact require LF A-movement, one might ask whether such movement is necessary in any language. If the claim of LF A-movement fails to find empirical support this would cast doubt on the feature strength approach advocated by Chomsky. This approach, especially combined with the principle of procrastination, predicts that LF A-movement should be rampant in the world's languages. This thesis addresses the first claim, that the empirical generalization that English needs LF A-movement is mistaken. In what follows I show that objects move overtly to Spec,AGRo.

The evidence is of various sorts. In Chapter 2 I begin by first arguing that various types of LF phenomena support the claim that the object is VP-external at least at that level. This evidence is consistent with Chomsky's (1991, 1993) proposal as well as the current one. It is inconsistent with the "standard" LGB account of object positions.

In chapter 3, I continue by first showing that the main verb has also left VP. This is shown by various tests which show the verb to be external to a constituent containing the object and other VP elements: AGRoP. Second, I then show that the verb and the object are both external to a constituent containing the remainder of the VP contents and adjoined elements: VP.

In chapter 4, adverb placement in VP suggests that VP contains only complement PPs, IPs, and CPs, as well as adjoined adverbials: everything but the verb and the object. In the process of arguing for the claim that the object has moved to Spec,AGRo in the overt syntax, I spend quite some time arguing that Larson's (1988) VP-shell account, though allowing in many cases the right constituency, finally fails when faced with the full range of adverb placement facts. Having shown Larson's account to be

Preliminaries 9

inadequate I show that Chomsky's (1993) account of the surface syntax of VP cannot handle the constituency and adverb placement facts pointed out above.

Chapters 5 and 6 take up other kinds of "objects". Chapter 5 argues that "ECM" is in fact overt raising of the embedded subject to Spec,AGRo. A number of phenomena favor the overt account, some of which had been brought up in Postal's (1974) book on the subject. The strongest kind of evidence is from cases in which clearly matrix material comes between the supposedly embedded subject and the rest of the embedded clause. On the view that either ECM involves no movement at all or that movement occurs at LF these phenomena pose a real challenge. On the overt raising account they follow straightforwardly. These phenomena include adverb placement of several types, floating quantifiers and particle verbs.

Chapter 6 provides an account of the double object construction. I propose that both objects move overtly to the specifiers of AGR projections external to VP. This is supported in part by tests for LF position, which show that both objects asymmetrically c-command VP and its contents. Then constituency tests show that both NP objects are external to a projection containing other VP-type material: VP, lacking objects and a verb. I show that while Larson's (1988) account gets the relationship between the two objects right it cannot be extended in such a way as to account for the second object's relation to other VP material without completely revising the proposal to look much more like the present one. Finally, I extend a proposal made by Johnson (1991) about the underlying structure of the double object construction: the two objects form a "clausal DP". Case requirements separate them placing each in its own Spec,AGR in the overt syntax. This clausal DP proposal ends up making several interesting and correct predictions about scope, binding and extraction.

Chapter 7 examines the LF positions of NPs. In Chapter 2, I examined definite objects and found them to be in Spec,AGRo at LF. Interestingly, it turns out that indefinite objects, as well as subjects, if interpreted existentially, are not in Spec,AGR at LF. The strongest evidence comes from their behavior in antecedent contained deletion contexts, and from the range of interpretations available with certain predicate types. They behave as if they can be VP-internal at LF. I attribute the relationship between the distribution of NPs at LF and their interpretation to Diesing's (1992) mapping hypothesis and take as my goal a syntactic account of how these NPs appear where they appear.

Having discussed why NPs appear in different positions at LF I examine the question of how. The question is the following: since overtly, objects and subjects are in VP-external Spec,AGR how can they end up in VP at LF? I follow Lasnik (1993) and Adger (1994) and develop a proposal in Chomsky (1993). Chomsky suggests that A'-movement follows a copy and delete strategy. This strategy allows an elegant account of reconstruction phenomena without actually moving downwards at LF. Lasnik (1993), Adger (1994) and I suggest that this strategy be available for A-movement as well. Thus an elegant account of A-movement "reconstruction" becomes available.

Copy and delete movement opens up a number of questions about when and where copies delete. Trying to maintain the null hypothesis that deletion should be free, subject to recoverability, I examine deletions at PF and LF. I propose essentially that if AGR is licensed at a level, its specifier must be filled. So, if AGR is licensed (to be defined below) at PF, its specifier must be filled at PF; this ends up constraining deletion independently.

In chapter 8, I examine some extensions of the copy and delete account by looking at *there* sentences and stylistic inversion, providing accounts of these constructions which do not suffer from the drawbacks of some earlier analyses.

1.5 COPYING AND A-MOVEMENT

Several important points can be made before continuing. First, the copy and delete strategy for movement, which very nicely accounts for the PF/LF mismatches observed, obviates any feature strength account of PF NP position. This is because, while the feature strength approach may serve to motivate the overt movement initially, it says nothing about deletion, allowing overt NP movement followed by upstairs deletion, satisfying the strong feature-checking requirement but without ensuring that the NP appears in the upstairs position. Thus, an account like the one

Preliminaries

I propose, which independently constrains the deletions, is preferable to one exploiting feature strength.

Secondly, I will assume, following Marantz (1994), that copying in copy and delete movement is in fact simply the independent building of identical structure, building phrases from lexical items. Given Chomsky's (1993) reasonable claim that lexical access is available only in the "overt syntax", that is before the split to PF and LF, this implies that all movement, A- and A'-, must occur in the overt syntax. If movement exploits the copy and delete strategy and copying requires lexical access for phrase-building, and lexical access is denied to the PF and LF components, then "movement" is restricted to the overt syntax. This implies, then, that A-movement, in particular, must be in the overt syntax universally. There is no LF A-movement, contra Chomsky's (1993) account of object movement in English. This thesis, in fact, shows that objects in English do move overtly to Spec,AGRo. Thus, the proposal defended here is consistent with the requirement that all A-movement precede the split to PF and LF, while other current proposals assuming LF A-movement are not. I take this to favor my account.

CHAPTER 2
Initial Motivation: "LF" Asymmetric C-Command

2.1 INTRODUCTION

As part of supporting one of the main goals of this thesis, that objects in English move overtly to a Case position external to VP, I will begin by examining some of the evidence that these objects are ever external to VP. The "standard" (e.g. LGB) VP places the object as sister to the verb in the VP at all levels of representation (unless QR moves it out for scope at LF). Thus, one of the first hurdles is to show that there are indeed indications that the object is external to VP at some level.

Larson (1988) accepts and extends the data examined in Barss & Lasnik (1986) suggesting that the object in English asymmetrically c-commands other VP-internal material. The sorts of data Barss & Lasnik discuss involve Binding Theory, Quantifier binding, Weak Crossover, Superiority, *each . . . the other* construal, and negative polarity items. While it is controversial exactly which level of representation each of these phenomena are sensitive to, taken together they do support the claim that the object asymmetrically c-commands VP-internal material at some level. Thus, we begin be reviewing and discussing these phenomena.

Two points need to be made before we begin. First, Larson (1988) rightly points out that these data simply show that the object in English asymmetrically c-commands other VP-internal material. They do not necessarily show that the object itself is not also within VP, or a higher VP. So, this chapter will not help us choose between the Larsonian "VP-shell" analysis and the present analysis placing the object in Spec,AGRo,

13

which I argue for. Choosing between these two accounts will be left for later chapters. However, the data discussed here do show, I think clearly, that the standardly assumed VP structure is simply not correct.

Second, Jackendoff (1990) in a reply to Larson's (1988) article calls into question the claim that the Barss & Lasnik (1986) facts illustrate asymmetric c-command. He instead argues that they show perhaps a combination of asymmetric c-command and linear precedence, which is more along the lines of the conclusions drawn by Barss & Lasnik themselves. However, I will defend the claim that asymmetric c-command is what is being probed for. To do so, though, I need to expand the data base and consider the predictions of the two sorts of accounts. In fact a good deal of the chapter is devoted to doing this. Ultimately, I believe I show that it is indeed asymmetric c-command that the phenomena in question are sensitive to.

I now turn to a brief illustration of the tree I will be arguing for throughout the next few chapters. Then we will turn to the Barss & Lasnik facts, as interpreted by Larson (1988). For the time being I illustrate only the relevant lower portion of the structure. This is what we will be dealing with in this chapter:

1. Jan envies Marcia.

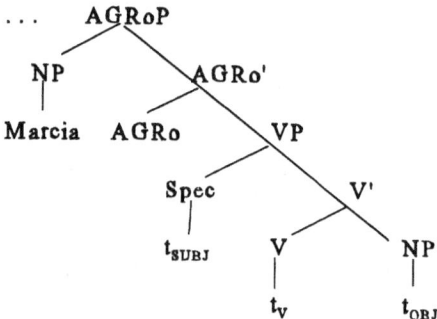

The object *Marcia* appears in Spec,AGRo, where it receives accusative Case. From this position it asymmetrically c-commands any material within VP. In this particular example there is no other material. But should there be PPs, or VP-adjoined adverbials, the NP *Marcia* will asymmetrically c-command them. This is what the Barss & Lasnik (1986) facts show. Let us turn to this now.

2.2 LF OBJECT POSITION(S)

Larson (1988) argues that a series of tests for "domainhood" assembled by Barss & Lasnik (1986) point to the conclusion that the first object in a VP asymmetrically c-commands the second object or prepositional phrase in VP. As he points out, this is not surprising in the case of NP PP, since if we assume m-command in the definition of domain, most versions of VP containing NP PP will predict the object of P to be in the domain of NP. What is striking is that on most views of the internal structure of a double object VP, the first object does not m-command the second object. Thus, Larson's task is to postulate a structure in which asymmetric m-command or c-command does hold between the two objects.

I will begin by reviewing the Barss & Lasnik tests (henceforth, B&L tests), showing the results for both double object and the NP PP verb phrases that Larson discusses. I will then present Larson's structures and how they account for the tests. I will then show how the structure I am arguing for in (1), above, as well as that of Chomsky (1993) account for the results of the tests just as well.

Barss & Lasnik (1986) assemble six tests for "domainhood". In every case the first NP in VP appears to have a second NP within its domain. Barss & Lasnik show this to be true in the case of V NP_1 NP_2; I have included Larson's examples showing the same asymmetry to be true of V NP_1 [P NP_2].

Binding Principles. NP_2 can be a reflexive or reciprocal and be bound by NP_1, satisfying Condition A of the binding theory. Note that NP_2 does not bind NP_1 or Condition C/B would be violated in (a). If NP_1 is an anaphor, it cannot be bound by NP_2 (b):

2. a.   I showed John/him himself (in the mirror)
   b. * I showed himself John (in the mirror)
3. a.   I showed the professors each other's students
   b. * I showed each other's students the professors

4. a.   I presented/showed Mary to herself
    b. * I presented/showed herself to Mary

Quantifier Binding. NP_1 as a quantified NP can bind a bound variable pronoun in NP_2 (a), but not vice versa (b):

5. a.   I denied each worker his paycheck
    b. * I denied its owner each paycheck
6. a.   I showed every friend of mine his photograph
    b. * I showed its trainer every lion
7. a.   I gave/sent every check to its owner
    b. ?? I gave/sent his paycheck to every worker
                                            [Larson's judgment]

Weak Crossover. NP_1 can be wh-moved and still bind a pronoun in NP_2 (a), but the reverse is impossible (b):

8. a.   Which worker did you deny his paycheck?
    b. * Which paycheck did you deny its owner?
9. a.   Who did you show his reflection in the mirror?
    b. * Which lion did you show its owner?
10. a.   Which check did you send to its owner?
    b. * Which worker did you send his check to?

Superiority. If both NPs are wh-words, NP_1 can be moved leaving NP_2 in situ, but not vice versa:

11. a.   Who did you give which book?   ["awkward"–B&L]
    b. * Which book did you give who?
12. a.   Which check did you send to who?
    b. * Whom did you send which check to?
          (* To whom did you send which check?)

Each ... the other. As (a) shows, NP_1 headed by *each* licenses *the other* in NP_2. If NP_2 contains *each* it does not license *the other* in NP_1 (b):

13. a. I have each man the other's watch
    b. * I gave the other's trainer each lion
14. a. I sent each boy to the other's parents
    b. * I sent the other's check to each boy

Negative Polarity Items. A negated NP_1 licenses a polarity item in NP_2, as in (a). The reverse is impossible (b):

15. a. I gave no one anything
    b. * I gave anyone nothing
16. a. I sent no presents to any of the children
    b. * I sent any of the packages to none of the children

Generalization: in V NP_1 (P) NP_2, NP_2 is in the domain of NP_1.

Putting aside for the moment the conceptual motivation for the structures Larson (1988) proposes, the syntactic motivation is clear: the first object must asymmetrically c-command the second object, or the object of P. This is because Larson takes the B&L tests to be tests for asymmetric c-command, contra Barss & Lasnik themselves, who conclude that linear precedence plays a role in the definition of domain. For the sake of the argument I will simply follow Larson in taking the B&L tests as tests for asymmetric c-command but I will devote the next section to showing that this must be the case, contra Jackendoff (1990).

The VP structures Larson (1988) proposes are the following:

17. Double Object (V NP NP)

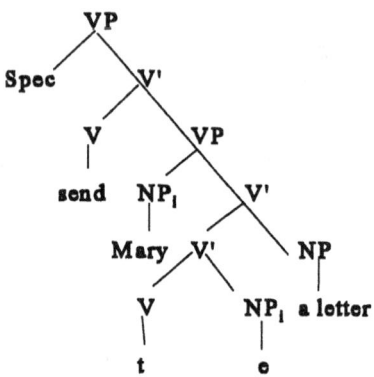

18. Object and PP (V NP [P NP])

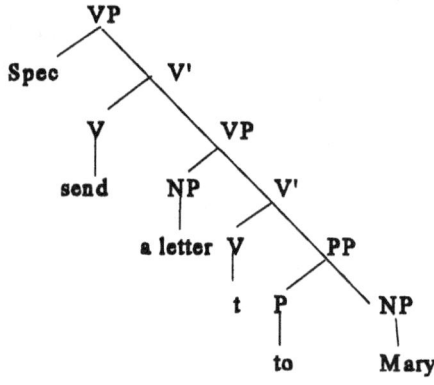

The crucial characteristic that these structures have which allows them to account for the B&L tests is that the first object is in a position higher than other material in the verb phrase. Thus the first object c-commands the second object or PP, and not vice versa.

Abstracting away from the details of Larson's structure, what makes it work is that in both cases we have the following schema:

19. Abstract Schema of What "Works"

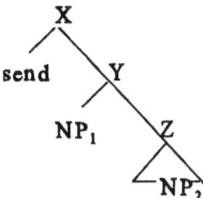

NP$_1$ asymmetrically c-commands NP$_2$, whether NP$_2$ is the second object or the object of a preposition. Larson identifies X as V' and Y as the maximal projection of a lower VP. Z is identified as V'. It is important to note that the B&L tests only test for the abstract configuration in (19), not for the labels Larson has given to X, Y and Z. This is important because I will argue for a structure which maintains the schema in (19) but with quite different node labels. And until we look into other properties of the structures, the B&L tests do not help us choose between the alternatives.

The structure I will support, which is essentially that of Chomsky (1993), is roughly the following. At this point in the chapter I do not wish to address the details of the double object construction, so it will be left open exactly where the second object actually lies; for now I will simply assume that it is somewhere in VP (though see Chapter 6 for the full proposal). What is crucial is that the first object is in Spec,AGRo, a position that asymmetrically c-commands VP and its contents:

20. Proposed Structure (S-structure)

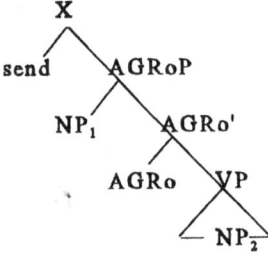

This is essentially the structure assumed in Chomsky (1993). However, Chomsky assumes this to be the LF representation. Before LF the verb and the object are in VP, only raising covertly in the mapping to LF. My claim is that (20) is derived in the overt syntax. That is, the verb and the object are VP-external at S-structure and remain so even at LF.

The B&L tests illustrated above all arguably test for LF configurations. If Chomsky (1993) is correct, the binding theory, quantifier binding, crossover, superiority, *each . . . the other* construal and NPIs are all relations which are checked at LF for appropriateness. This being the case, what the abstract schema in (19) shows is the correct LF configuration the B&L tests point to. Thus, my claim that this is the S-structure configuration as well as the LF one is neither confirmed nor denied by the B&L tests (see Chapter 3 for details).

What the B&L tests rule out are any proposals which do not end up with the configuration in (19) at LF. Such proposals include the following commonly assumed structures (discussed in Larson 1988; (a) is from Oehrle 1976, (b) is from Chomsky 1981):

21. a.   b.

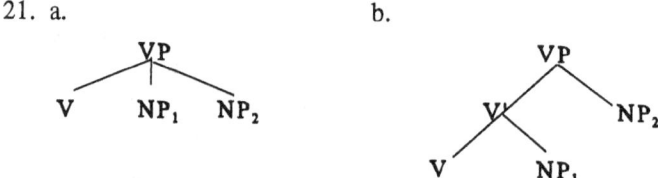

The structure in (a) predicts that NP_1 and NP_2 should c-command each other. The one in (b) predicts that NP_2 should c-command NP_1. Neither of these proposals, if assumed to hold of LF configurations, accounts for the fact that NP_1 appears to c-command NP_2 for the LF conditions that the B&L tests are pointing to.

My account, which places the object in Spec,AGRo at S-structure and LF, Chomsky's account, which does so at LF only, and Larson's account, which places the object in a high VP-internal position at S-structure (and presumably LF), are each consistent with the B&L tests and thus should be preferred over accounts assuming LF structures like those in 21.[1]

2.3 PREPOSITIONAL OBJECTS AND ASYMMETRIC C-COMMAND

Jackendoff (1990) points out that verbs with two PP objects behave unexpectedly with respect to the B&L tests; his goal is to show that the B&L tests do not in fact test for asymmetric c-command but rather, linear precedence. According to the B&L tests, the NP in the first PP has the NP in the second PP in its domain. If we accept that the tests are for asymmetric c-command then we have to explain how an NP in a PP c-commands something outside of its PP. If we accept that the B&L tests are for linear precedence then no further explanation is necessary.

Ultimately I will show that the B&L tests do test for asymmetric c-command so I must explain the data that follows. The explanation I give will essentially be an account which does in fact put the NP in the first PP in a position to asymmetrically c-command the second. The account will be motivated by expanding the data base even further, showing that linear precedence will not account for what is found. But asymmetric c-command, combined with my account of the interesting "exceptions", will.

2.3.1 The Data and the Problem

I will begin by displaying the data (from Jackendoff 1990):

Anaphors.

22.	a.		I talked to John and Bill about themselves/each other
	b.		I heard from John and Bill about themselves/each other
23.	a.	*	I talked to themselves/each other about John and Bill
	b.	*	I heard from themselves/each other about John and Bill
24.	a.	??	I talked about John and Bill to themselves/each other
	b.	??	I heard about John and Bill from themselves/each other
25.	a.	*	I talked about themselves/each other to John and Bill
	b.	*	I heard about themselves/each other from John and Bill

QNP-Bound Pronoun Relations.

26. a. I talked to every girl about her mother
    b. I heard from every mother about her child
27. a. * I talked to her mother about every girl
    b. * I heard from her mother about every girl
28. a. I talked about every girl to her mother
    b. I heard about every girl from her mother
29. a. ?* I talked about her mother to every girl
    b. ?* I heard about her mother from every girl

Wh-Movement and Weak Crossover.

30. a. Which girl did you talk to about her mother?
    b. ?* Which mom did you talk to her daughter about?
31. a. Which mom did you talk about to her daughter?
    b. ?* Which girl did you talk about her mother to?

Superiority.

32. a. Which girl did you talk about to which boy?
    b. ?* Which boy did you talk about which girl to?
33. a. Which boy did you talk to about which girl?
    b. ?* Which girl did you talk to which boy about?

Each ... the other.

34. a. I talked about each boy to the other
    b. * I talked about the other to each boy
35. a. I talked to each boy about the other
    b. * I talked to the other about each boy

Polarity *any*.

36. a. I talked about none of the boys to any of the girls
    b. * I talked about any of the boys to none of the girls

"LF" Asymmetric C-Command

37. a. I talked to none of the girls about any of the boys
    b. * I talked to any of the girls about none of the boys

Generalization: in V [P NP$_1$] [P NP$_2$], NP$_2$ is in the domain of NP$_1$.

In every case the B&L tests show that the NP in the first PP of a two PP VP has the second in its domain. If I want to maintain the claim that the B&L tests test for asymmetric c-command then these examples do pose a problem. I will consider them with respect to this problem.

An account assuming linear precedence to be relevant to the definition of domain (henceforth, a precedence account) can explain these data straightforwardly. In every case it is a preceding NP which has another NP in its domain. An account assuming asymmetric c-command (henceforth, a c-command account), on the other hand, must explain why the object of the first preposition appears to asymmetrically c-command an NP in a subsequent prepositional phrase. Standard structures assumed include the following (adapted from Jackendoff 1990, p.430-431):

38.

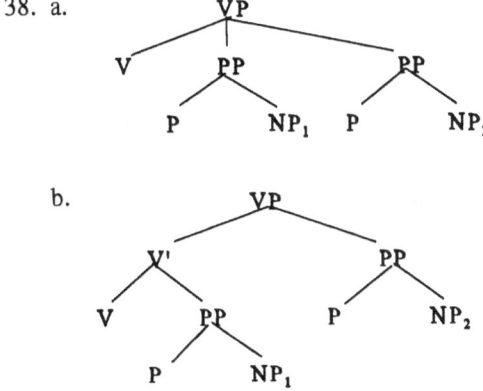

In neither structure, on any definition of c-command, does NP$_1$ c-command NP$_2$.

2.3.2 A C-Command Account

Recall what the B&L tests are testing for: domainhood *at LF*. What that means is that at LF NP_1 must be in a position which asymmetrically c-commands NP_2. Suppose this is correct. Then either of the above structures might be correct for S-structure. The c-command account requires something like the following at LF, however (assuming an S-structure like that of (b)):

39.
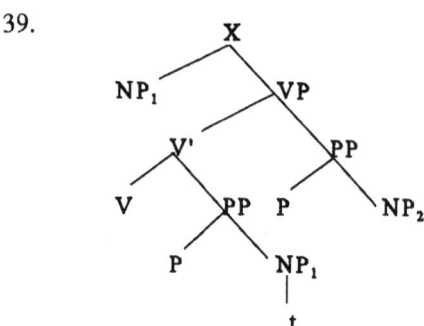

This structure represents the LF of an S-structure like (b) above, in which NP_1 has been moved to a position which asymmetrically c-commands NP_2 as well as other VP material. If this structure could be motivated as the correct LF for the Jackendoff examples, then an explanation adhering to the c-command account can be maintained.

What kind of motivation could be given for this structure? The first question to ask is *why* NP_1 might move to such a position. Phrases move for various reasons, including at least the following: wh requirements, scope requirements, and Case. It is unlikely that this is wh-movement since most any kind of NP can undergo it (review the data: names, definite and indefinite NPs and pronouns are what we find). It is unlikely as well that such a movement is motivated for scope, since again the types of NP that undergo it are not the types normally required to take scope. What about Case? It is usually assumed that a preposition assigns Case to its object. So, unless something else is going on, the preposition heading the PP containing NP_1 at S-structure should be able to Case-mark NP_1.

2.3.2.1 What Position does NP Move to?

Let us consider the possibility that something else is going on and that the movement of NP_1 is, in fact, for Case. The first question is, why can't it get Case from P? But the second question is, why is the position it is moving to a Case position? I would like to consider the second question first. Recall that I am arguing that "normal" direct objects move to the specifier of a functional projection, AGRoP, dominating VP. This movement is motivated by Case requirements. I would like to suggest that the position in which NP_1 resides in (39) is also Spec,AGRo. That is, I propose that the label X in (39) is AGRoP:

40. Proposed Structure

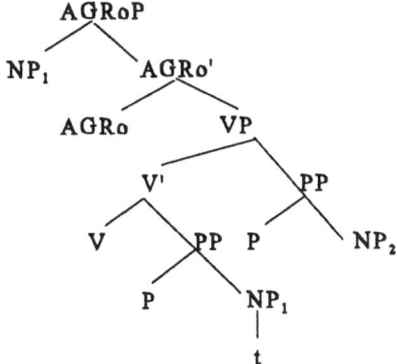

Is it reasonable to assume that there might be an AGRoP node in the examples in question? AGRo is the head which, in combination with V, assigns accusative Case to an NP in its specifier. This usually only happens with transitive verbs since intransitive verbs do not have an object NP needing Case. My claim is that AGRo is present and can assign accusative Case in combination with the verbs in question.

I would like to state some conceptual motivation for such an assumption. Burzio (1986) claimed to be universal the following generalization regarding thematic roles and Case-assignment properties:

41. *Burzio's Generalization* (paraphrased): A verb assigns structural accusative Case if and only if it assigns an external theta role.

According to this generalization, transitive verbs, because they assign an external theta role, can assign accusative Case. Unaccusative verbs, which do not assign an external theta role, do not assign accusative Case. It also implies that unergative verbs, which assign an external theta role, should assign accusative Case.

Now, since unergative verbs do not normally have objects,[2] whether or not they assign accusative Case might seem irrelevant. However, it is in fact unergative verbs which we are now considering. And Burzio's claim is, essentially, that they do assign accusative Case. On an account which associates accusative Case with a Case feature in V which is checked against AGRo, this means that unergative verbs should license an AGRo projection with which to combine and assign accusative Case on an NP in its specifier. Thus, if this interpretation of the generalization is correct, we may have found reason to think that the verbs in question can in fact provide a Spec,AGRo for the object of the preposition below them to move to for Case.

Burzio's generalization is just a generalization. It does not explain *why* such a correlation should exist. I do not plan to explain this either. However, I would like to update the generalization slightly given my assumptions about structural Case assignment. On my account, following Chomsky (1991, 1993), structural accusative Case is checked on an NP in Spec,AGRo. AGRo, in combination with a verb with the appropriate Case feature, licenses the NP in its specifier. If Burzio's generalization is a generalization about which verbs have the relevant Case feature, it can be reformulated in the following way:

42. *Burzio's Generalization (Revised)*: A verb bears a structural Case feature iff it assigns an external theta role.

Following Chomsky, I assume that in unaccusative sentences, AGRoP is either present and simply not activated (resulting perhaps in there being no specifier generated), or it is absent completely. If a verb has a Case feature it needs to check, AGRo will have to be present and active. Thus, an unergative verb, which since it assigns an external theta role has a structural Case feature to check (according to (42)), will have an active/present AGRoP dominating VP. Standardly with unergative verbs, no object will end up in Spec,AGRo, presumably, so the Case feature born by such a verb must not be obligatorily checked. However, in the cases at hand, an object does appear in Spec,AGRo, having its Case checked by AGRo plus the unergative verb:

43.

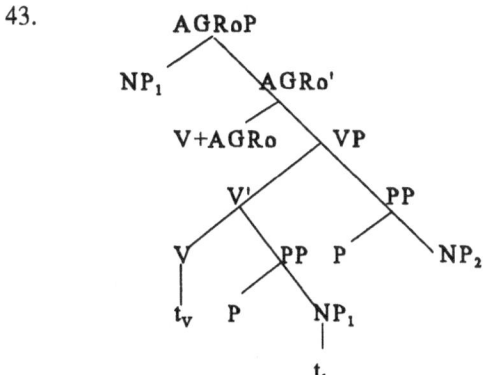

2.3.2.2 Why Move at All?

Having given some conceptual motivation to the claim that the verbs in question might actually have Case-assigning AGRo projections, we are still left with the question of why the NP moves to Spec,AGRo. It may be the case that Spec,AGRo is a Case position, but why doesn't the NP simply remain *in situ* being assigned Case by P?

A couple of answers seem plausible. One possibility is that the Case assigned by P is only *optionally* assigned. If this is true, then the NP can move to Spec,AGRo to check Case there, or remain in PP to check Case *in situ*. The optionality flavor of this proposal conflicts with Chomsky's (1991, 1993) claim that there is no optionality in grammar. This claim, of course, is more of a methodological than empirical claim so I will not put too much weight into it. However, we will see below that in fact there are reasons to believe that this is not an optional movement. NP_1 is in

Spec,AGRo obligatorily. Thus, I will set aside this possibility, to be discussed and discarded more carefully below.

A second possibility is that for some reason P in (43) does not have Case-assigning capability. Let us seriously consider this possibility. Now, normally it is assumed that P has a Case to assign, thus licensing an object NP. Why would P apparently be "stripped" of its Case-assigning capability in (43)? Once again, there are several possibilities, one of which has been proposed in the literature, the other of which I believe has not.

2.3.2.2.1 P has no Case

This subsection will concentrate on the hypothesis that P has no Case to assign. Two basic types of analysis will be outlined: a "reanalysis" account and an "unaccusative" preposition account. The former account comes in two varieties: a syntactic and a lexical variety, each of which is supported by empirical arguments. The latter account, while technically feasible, finds little empirical support and conceptually seems to make the wrong predictions. Thus, a version of the reanalysis account will be supported.

2.3.2.2.1.1 "Reanalysis" as P-Incorporation

The first possibility for why the P has no Case to assign is that it has "reanalyzed" as part of the verb. That is, in examples like *talk about Bill*, [talk-about] has reanalyzed as a complex verb. Technically, this could be accomplished syntactically by head movement of P into V, as argued by Baker (1988) and references therein. If P is actually incorporated into V then the former object of P comes to be the object of the complex verb [V+P]:

44. Preposition Incorporation

```
        V'
       / \
    V+P   PP
         /  \
        P    NP
        |
        t_p
```

Baker proposed this operation to account for pseudopassives like the following:

45. a. George Washington slept in this bed
    b. This bed was slept in t by George Washington
46. a. The Smiths and the Joneses have fought over this piece of land for centuries
    b. This piece of land has been fought over t for centuries
47. a. We talked about John after he left
    b. John was talked about t after he left

E.g. *slept in* is a complex verb in (a), assigning Case to *this bed*. The complex verb is passivized in (b), thus losing Case-assigning capability. The "object" of the complex verb moves to subject position for Case, as in plain passive.

The structure in (44), combined with my assumptions about Case-assignment, would be the following. VP is embedded in AGRoP, so due to P-incorporation the NP object of P must move to Spec,AGRo for Case:

48. P-Incorporation and AGR

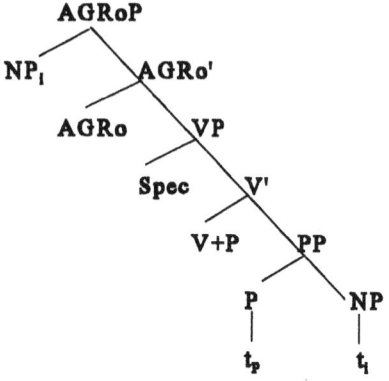

P-incorporation is assumed by Baker (1988) to be a case of LF head-movement. This proposal is consistent with our need for NP_1 to be in Spec,AGRo at LF.

2.3.2.2.1.2 "Reanalysis" as a Lexical Operation

A second possibility for explaining the "reanalysis" operation would be to assume a lexical operation deriving a complex transitive verb *talk about* lexically. On this type of account the object of *about* is in fact the object of the complex verb *talk about*. As an object, it would appear in Spec,AGRo for Case reasons, thus would asymmetrically c-command elements within VP, as required:

49. Lexical Reanalysis

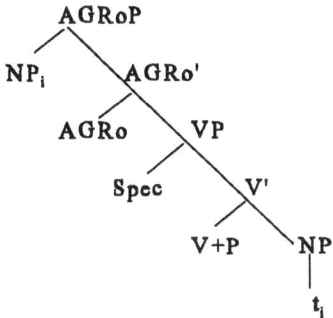

This proposal would also account for the pseudopassives pointed out above. If the complex verb is passivized, as with other verbs, its Case feature is suppressed and its object must move to Spec,AGRs for Case. Those two possibilities for accounts of "reanalysis" have the property that the verb and preposition are a unit at some level. They just differ on which level. Another possibility for why the preposition in V PP might not have Case to assign to its object takes us into a closer look at Case-assignment by prepositions, to which we now turn.

2.3.2.2.1.3 Unaccusative Prepositions

Prepositions have been assumed to assign Case to their objects. What kind of Case do they assign? Some have argued that they assign *structural* Case; others have argued that they assign *inherent* Case. In favor of inherent Case is the fact that quite often a specific theta role is assigned to the complement by P. Since inherent Case is thought to be linked to theta role assignment (Chomsky 1981) we might claim that prepositions assign inherent Case. Is there always a particular theta role born by the object of a preposition? Against the inherent Case case are cases like the objects of *by*-phrases in English:

50. a. Hortense was pushed by Elmer [agent]
    b. Elmer was seen by everyone who entered [experiencer]
    c. The intersection was approached by five cars at once [theme]
    d. The porcupine crate was received by Elmer's firm [goal/recipient]
    e. The house was surrounded by trees ["something else"]

Baker (1988, p.335)

The theta roles born by these NPs vary greatly, while the preposition remains constant. If we assume that the Case assigned by such a preposition is inherent we are at a loss to explain why the same preposition appears to be able to assign inherent Case to NPs with such a variety of theta roles. If the Case assigned by P is structural this is expected. Let us then assume that prepositions assign structural Case.

One of Chomsky's (1991) most intriguing claims is that structural Case is assigned uniformly in a Spec-head relation with AGR. Nominative Case is assigned in Spec,AGRs (with T); accusative Case is assigned in Spec,AGRo (with V). What about the structural Case assigned to objects of prepositions? Let us explore the possibility that Chomsky's claim about structural Case should extend to PPs. If that is the case then we must assume that there is an AGRP projection dominating PP, call it AGRpP. The preposition will move to AGRp to check its Case feature there. The object of the preposition will move to the specifier of the AGRp phrase to check its structural Case:

51. Prepositional AGR

```
            AGRpP
           /    \
        NP_i    AGRp'
               /    \
          P+AGRp    PP
             |     /  \
             P    NP
             |     |
             t_P   t_i
```

(51) represents presumably the LF of a regular prepositional phrase. This would be the structure of a P that "assigns Case".[3]

The structures we are interested in are of the form V PP in which the P apparently does not assign Case, thus forcing its object to move to Spec,AGRo for Case. One way to technically implement this idea would be to reduce it to a c-selection difference. In *talk about*, *talk* c-selects a PP instead of an AGRP containing a PP. S-selection would be the same in both cases; the difference would simply be a syntactic one. The relevant structure would be the following:

52.

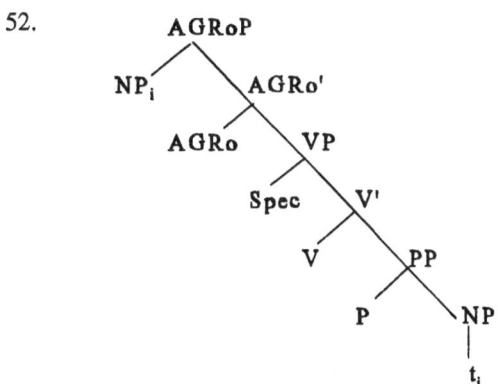

In the standard PP, as represented in (51), there is an AGRP, the specifier of which the object of P can move to at LF for Case. In (52), however, PP has been selected without an AGRP. Thus, the object of P must move elsewhere for Case. It moves to Spec,AGRo dominating VP. This derives the result that the object of P is in the higher Spec,AGRo position.

This account as well can deal with the pseudopassive facts. If the main verb is passivized, which presumably means removing its AGRo from candidacy as a Case position, the object of P will simply move to Spec,AGRs just like the object of a transitive passivized verb.

I would like to provide a bit of conceptual motivation for this type of account. As is well known, there are transitive and unaccusative verbs. What that means, according to the interpretation assumed here involving AGR for Case-assignment, is that VPs differ with respect to whether or not they have an (active) AGR projection dominating them. Transitives have an object argument and have an AGR projection for the argument to get case in. Unaccusatives have an object argument but have no AGR projection (or it is inactive), so their argument must move elsewhere for Case. I would like to suggest that the same is true of prepositions. There are prepositions with objects in PPs embedded in AGRP. These objects can get Case by moving to Spec,AGR. Then there are prepositions with objects in PPs without an (active) AGRP. These objects, like the objects of unaccusative verbs, must move elsewhere for Case, in this case to Spec,AGRo.

However, as opposed to the unaccusative/unergative split which has clear semantic correlates, the most obvious of which is the correlation between external theta role and accusative Case-assignment, the "unaccusative" prepositional phrase account seems to be simply a technical implementation to force NP movement, with no other obvious semantic correlates.

2.3.2.2.2 Suggestive Bases for a Choice

We have now discussed two basic possibilities to account for why the P in V P NP might not be able to assign Case to NP, thus motivating movement to a higher Case position. The first, reanalysis, comes in two flavors, a syntactic version resulting in a complex verbal unit at LF, and a lexical version starting out lexically as a complex verbal unit. The second possibility is that there are essentially unaccusative prepositions whose object must move to Spec,AGRo for Case because the PP does not provide it with a Case position.

We are not short of possibilities. Are there empirical bases on which we can make a choice? It turns out that there are some considerations.

There are some hints that the lexical account might be on the right track. If the reanalysis that gives us V+P is lexical, then we predict that the V+P unit might undergo lexical processes. Pseudopassive participles can be prenominal adjectival modifiers.

53. a. the slept-in bed
    b. the fought-over piece of land
    c. the talked-about TV show

The derivation of these forms would presumably be first, complex verb formation (=[$_V$sleep+in]) which can undergo adjectival passivization, the participle of which can then be used as an adjectival modifier. Also suggestive is that they can undergo lexical rules applying to adjectives, not verbs:[4]

54. the untalked-about problem

Thus, whatever process makes V+P a unit for phenomena like pseudopassive appears to be able to occur lexically. However, there is also evidence that the process can be syntactic, to which we now turn.

Only the syntactic P incorporation in (48) predicts that certain syntactic material might interfere with such a process. The lexical unit account and the unaccusative preposition account, since they do not depend on any special syntactic operations should not be blocked by syntactic material. As is well known, pseudopassive is blocked by certain adverbs:

55. a. George Washington slept frequently in this bed
    b. This bed was slept (*frequently) in t by George Washington
56. a. The Smiths and the Joneses have fought constantly over this piece of land for centuries
    b. This piece of land has been fought (*constantly) over t for centuries
57. a. We talked quietly about John after he left
    b. John was talked (*quietly) about t after he left

These facts suggest that whatever pseudopassive is, it is blocked by adverbs. Facts like these have been used to argue in favor of a syntactic derivation such as LF preposition incorporation (Baker 1988).

If P-incorporation is blocked by the adverb, then that suggests P-incorporation is the correct way to derive pseudopassives. It also tells us something about our own cases. As it turns out, adverbs do not block whatever process is allowing NP_1 in P NP_1 P NP_2 to move to a higher position to asymmetrically c-command NP_2 at LF. The following are the B&L tests applied to some of Jackendoff's examples with adverbs inserted into them:

Anaphors.

58. a. I talked quietly to John and Bill about each other
    b. I heard frequently from John and Bill about themselves

QNP-Bound Pronoun Relations.

59. a. I talked loudly to every girl about her mother
    b. I heard sometimes from every mother about her child

Wh-Movement and Weak Crossover.

60. a. Which girl did you talk quietly to about her mother?
    b. Which mom did you talk loudly about to her daughter?

Superiority.

61. a. Which girl did you talk loudly about to which boy?
    b. Which boy did you talk loudly to about which girl?

Each ... the other.

62. a. I talked quietly about each boy to the other
    b. I talked quietly to each boy about the other

Polarity any.

63. a. I talked quietly about none of the boys to any of the girls
    b. I talked loudly to none of the girls about any of the boys

Generalization: in V ADV [P NP_1] [P NP_2], NP_2 is in the domain of NP_1.

The B&L tests show that whatever the LF process is that brings NP_1 to Spec,AGRo, intervening adverbs are not a problem. If intervening adverbs block P-incorporation, as argued by Baker (1988), then P-incorporation is not what we are studying here.

"LF" Asymmetric C-Command 37

On the other hand, since we have some evidence that pseudopassive participles can be formed lexically (e.g. (53) and (54)), perhaps we should assume it to be a lexical formation. In favor of this is the lurking question of why adverbs might block P to V movement in the first place. Adverbs do not block such movement of V to e.g. I. So in general head movement is not blocked by adverbs. If, however, pseudopassive participle formation is a lexical process, insertion of an adverb between V and P would be word-internal adverb placement, which is presumably ruled out.

Borer (1991) has argued that certain morphological processes can take place either pre- or post-syntactically. Let us consider the possibility that pseudopassive is the incorporation of P into V at the pre-syntactic level while the incorporation of P into V in the cases above ((58)-(63)) is a post-syntactic process. That would account for why intervening adverbs are not possible in the former, but are acceptable in the latter.

Adopting this account of double PP complements also avoids the conceptually unappealing "unaccusative" P approach, outlined above, while being able to handle all of the facts surrounding pseudopassive participles and adverbs.

2.3.3 Summary

This section has outlined an account of double PP complement verbs which takes as its goal an explanation of why the first NP asymmetrically c-commands the second at LF. The required structure follows. The motivation for such a structure comes from mainly conceptual sources, as well as the asymmetric c-command facts pointed out by Jackendoff (1990):

64. Structure of V P NP at LF

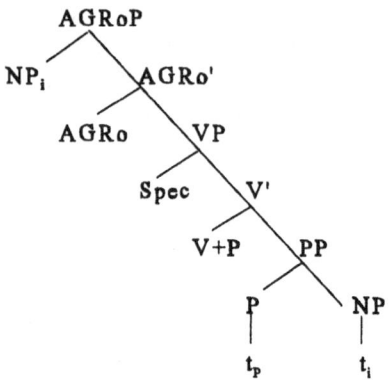

Summary: I will assume, then, that there is a syntactic process of P-incorporation the results of which include the following: the original object of P is not Case-marked in PP; this NP moves to Spec,AGRo above VP for Case; this incorporation and NP movement, however, are not part of the overt syntax.

A comment is in order. I began this thesis making the claim that all A-movement must apply before LF. Does the above account of P-incorporation and NP movement threaten this claim? It appears to do so at first. However, as we will see in chapter 7, employing the copy and delete strategy for movement allows the required syntactic process to apply before the split to PF and LF, but still to appear as if covert.

Anticipating a bit, I will outline the basic idea. Before the split to PF and LF, the object of P moves to Spec,AGRo, leaving a copy in PP. The NP chain is Case-checked and licensed with respect to the Case Filter/Visibility Condition. Still before PF and LF, the top copy of NP deletes, leaving only the PP-internal one to appear at PF. What this sort of account allows, essentially, is two types of "covert" movement: LF movement, and movement in the syntax preceding the split to PF and LF that involves deleting the top copy of NP. The result in both cases is that at PF only the downstairs copy of NP appears. As I also pointed out above, I will in fact suggest that the copy and delete pre-split "movement" is in fact the only type of A-movement available. The required derivation outlined in (64), above, fits right in with such a proposal.

"LF" Asymmetric C-Command

The remainder of this chapter will be devoted to further motivating the claim that the B&L tests are in fact tests for asymmetric c-command. Since, as Jackendoff (1990) argues, double PP complement verbs provide one of the stiffest challenges to this claim, they and the structure above will remain the focus of attention. I will show, by bringing in more data, that only asymmetric c-command and not linear precedence is what the B&L tests determine.

2.4 PRECEDENCE VS. C-COMMAND: MORE DATA

Thus far we have seen that the B&L tests show that in each of the following schemata:

65. a. V NP_1 NP_2,
    b. V NP_1 P NP_2
    c. V P NP_1 P NP_2

NP_2 is in the domain of NP_1. Larson (1988), who considers only (a) and (b), assumes that the B&L tests test for asymmetric c-command. He proposes a VP structure that then predicts that NP_1 asymmetrically c-commands NP_2 in schemata like (a) and (b). Jackendoff (1990), based in part on (c), argues that what the B&L tests show is a linear precedence restriction on the definition of domain, not asymmetric c-command.

I hope to maintain the claim that the B&L tests show asymmetric c-command. Towards that end, I proposed a plausible account of (c) which, at the level at which the B&L tests apply, has NP_1 in a position which does, in fact, asymmetrically c-command NP_2. Of course, it is not enough to stop here. I will now continue by expanding the data set, showing that there is a set of exceptions to the definition of domain if it contains linear precedence. These exceptions are predicted by the definition of domain employing asymmetric c-command.

Contreras (1984) noticed that direct objects in English create Condition C effects on phrases embedded within certain adjoined adverbials:

66. * John filed them$_i$ without reading [Mary's articles]$_i$

On the standard view, the adverbial was adjoined to VP or higher so the object, which was assumed to be in VP, was not supposed to c-command into the adverbial. (He was using this as an argument against the anti-c-command requirement for parasitic gap constructions). Adverbials of various types show this sensitivity to objects. I use both pronouns and epithets to make the point to avoid the argument that the pronoun might be in a higher position due to cliticization to the verb (Johnson 1991).

Condition C.

67. a.   I saw John$_i$ before he$_i$ left
    b.   I saw John$_i$ before the bastard$_i$ left.
    c. * I saw him$_i$ before John$_i$ left
    d. * I saw the bastard$_i$ before John$_i$ left
68. a.   I called John$_i$ without dialing his$_i$ number
    b.   I called John$_i$ without dialing the bastard$_i$'s number
    c. * I called him$_i$ without dialing John$_i$'s number
    d. * I called the bastard$_i$ without dialing John$_i$'s number
69. a.   I visited John$_i$ at his$_i$ office
    b.   I visited John$_i$ at the bastard$_i$'s office
    c. * I visited him$_i$ at John$_i$'s office
    d. * I visited the bastard$_i$ at John$_i$'s office

In fact, all the B&L tests which can be applied point to the same conclusion. The direct object has these adverbial expressions in its domain, whatever the definition of "domain" turns out to be. The B&L tests all work for these examples except for the Weak Crossover and Superiority tests, presumably because they would require movement out of an adjunct, something not permitted independently of these tests.

Condition A.

70. a.   I saw Mary and Sue in each other's yard
    b. * I saw each other in Mary and Sue's yard

71. a. ? The DA accused the defendents during each other's trial
   [Lasnik 1993]
   b. * The DA accused each other at the defendents' trial

QNP-Binding.

72. a. I saw every boy after he left
   b. * I saw him after every boy left
73. a. Gilligan visited every maternity patient while she slept
   b. * Gilligan visited her while every maternity patient slept
74. a. Marcia called each boy at his grandmother's house
   b. * Marcia called him at each boy's grandmother's house

Each ... the other.

75. a. I saw each boy after the other left
   b. * I saw the other after each boy left
76. a. I called each boy without dialing the other's number
   b. * I called the other without dialing each boy's number
77. a. I visited each child at the other's house
   b. * I visited the other at each child's house

Negative Polarity Items.

78. a. The DA accused none of the defendents during any of the trials [Lasnik 1993]
   b. * The DA accused any of the defendents during none of the trials
79. a. I saw none of the children after any of their parents left
   b. * I saw any of the children after none of their parents left
80. a. I visited none of the patients at any of the hospitals
   b. * I visited any of the patients at none of the hospitals

Generalization: in V NP_1 [$_{Adv}$ ... NP_2 ...], NP_2 is in the domain of NP_1.

These facts on their own do not help us choose between linear precedence and asymmetric c-command but they do show that whatever the B&L tests test for it is true of a direct object and material within an adjoined adverbial phrase. Linear precedence would clearly work in these cases since it is in just the cases where linear precedence fails to hold that the result is ungrammaticality. All three c-command accounts, I believe, predict this behavior as well. I assume the adverbials like *during/after/before* ... are all VP-adjoined; the *at* ... PPs are probably within VP. On my account, since direct objects are in Spec,AGRo at S-structure it comes as no surprise that they asymmetrically c-command VP-adjoined and VP-internal phrases. The same can be said of Chomsky's account. Larson (1988) assumes a rather nonstandard view of adverbial placement. He assumes that, "adverbs are not the outermost adjuncts of V but rather its innermost complements." (fn.11, p.346). Thus, I suppose these adverbial phrases would also be asymmetrically c-commanded by the direct object.

Jackendoff pointed out that when there are two PPs present, the NP in the first has the second in its domain. I accounted for this fact on the c-command analysis by proposing that at LF the first NP is in Spec,AGRo, thus asymmetrically c-commanding VP and its contents. We predict then that generally, an NP in PP can have the adjoined adverbials just discussed in its domain. This is true, as the following data show:

Condition A.

81. a. Cindy laughed at Greg and Bobby at each other's performance
　　b. * Cindy laughed at each other at Greg and Bobby's performance
82. a. ? I talked to the boys after each other admitted they were wrong
　　b. * I talked to each other after the boys admitted they were wrong

QNP-Binding.

83. a. Alice played with each boy before his mother picked him up
　　b. * Alice played with him before each boy's mother picked him up

84. a.   I struggled with each problem until it was solved
    b. ?* I struggled with it until each problem was solved
85. a.   Mike talked to every child before putting her to bed
    b. * Mike talked to her before putting every child to bed

Each ... the other.

86. a.   I laughed at each boy while the other just sat and watched
    b. * I laughed at the other while each boy just sat and watched
87. a.   Greg slept in each bed after the other got dirty
    b. * Greg slept in the other after each bed got dirty

Negative Polarity Items.

88. a. ? I talked to none of the children while putting any of them to bed
    b. * I talked to any of the children while putting none of them to bed
89. a.   I've slept in none of the beds at any of my homes
    b. * I've slept in any of the beds at none of my homes

Generalization: in V [P NP_1] [$_{Adv}$ ... NP_2 ...], NP_2 is in the domain of NP_1.

These facts simply mirror Jackendoff's facts pointed out above combined with Contreras' observation that material in an adverbial can be in the domain of a preceding noun phrase. Linear precedence would explain this straightforwardly since once again it's a preceding NP that is apparently triggering the effects found in the adverbial. And our account also predicts these facts since NP is in Spec,AGRo asymmetrically c-commanding the adjoined adverbials.

Recall that above, in discussing why P in P NP_1 might not assign Case to NP_1 I suggested but discarded the possibility that P optionally chooses not to assign Case. In fact, the movement of NP_1 to Spec,AGRo is obligatory as the following examples suggest:

90. a. ?* I slept in it after the bed was made
    b. * I slept in the fucker after the bed was made
91. a. * I talked to him before John came out of the bathroom
    b. * I talked to the bastard before John came out of the bathroom

These examples show Condition C being triggered by the object of the preposition. This can be explained on my account, which puts the object of P in Spec,AGRo at LF. However, if this were an optional movement there would be an alternative derivation in which the movement did not occur and no Condition C violation is incurred. Since the violation is quite strong, I conclude that the movement of NP to Spec,AGRo is obligatory.

We have now examined the following schemata:

92. a. V NP_1 NP_2,
    b. V NP_1 P NP_2
    c. V P NP_1 P NP_2
    d. V NP_1 [$_{ADV}$ ... NP_2 ...]
    e. V P NP_1 [$_{ADV}$ ... NP_2 ...]

In every case NP_1 has had NP_2 in its domain. These results are equally predicted by both the precedence account and the c-command account. For the precedence account they follow because in every case NP_1 precedes NP_2. For the c-command account they follow because in every case NP_1 c-commands NP_2.

As we have seen it is possible to adjoin an adverbial phrase (as in (d) and (e)) and test preceding NPs. So far all the tests have shown that any preceding NP_1 has an NP_2 embedded in the adverbial in its domain. This has been predicted by both types of accounts since the NP_1s tested have all *preceded* NP_2 (thus clearly satisfying the precedence account) and have all arguably *c-commanded* NP_2 (thus satisfying the c-command account). Consider now cases like those represented in (b) and (c), but with an adjoined adverbial:

93. a. V NP_1 P NP_2 [$_{ADV}$ ... NP_3 ...]
    b. V P NP_1 P NP_2 [$_{ADV}$ ... NP_3 ...]

Let us consider the predictions made by the two accounts. The precedence account predicts that NP_1 will have NP_2 and NP_3 in its domain. We already saw that it is true that NP_2 is in the domain of NP_1. It also predicts that NP_2 will have NP_3 in its domain since NP_2 precedes NP_3. The c-command account, which places NP_1 in Spec,AGRo, predicts something subtly different: NP_1, in Spec,AGRo, is predicted to have NP_2 and NP_3 in its domain. It does not, unlike the precedence account, predict NP_2 to have NP_3 in its domain:

94.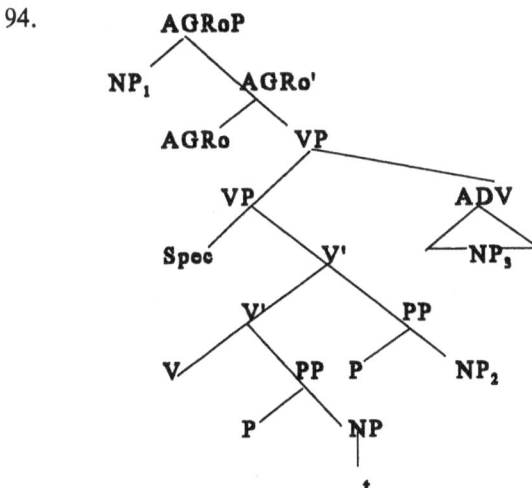

NP_2 is embedded in a PP and NP_3 is embedded in the adverbial phrase. Neither c-commands the other and no B&L effects are predicted.[5]

Let's look at the facts:

Condition A.

95. a. ?? I talked to Mary about the boys at each other's performance
    b.   I talked to the boys about Mary at each other's performance
96. a. *   I heard from Bill about John and Mary after each other's evening out
    b.   I heard from John and Mary about Bill after each other's evening out

QNP-Binding.

97. a. I talked to Mary about each boy at his mother's house
    b. I talked to each boy about Mary at his mother's house
98. a. I heard from Carol about every song after it played on the radio
    b. I heard from every mother about that song after she recognized it on the radio

Each ... the other.

99. a. * Cindy talked to Marcia about each book after reading the other
    b. Cindy talked to each boy about the book after the other red it
100. a. * Sandy heard from Lance about each date before the other called
     b. Sandy heard from each date about Lance before the other called

Negative Polarity Items.

101. a. ?* Sarah talked to Mary about none of the books instead of mingling with anyone
     b. ? Sarah talked to nobody about the party instead of mingling with anyone
102. a. ?* I heard from Sandy about none of the parties during any dinner
     b. I heard from nobody about the party during any dinner

Generalization: in V [P NP$_1$] [P NP$_2$] [$_{Adv}$ ... NP$_3$ ...], NP$_3$ is in the domain of NP$_1$, but not in the domain of NP$_2$.

The B&L tests, except for the QNP test, show quite clearly that NP$_2$ does not have NP$_3$ in its domain. This is unexpected on the precedence account. It is predicted on the c-command account since NP$_2$ does not c-command NP$_3$ as represented in (94), above.[6]

I would like to conclude, then, that the B&L tests do not test for linear precedence as the above evidence makes clear. If they test for asymmetric c-command the preceding contrasts are accounted for straightforwardly.

2.5 CONCLUSION

The B&L tests show that an object in English asymmetrically c-commands VP at LF. This is true of a "pure" object, as well as a derived one, derived by P to V incorporation at LF. This is accounted for by the present proposal: object NPs move to Spec,AGRo, a VP-external Case position. From there they asymmetrically c-command VP. These results are consistent with Larson's (1988) and Chomsky's (1991, 1993) proposal for the structure of the clause, as well as the current proposal. It is inconsistent with more "standard" views, such as the LGB view that objects are unmoved sisters of V at all levels of representation.

The next task, taken up in Chapter 3, will be to show that object movement occurs in the overt syntax. This result is contra Chomsky (1991, 1993) but still consistent with Larson (1988). Thus, Chapter 4 will discuss Larson's account in more detail.

CHAPTER 3
Constituency: the Surface Position of the Verb and the Object

3.1 INTRODUCTION

This chapter has two main goals. First, I will show that at S-structure the main verb in English is external to a constituent containing the object and other verbal material. I will argue that this shows the verb to have escaped VP in the overt syntax. I will suggest that the verb has moved to a functional head position at least above AGRoP but below the position to which the e.g. French main verb moves overtly, thus maintaining the well-known distinguishing characteristics of English vs. French verb movement. This having been determined, we can move on to the second question: the position of the object at S-structure. I will show that the object and the main verb are both external to a constituent containing the remainder of the verbal elements. I will argue that this is VP. This will lead to the conclusion that the object has moved to a VP-external position in the overt syntax of English, which I analyze as the Case position Spec,AGRo. These results are incompatible with the standard view of the structure of the clause (e.g. Chomsky 1981) as well as more recent views in which the verb and the object remain *in situ* throughout the overt syntax, moving to VP-external positions at LF (e.g. Chomksy 1991, 1993). However, the arguments I give will be consistent with both my account and that of Larson (1988). Thus, choosing between these two accounts will be left to the following chapter.

3.2 THE SURFACE POSITION OF VERBS AND OBJECTS

Recall the account I am arguing for. The direct object is in Spec,AGRo, a position external to VP, at S-structure. Given the SVO surface word order this implies that the verb itself has also escaped VP. In particular, the verb must have moved to a position above Spec,AGRo, the position of the object:

1.

```
          X
         / \
        V   AGRoP
           / \
         NPᵢ   AGRo'
              / \
           AGRo   VP
                 / \
              Spec   V'
                    / \
                   V   NP
                   |   |
                   tᵥ  tᵢ
```

I would now like to spend some time arguing for two claims made by this structure. First, that the verb is overtly external to a constituent containing the object and the VP–AGRoP. Second, that the verb and the object are both overtly external to a constituent containing other VP-material–VP itself.

I will, along the way, point out how Larson's (1988) structure makes the same predictions. Thus, this chapter will not help us choose between the alternatives, but rather just explicate and motivate them a bit more.

3.2.1 V is External to VP at S-structure

The claim that the verb has moved to a position above AGRoP predicts that there should be a constituent containing the direct object and other VP material but not a verb. This constituent would be AGRoP.

3.2.1.1 Coordination

Johnson (1991), citing Larson (1988, p. 345, n. 11), discusses the following examples:

2. a. Gary put [the book on the table] & [the lamp on the sofa]
   b. Chris ate [the meat slowly] but [the vegetables quickly]
   c. Sam talked [to Mittie yesterday] & [to Betsy the day before]

In (a) we have what looks like a constituent containing the direct object and an argument PP. (b) and (c) have a constituent containing the object and an adverbial. Independently of the question of whether the object is in VP or in Spec,AGRo, the constituent we find coordinated is clearly something like a VP without the verb. If the object were assumed to be VP-internal, along with the PP, then this looks like VP-coordination. If the object is in Spec,AGRo, and the PP in the VP, this looks like AGRoP-coordination. In either case, a coherent consituent is found only if the verb has moved out of the VP and to some higher VP-external position. My account posits the following structure:

3. Coordinated AGRoP

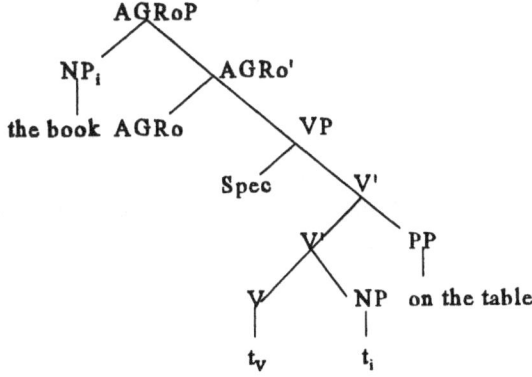

These coordinations make sense on the account assumed here. They simply involve AGRoP coordination. An account which places V in VP at S-structure will have difficulty.

Jackendoff (1990), arguing against the verb movement account, suggests that these coordination facts are really the result of gapping. There are two considerations to take into account, suggesting that these examples are in fact not examples of gapping.

Larson (1990) points out that the plausibility of the coordination account is increased by the fact that similar coordination constructions are possible due to verb movement in languages where such movement is uncontroversial. He points out that Neijt (1979) analyzes the following examples as across-the-board V2 (b-d attributed to Riny Huybregts):

4. a. Jan gaf$_V$ [Marie een appel t$_V$] én [Piet a peer t$_V$]
'John gave Mary an apple and Pete a pear.'

 b. Jan legde$_V$ [de worteltjes in de gootstee t$_V$] én [het brood op tafel t$_V$]
'John put the carrots in the sink and the bread on the table.'

 c. Jan vindt$_V$ [Felix intelligent t$_V$] én [Max vlijtig t$_V$]
'John considers/finds Felix intelligent and Max hardworking.'

 d. Jan zag$_V$ [Willem studeren t$_V$] én [Marie uitflippen t$_V$]
'John saw Bill study and Mary goof off.'

This is suggestive that this type of account should be available in principle.

Secondly, gapping requires a certain type of background-focus information structure, such that the non-gapped material is focused. This can be but is not necessarily part of the information structure of the types of coordination I have exemplified above, suggesting that they are not examples of gapping.[7]

3.2.1.2 Right Node Raising

Right Node Raising (RNR), while not very well-understood, has often been used as a constituency test. The relevant property of RNR is that it targets (right-peripheral) constituents only. There has been a class of exceptions to this generalization, discussed in Abbott (1976) and later Larson (1990), which I believe can be explained nicely if we assume the verb moves out of VP at S-structure. Consider the following examples (from Abbott 1976):

5. Smith loaned, and his widow later donated, a valuable collection of manuscripts to the library
6. I borrowed, and my sister stole, large sums of money from Chase Manhattan Bank
7. Leslie played, and Mary sang, some Country & Western songs at George's party
8. Mary baked, and George frosted, twenty cakes in less than an hour

What was difficult about these examples was that the apparently right node raised material didn't form a coherent constituent on the standard assumption that the verb remains in the VP at S-structure. However, if the verb is outside of the VP (independently of the position of the object), then the VP (or AGRoP) is the constituent which is right node raised. For concreteness I will assume the object is in Spec,AGRo but that is not crucial to the argument; what is crucial is that V has escaped VP:

9. Smith loaned [e], and his widow later donated [e], [$_{AGRoP}$ a valuable collection of manuscripts [$_{VP}$ t$_V$ t$_{NP}$ to the library]]

This class of exceptions disappears if we assume that the verb is VP-external at S-structure. On the assumption that it is VP-internal at S-structure these examples remain problematic.[8]

3.2.1.3 Stylistic Inversion

From Rochemont & Culicover (1990, p.74), and also discussed in Johnson (1991), are the following ((a) sets up the context a bit, and (b) is the example in question):

10. a. They said John would walk into the room nude, and
    b. into the room nude John walked/walked John

Rochemont & Culicover argue convincingly that the fronted constituent is indeed a VP. This suggests something like the following, which is unexpected if V does not move out of VP:

11. [$_{VP}$ t$_V$ Into the room nude] John walked t$_{VP}$

12. Fronted VP

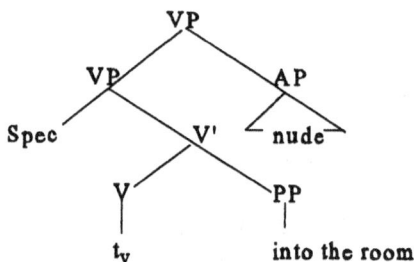

If V were in its standardly assumed VP-internal position it is not clear what would have fronted in this case. On the assumption that V is in a position external to VP, the example finds an explanation. See chapter 8 for a complete account of stylistic inversion.

3.2.1.4 The Surface Position of V

We have seen reasons to believe that the main verb escapes VP at S-structure. It is seen to move to a position at least higher than the S-structure position of the object. Where is it moving to?

Chomsky (1993) follows Emonds (1978) and Pollock (1989) in assuming that the main verb in English does not move at all in the overt syntax, while the main verb in French moves to the highest inflectional head position in the tree. One type of evidence for this claim is based on the assumption that certain adverbs are adjoined to VP. The English verb follows these adverbs while the French verb precedes them. The Chomsky-Pollock structures are roughly as follows:

13. a.   Jean embrasse souvent Marie
    b.   NP verb [$_{VP}$ ADV [$_{VP}$ t$_V$ NP]]   [French]

The Surface Position of the Verb and the Object 55

14. a. John often kisses Mary

b. NP [$_{VP}$ ADV [$_{VP}$ verb NP]]   [English]

If the adverbs in question appear in identical positions in both French and English then clearly the French verb is higher than the English one. However, that the verb in English has not moved at all only follows from the <u>assumption</u> that the adverbs in question are adjoined to VP.

Since the previous few arguments established that the English verb is indeed external to VP, I will assume that the adverbs in question are adjoined to a higher VP-external functional projection, labeled FP:

15. a. NP verb [$_{FP}$ ADV [$_{FP}$ t$_V$ [$_{AGRoP}$ NP [VP]]]]   [French]

b. NP [$_{FP}$ ADV [$_{FP}$ verb [$_{AGRoP}$ NP [VP]]]]   [English]

I leave open exactly what the label of FP is but note that it is higher than AGRoP.[9]

16.

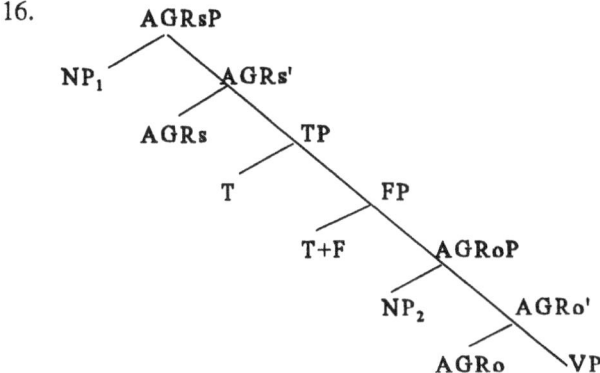

Maintaining the claim that French main verbs move all the way to AGRs at S-structure (Emonds 1978, Pollock 1989), combined with the fact that we see a surface distinction between English and French, I will claim that the English verb moves to F, the projection just above AGRoP. Instead of assuming that adverbs like *often* are adjoined to VP, I will assume they are adjoined to FP. On either account (the Chomsky/Pollock one, or the present one) an assumption needs to be made about the location of these adverbs. I suggest that the assumption that they are adjoined to FP, and that the main verb moves to F in English and to AGRs in French, is correct given the arguments made in the previous section.

The following well-known contrast is accounted for on this analysis:

17. a.   *   John kisses often Mary
    b.   John often kisses Mary

The adverb is adjoined to FP. The verb only moves to F, so (a) is out. Since F is below the adjunction site to FP, the order *often V* is found.

As for negation, I assume that a negative-headed phrase dominates FP. The following contrast is thus accounted for:

18. a.   *   John loves not Mary
    b.   John does not love Mary

The main verb does not move above F, so (a) is out. F is below NegP so the order *not V* is found, as in (b).

Putting both the adverb and the negation together, we get the following: NegP is above FP, so negation precedes the adverb; the adverb is adjoined to FP so it precedes the verb, which is in F:

19. John does not often kiss Mary

The Surface Position of the Verb and the Object 57

Consider the tree:

20. Complete Tree with Negation and Adverb

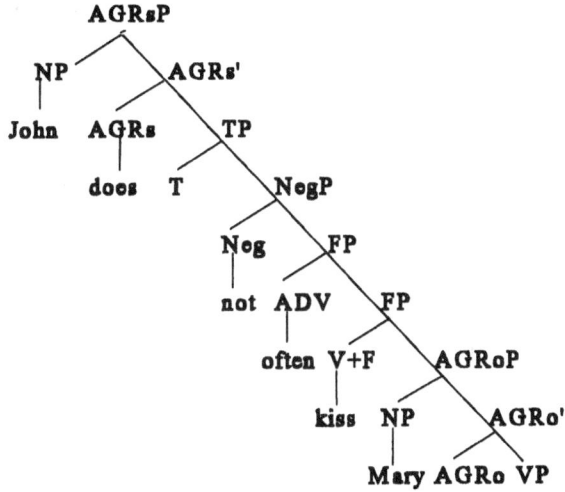

3.2.2 V and DO are external to VP at S-structure

Besides claiming the V escapes VP, my structure claims that both the verb and the object are VP-external at S-structure. Thus, constituency tests should show that VP minus V and DO is a constituent.

3.2.2.1 Coordination

The following can behave like a constituent for coordination:

21. Mary told the story [$_{VP}$ to Bill before breakfast] and [$_{VP}$ to Sam after dinner]
22. I showed the office [$_{VP}$ to the prospective students during their interviews] and [$_{VP}$ to the faculty after cleaning it up]

58   Noun Phrase Licensing

23. Ginger saw Mary Ann [vp in the park after dinner] and [vp at the dock around sunset]

Without the assumption that the verb and the object move out of VP at S-structure these examples are a bit of a surprise. On my account, these are VP-coordinations. Consider the VP on my account:

24. Coordinated VP

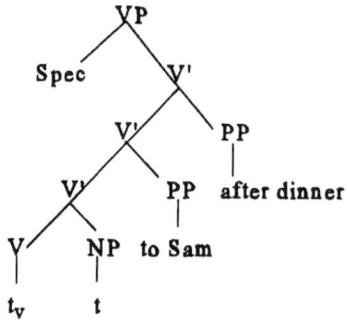

VP is a constituent containing all VP-material except the verb and the object.

3.2.2.2 Right Node Raising

If it is the case that a verb and its object are both VP-external at S-structure, we expect the whole VP (minus V and DO) to be able to undergo RNR. It should satisfy the restriction: being a right-peripheral constituent. I have constructed what I think are the relevant examples:

25. a. Mary told the story, and Sam explained the problem, to Bill after dinner
    b. [vp[vp t$_V$ t$_{NP}$ to Bill] after dinner]

26. a. I showed the office, and Mary showed the computer lab, to the prospective students during their interviews
    b [$_{VP}$[$_{VP}$ t$_V$ t$_{NP}$ to the prospective students] during their interviews]

27. a. Ginger saw Mary Ann, and Thurston saw Lovey, in the park after dinner
    b. [$_{VP}$[$_{VP}$ t$_V$ t$_{NP}$ in the park] after dinner]

The (a) examples are all grammatical RNR examples. These superficially appear to be in violation of the "constituent" restriction on the operation, if one assumes that the verb and the object are in the VP at S-structure. If that were the case no coherent constituent would be raising in these examples. However, on the current account direct object NPs and their verbs are VP-external at S-structure; left behind is a VP containing only VP-internal and VP-adjoined elements. Thus RNR affects a VP constituent as the (b) examples show.

3.3 CONCLUSION

The main verb in English moves to a position external to a constituent containing the object and other verbal material, which I analyze as AGRoP. Also, the object moves to a position external to a constituent containing the remainder of the verbal material, which I analyze as VP.

The data discussed are all consistent with Larson's (1988) "VP-shell" account, which would assign a structure like (29) to (28):

28. I wrote a letter to Mary in the morning

29.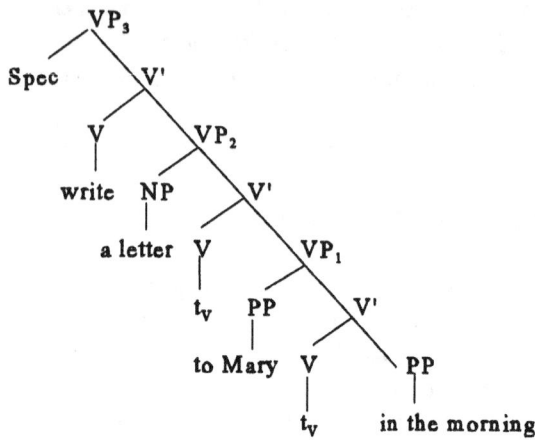

The VP-shell tree in (29) can account for the constituency tests discussed above: the constituent which the verb is external to is VP_2; the constituent which the verb and object are both external to is VP_1. The main difference is that neither the verb nor the direct object is external to a VP. While the constituent structure of (29) is identical to that of the structure I argue for, it is the labels on the nodes that differ.

To proceed, then, it will be necessary to consider evidence for the choice of node labels. The following chapter will turn to this task.

CHAPTER 4
VP-Shell or No VP-Shell: the Case of Adverb Placement

4.1 INTRODUCTION

As pointed out in the previous chapter, Larson's (1988) VP-shell account fares well with the constituency tests discussed. The choice of node labels is the biggest difference between the VP-shell account, which has several layers of VP containing the verb, the object and the other VP-material, and the current account, which divides the tree into the functional domain containing the subject, verb and object, and the verbal domain containing the remaining verbal material. I believe that the node labels are also the relevant difference between the two accounts, the difference that will help choose between them.

I will begin by showing how my account deals with adverb placement. I will argue that the adverbs in question are sensitive to the labels of the projections to which they adjoin. Only by distinguishing among the various projections can an adequate statement of adverb placement be given. Since the VP-shell account labels projections VP which my account labels as functional projections, it cannot adequately distinguish among the VPs, which turns out to be necessary.

I then turn to several alternative accounts of adverb placement which assume no overt V movement. Besides the constituency problems they face, I argue that no coherent account of adverb placement is available to them, either.

Finally, I turn to Larson's own (1988) proposal for adverb projection. His account projects adverbs as the innermost complements of V. By the rules of V' Reanalysis and Light Predicate Raising he is able to derive variations on the underlying basic structures. I examine these rules in detail, showing that Larson's formulation of them will not cover all the relevant cases, and that the necessary reformulations suggest a generalization is missing. I argue that the problem is that the VP-shell account labels too many projections as VP, wrongly masking important functional differences among them. Once the labels are changed, as in the present proposal, Larson's account of adverb projection is workable.

4.2 ADVERB PLACEMENT

4.2.1 Adverb Placement and Functional Projections

We will begin by examining the placement of Jackendoff's (1972) Class II adverbs (*quickly, slowly, quietly, frequently*, etc.) according to the structure I am arguing for, repeated here:

1.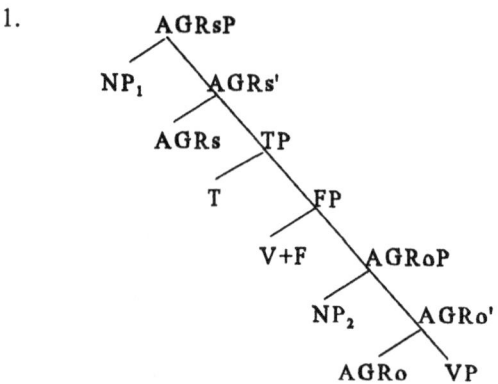

Assuming my structure in (1), these adverbs are highly constrained in the functional area of the tree, but are freely distributed within the VP area of the tree. Let us begin by examining the functional part of the tree. Consider the following examples (adapted from Johnson 1991):

2. a. (Quietly) Mikey (*quietly) has (*quietly) not (?quietly) been (quietly) visiting (*quietly) his parents (quietly)
   b. (Loudly) Betsy (*loudly) has (*loudly) not (?loudly) been (loudly) singing (*loudly) the anthem (loudly)
   c. (Quickly) Chris (*quickly) has (*quickly) not (?quickly) been (quickly) hitting (*quickly) the dog (quickly)

The distribution of Class II adverbs can be described as follows:

3. Adjunction status (with reference to example (2a)):

- AGRsP = okay (before *Mikey*)
- AGRs' = * (before *has*)
- NegP = * (before *not*)
- TP = ? (before *been*)
- FP = okay (before *visiting*)
- AGRoP = * (before *his parents*)

The point of these examples is that in the functional area of the tree Class II adverb placement is highly constrained. Reference to particular functional heads/projections seems necessary to adequately constrain adverb distribution.[10]

Consider VP-internal adverb placement; Class II adverbs freely mingle with VP-internal elements:

4. Sam talked (quietly) to Carol (quietly) about Oliver (quietly)

Thus, on an account incorporating (1), which distinguishes VP from other functional projections, it is possible to state the distribution of the Class II adverbs. In fact it seems necessary to be able to refer to individual functional projections in such a statement.

4.2.2 Adverb Placement and Larson's (1988) VP-Shell Account

I will focus on one crucial example to make my point. Double complement verbs, either those taking NP PP or PP PP, require two VPs according to the VP-shell account. Let us take the following examples as illustrative:

5. a. Sam talked to Carol about Oliver
   b. Cindy showed the book to Jan

The tree for (5) would be the following:

6. Double Complement Verb

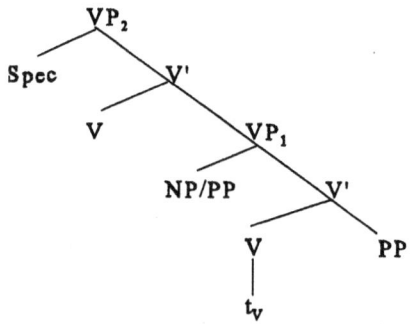

Now consider (7):

7. a. Sam talked quietly to Carol about Oliver
   b. *Cindy showed quietly the book to Jan

On the current account, *quietly* in (a) is acceptable because it appears in VP; however, it is unacceptable in (b) because, as noted above, this adverb cannot adjoin to AGRoP.[11]

Now let us consider adverb placement in the VP-shell structure:

VP Shell or No VP Shell: Adverb Placement

8. Double Complement with Interpolated Adverb

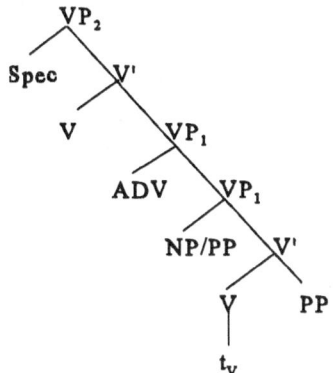

The generalization according to the VP-shell account seems to be that the adverb: (a) must not adjoin to VP_1 if the first complement is NP; but (b) may adjoin to VP_1 if the first complement is PP. Short of invoking Case-adjacency, which is a now dubious solution (and see below for more discussion), it is not clear what the generalization really is.

The present analysis, which removes the object from VP and places it in a Case position external to VP, can account for the freedom of adverb placement within VP, while also being able to stipulate which functional projections it can and cannot be adjoined to. Without labeling the functional projections differently from VP labels it is difficult to state the adverb restrictions.

4.3 ALTERNATIVES

Several conceivable alternative accounts which do not involve V or object movement can be suggested immediately. I will spend a moment dispensing with them. I turn to these now.

4.3.1 Adjacency for Case Assignment

Stowell (1981) proposes that the reason no adverb can intervene between the verb and its object is that the verb must be adjacent to the object in order to assign it Case. The problems for this proposal have been documented in the literature so I will just point out two, and add a third.

First, Johnson (1991) points out that the claim that adverbs block Case-assignment is directly disconfirmed by the facts surrounding nominative Case-assignment. Whether one believes that Comp assigns nominative Case (see (9)), or that INFL does so (see (10)), an intervening adverb appears to have no effect on it:

9. a. I knew that probably Gary had left
   b. I wonder whether in fact Gary left
10. a. Gary probably has left
    b. Gary in fact will leave

If Case-adjacency is used to derive the ban on V-ADV-NP order then it needs to be stipulated that it only holds of accusative Case-assignment. As such it is a mere stipulation whose only effect is to rule out an adverb in one position. (Recall that the same adverb will have to be banned from other positions so a statement of its distribution is independently needed.)

Second, Case-adjacency appears not to hold of every language. So, for example, it is well known that French allows an adverb to intervene between the main verb and its object (Emonds 1978, Pollock 1989):

11. Jean embrasse souvent Marie
    'John kisses often Mary.'

Thus, if Case-adjacency is invoked to rule out such an order in English, it must be invoked as a stipulation for English.

Third, if accusative Case is not in fact assigned under government by the verb, as proposed in Chomsky (1991, 1993) and defended here, then Case-adjacency makes no sense. It should not matter if at S-structure the verb and the object are separated by an adverb, since the verb will have checked the object's accusative Case feature in a Spec-head relation in the AGRo projection, at which point the adverb's presence should be irrelevant.

4.3.2 PP/CP Extraposition

Johnson (1991) argues against another alternative account for the following paradigm:

12. a. * Mikey visited quietly his parents
    b. * Betsy sung loudly the anthem
    c. * Chris hit quickly the dog
13. a. Chris walked quickly down the street
    b. Mikey talked slowly to Gary
    c. Betsy spoke loudly with everyone
    d. Sam said suddenly that we must all leave
    e. Gary tried diligently to leave

The alternative would claim that the ungrammatical examples are out because of a violation of the Projection Principle, which requires complements to be sisters to verbs (Chomsky 1981, p.38 and Jackendoff 1977, pp.55-72). This alternative would assume the verb and object to be in VP at S-structure; what you see is what you get. (Note, of course, that this has the now familiar problem of dealing with the constituency tests discussed above.) Thus (12) would be ruled out by the Projection Principle since the adverb has been generated as sister to V. The question, then, would be, why are the examples in (13) acceptable?

A possible claim would be that the PP/CP complements of V have undergone some sort of rightward movement, or extraposition. Johnson offers the possible tree (simplified for the present discussion):

14. Projection Principle Alternative

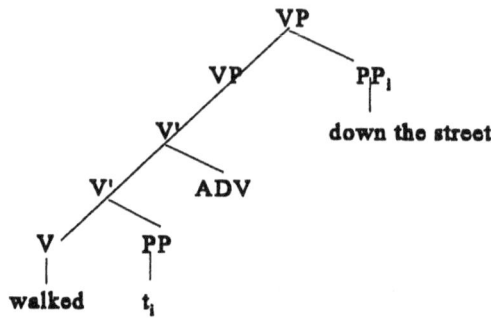

Johnson then provides several arguments against such an approach, which I will just reiterate here.

First, one wonders why whatever the operation is, it is unavailable for the objects in (12). The operation is apparently sensitive to the NP/non-NP distinction.

Second, if such a process is generally possible for non-NPs, why is there a contrast in the following examples? (Johnson 1991, p.581):

15. a.   Mittie went with it to her quickly
    b. ?* Mittie went with it quickly to her
16. a.   Gary said to her to leave
    b. ?* Gary said to leave to her
17. a.   Sam talked about it to her calmly
    b. ?* Sam talked about it calmly to her

Johnson also points out that should the PP be heavy enough such rightward movement becomes acceptable. Heaviness is not a factor in examples like (13).

Third, the rightward movement account has trouble with examples like the following (Johnson 1991, p.582):

18. a.   Sam Spoke loudly to everyone in falsetto
    b.   Betsy walked quickly down the street naked

Assuming that *in falsetto* is adjoined to V' (as in Jackendoff 1977, sec.4.3) and that adjunction of a maximal projection is to a maximal projection, we end up with no explanation for where e.g. *to everyone* might have moved to. Since *in falsetto* is at the V' level, and the PP is a maximal projection, it should move to adjoin to VP, outside of the V'-adjoined phrase.

Johnson (1991) presents three further arguments against the hypothesis that the PP/CP arguments have moved rightward in (13). It seems highly unlikely that such a proposal will be successful.

4.4 V' REANALYSIS AND LIGHT PREDICATE RAISING

Larson (1988) makes a strong and interesting claim about the projection of verbal material. Projection follows a thematic hierarchy. Adverbial expressions are projected as the innermost arguments of the verb, while goal, theme and agent are respectively the three outermost arguments. He gives an example of a VP containing a theme, goal and adverbial (Larson 1988, p. 346, fn. 11):

19. I wrote a letter to Mary in the morning

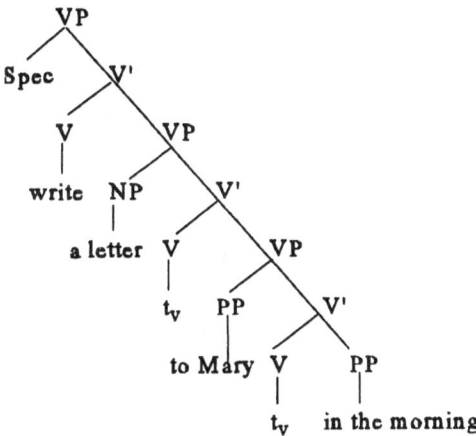

The default S-structure, then, will have all the arguments in decreasing order on some thematic hierarchy, with adverbial expressions at the end.

According to Larson's account there are two ways in which this thematic ordering can be interrupted. First, Case requirements on NP can force it to move from its base position to a higher position. This is standard in the case of the subject argument, but without reordering the arguments. This device is also used as part of his derivation of the dative "shifted" VP: a thematically lower (the goal) NP moves to a higher Spec,VP position for Case. The resulting order of complements is then goal > theme, as opposed to the basic, reversed order. The double object construction will be discussed in detail in the following chapter.

The second way for the complements to get reordered is through Larson's rule of V' Reanalysis and "Light Predicate Raising" (henceforth, V'R and LPR, respectively). What this rule does is reanalyze a V' as a V and then head-move the former V' (and its contents) to a higher head position. The result is a VP in which a basically lower thematic element ends up preceding a higher one. This device is found in Larson's treatment of Heavy NP Shift.

Let us examine this process a bit more carefully. Larson proposes to account for sentences like (20) with the optional rule of V'R (Larson 1988, p. 347-348):

20. a. I gave to John everything that he demanded
    b. Max sent to me the longest letter anyone had ever seen

21. **V' Reanalysis**: Let α be a phrase $[_{V'} \ldots]$ whose θ-grid contains one undischarged internal θ-role. Then α may be reanalyzed as $[_V \ldots]$.

What this rule does is take a V' containing a verb and everything up to but not including the highest internal argument and reanalyzes it as a V. Then, once it is a V it can head-move to the next highest V, carrying along with it the material in the former V'.

VP Shell or No VP Shell: Adverb Placement

Here is an example (Larson 1988, p. 348):

22. Light Predicate Raising

a. Before Reanalysis:

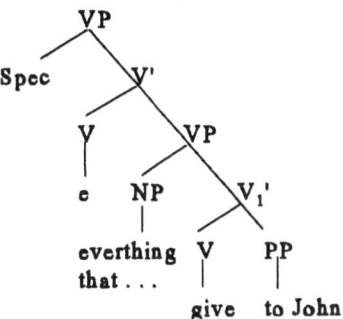

b. After Reanalysis and V movement:

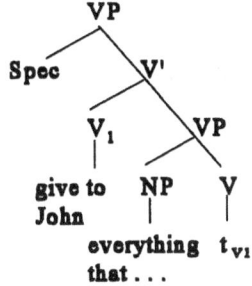

The phrase marked V_1' in (a) is a V' containing one undischarged internal θ-role, that of the theme (the "heavy" NP). According to the Reanalysis rule, V_1' can reanalyze as a V. It does so, and then, like a typical V, moves to the upper V position, carrying along with it the PP *to John* to the position in (b) marked V_1. In this way Larson accounts for "Heavy NP Shift" without actually shifting any NPs. He instead moves the light predicate forward over the heavy NP.

He calls this rule "optional" without specifying very carefully when it can and cannot apply. For one thing, we do not want it to apply when the theme is *not* heavy:

23. * I [[_V gave to John] the book t_V]

The rule, then, is clearly not optional. It just applies under some yet-to-be-determined circumstances. Assuming that the rule's application can be specified, let us continue.

What we will be exploring now is Larson's treatment of adverbs and the question of how his account is to generate them in all and only the correct positions. Let us begin with the simplest examples (adapted from Johnson 1991):

24. a. Mikey visited his parents quietly
    b. Betsy sung the anthem loudly
    c. Chris hit the dog quickly
25. a. Chris walked down the street quickly
    b. Mikey talked to Gary slowly
    c. Betsy spoke with everyone loudly

In (24) we have examples of transitive sentences with one adverb after the object. In (25) we have intransitive sentences with an argument PP followed by an adverb. Larson's account handles these straightforwardly. In fact, these are the predicted default cases:

26. Mikey visited his parents quietly

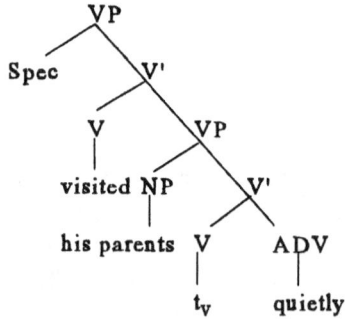

Since the projection of complements begins from the lowest role, the adverb *quietly* is projected as the innermost complement of V. In case there is any doubt that adverbs are meant to undergo this type of

VP Shell or No VP Shell: Adverb Placement

projection, I quote from Larson (1988), "Under the semantic analysis of adverbs assumed here (essentially that of McConnell-Ginet 1982), adverbs are not the outermost adjuncts of V but rather its innermost complements." (p. 346, fn. 11).

Next, the theme *his mother* is projected (and ultimately the external argument, which I ignore throughout). The verb moves from its base position to the higher V position by S-structure deriving the observed order.

Let us consider some examples in which the default order is no longer observed and one of the devices for interfering with the basic order must be invoked:

27. a. Chris walked quickly down the street
    b. Mikey talked slowly to Gary
    c. Betsy spoke loudly with everyone
    d. Sam said suddenly that we must all leave
    e. Gary tried diligently to leave

In these examples we find the adverb interpolated with the PP and CP complements of the verbs in question. Since we already know from the above discussion that the base form for e.g. (a) is:

28. Chris walked down the street quickly

we need to somehow arrive at the surface order of (a). Recall the two possibilities for interfering with the basic order: NP movement to a higher position for Case (as in the double object construction) and LPR. Since the examples in question do not contain NPs in search of Case, the former device is probably not where we should look. Let us consider a LPR account of these examples.

LPR follows V'R, which is possible just in case we come upon a V' whose θ-grid contains one undischarged internal θ-role; the V' can then be reanalyzed as V. As I pointed out above it is not optional; it can only apply under certain circumstances. Is this one of those circumstances? Consider the base structure of (a):

29. Chris walked quickly down the street [Base Structure]

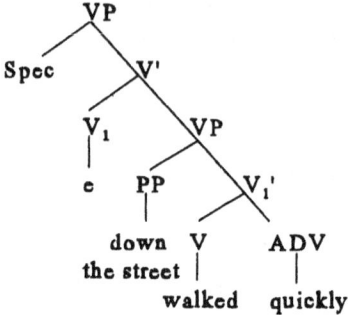

If we allow V_1' to undergo V'R, followed by LPR to the position of V_1, we can derive the observed surface order. Note that to do so we must interpret the role born by the PP *down the street* to be the "one undischarged internal θ-role". So, after V'R and LPR we get the following:

30. Chris walked quickly down the street [S-structure]

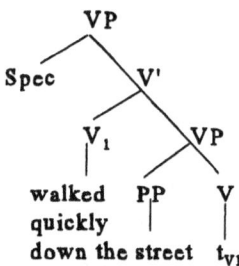

V'R followed by LPR, then, seems to be a reasonable way to account for variations in VP complement order.

One thing that should be pointed out is, that to make this example work we needed to allow V'R and LPR to apply. In this particular case the conditions were different from the case of heavy NP shift. Here the phrase the light predicate raises over is not terribly heavy: *down the street*. And reexamining the examples in (27), we see some in which the phrase is even "lighter", for example *to Gary* in (b) and *with everyone* in (c). Thus, we seem to have identified two types of environment in which V'R may

VP Shell or No VP Shell: Adverb Placement

apply: when the one undischarged θ-role is born by a heavy noun phrase, or by a PP (or CP–which might or might not be considered heavy).

One comment on "heaviness" is in order. Larson (1990) proposes to derive (b) from (a) by V'R and LPR (p. 607):

31. a. John talked to Mary about Bill
    b. John talked about Bill to Mary

The derivation of (b) would be the following:

32. a. John e to Mary [talked about Bill]
    b. John [talked about Bill] to Mary

Larson claims to find a "heaviness effect present . . . in the form of relatively greater stress borne by *Mary* in [(b)] than by *Bill* in [(a)]" p. 607. He finds a contrast in pronoun reduction in the following examples, suggesting the heaviness of the *to NP* phrase:

33. a. John talked to Mary about him\'m
    b. John talked about Mary to him*'m

First, I would have to say that I can get the pronoun reduction on both examples without any problem. Second, the examples that I just showed to involve LPR with the adverb also do not show any pronoun reduction problems, at least to my ear:

34. a. Mikey talked slowly to'm
       (cf. Mikey talked to'm slowly)
    b. Betsy spoke loudly with'm
       (cf. Betsy spoke with'm loudly)

Later in the article, however, while countering one of Jackendoff's (1990) comments, Larson (1990) suggests that maybe the PPs in examples like these bear unordered θ-roles. Then, he points out, (a) and (b) in (31) would be freely generated alternative structures. If this is the route he ends up taking, it is not clear what is to become of his observation about the "heaviness" of the (b) example. He apparently does not consider it so heavy that he is not willing to entertain an alternative analysis not involving LPR, and thus no "heaviness" requirement.

Notice that the "unordered θ-role" idea cannot extend to the adverb cases in (34). To derive the two alternants of (34) that way would be to assume that the PP and the adverb have roles that are unordered on the thematic hierarchy, a dubious assumption since the PP behaves much more like a real argument than the adverb.

The reason Larson is intent on drawing out the heaviness character of such examples is that he, I believe, wants the heaviness of a phrase to be what ultimately licenses LPR. I think that the wide range of examples already discussed (along with those in Larson 1990, above) suggest that heaviness is not a necessary condition for LPR.

If the full range of adverbs are to be accounted for under Larson's assumptions about projection, reanalysis and raising, it needs to be admitted that the processes of reanalysis and raising are not sensitive to heaviness alone.

To continue, then, things get more interesting when we consider examples with more complements:

35. a. Greg explained the problem slowly to Marcia
    b. Cindy put her books carefully into her backpack
    c. Bobby gave the towels lovingly to Jan

These verbs each have two internal arguments, an NP and a PP. Thus, the base structure will have the adverb at the end:

36. Bobby e_2 the towels e_1 to Jan [gave lovingly]

What we need, then, is for the adverb to get raised with the verb to a position preceding *Jan*, e_1:

37. Bobby e_2 the towels [gave lovingly] to Jan

This move, followed by head movement of the verb to e_2 will give us the correct surface order:

38. Bobby gave the towels lovingly to Jan

VP Shell or No VP Shell: Adverb Placement

However, though this derivation gets us the result we want, it's not allowed because of the formulation of V′R. V′R is only possible if the θ-grid of the V′ contains *one* undischarged internal θ-role. Consider the V′ in question: [gave lovingly] is a V′ containing the verb *give*, which contains *two* undischarged θ-roles: goal (*to Jan*) and theme (*the towels*). Intuitively, this is the operation we want, but the formulation of the rule will not allow it.

In fact, V′R must be loosened up a bit if we want to capture the following clear case of "Heavy NP Shift":

39. I explained to John carefully the hardest problem either of us had ever encountered

The base structure has the adverb at the end after the verb:

40. I e_2 to John e_1 [the hardest problem . . .] [explained carefully]

If we want this case of heavy NP shift to be accounted for by V′R and LPR, we need to allow V′R to apply even when there is more than one undischarged internal θ-role. At the point of reanalysis in this example, *explained* still has both of its internal roles undischarged. Allowing V′R in this case would allow the V′ [explained carefully] to raise to the position of e_1, followed by movement of the verb alone to the position of e_2, deriving the correct surface order.

We should consider reformulating V′R. Given the above facts, let us state it this way:

41. **V′ Reanalysis** (Revised): Let α be a phrase $[_{V'} \ldots]$ whose θ-grid contains one or more undischarged internal θ-roles. Then α may be reanalyzed as $[_V \ldots]$.

Why restrict V′R to θ-grids with at least one undischarged θ-role? Larson (1988) argued that the original formulation, which mentioned one and only one undischarged role, was meant to rule out a particular case of V′R in which the V′ contained *no* undischarged roles.

Larson wanted V'R not to apply to the V' containing the second object and the trace of the first in the double object construction. Consider the following examples (Larson 1988, p. 354):

42. a. * John sent a letter [every musician in the orchestra]
    b. * Max gave a book about roses [the tall man in the garden]
    c. * Mary promised to win [some spectator in the grandstands]

What appears to have happened here is that LPR has moved the V' containing the verb and the theme over the heavy goal. Here is Larson's tree (p. 355)

43.

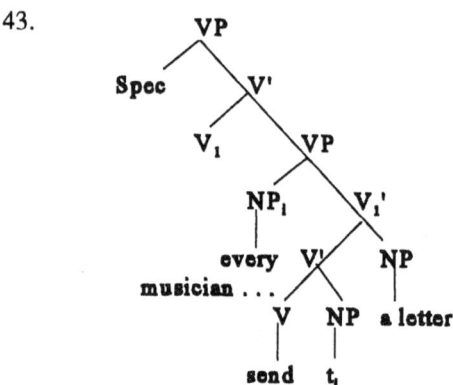

If V'R were not restricted to applying to V's with *at least* one undischarged θ-role it would be predicted that the V' marked V_1' could be reanalyzed as a V, followed by LPR to the V position marked by V_1. Such a reanalysis plus verb movement would result in the unattested examples in (42) above.

This formulation then seems to be a way of excluding (42). Unfortunately, we will now turn to examples which suggest that the current formulation of V'R is still inadequate and that the θ-grid phrase has to be removed altogether. At that point (42) and its structure will have to be reevaluated.

Larson (1990), in defense of his claim that "adjuncts" are the innermost complements to V, gives the following example (p. 624):

VP Shell or No VP Shell: Adverb Placement

44. John buttered the toast carefully, in the bathroom, at midnight, because he didn't want to awaken his wife

Then he states, "this order seems to track rather closely the criteria that philosophers have suggested for individuating events, where the causes and effects of events are preeminent, followed, in descending order, by their time of occurrence, their place of occurrence, their manner of execution, and their participants (see Davidson (1967) for discussion). Under this view, complements would thus be positioned with respect to V at D-structure in a way that mirrors their relative prominence in event individuation" (p. 624).

I point this out because what that ends up meaning to syntacticians is that if the S-structure order differs from the D-structure order (as described above), it must have undergone some process to reorder it. Consider (44) again. While it is perhaps the most natural ordering of complements, it is by no means the only S-structure order possible. A number of alternatives are available with varying degrees of naturalness:

45. a. John buttered the toast carefully, at midnight, in the bathroom, because he didn't want to awaken his wife
    b. John buttered the toast at midnight, carefully, in the bathroom, because he didn't want to awaken his wife
    c. John buttered the toast at midnight, in the bathroom, carefully, because he didn't want to awaken his wife
    d. John buttered the toast in the bathroom, carefully, at midnight, because he didn't want to awaken his wife
    etc.

As we know from above, this is not a problem for Larson because he has a mechanism for rearranging the internal structure of VP: V'R plus LPR. Assuming (44) to be the base order, as Larson suggests, I believe each of these reorderings can be derived by taking different V's and reanalyzing them and moving them to higher verb positions. And since there is always that one internal θ-role, the one for *the toast*, still undischarged, the process applies without violating the V'R rule as formulated above.

The problem arises when you have a sentence like (44) with one minimal difference: the verb is intransitive and has no internal θ-role. According to Larson, V'R should be blocked and the VP should essentially be "frozen" as is. I have constructed what I think is the relevant example:

46. I laughed loudly, at the party, for ten minutes, because of the crazy joke Bill told

In this example the verb never bears an internal θ-role. Therefore it should never appear in a V' with one undischarged role. Thus, V'R will be blocked and this order should be the only order of complements. This is, of course, not the case as the following manipulations show:

47. a. I laughed loudly, for ten minutes, at the party, because of the crazy joke Bill told
    b. I laughed for ten minutes, at the party, loudly, because of the crazy joke Bill told
    c. I laughed for ten minutes, loudly, at the party, because of the crazy joke Bill told
    d. I laughed at the party, loudly, for ten minutes, because of the crazy joke Bill told
    e. I laughed at the party, for ten minutes, loudly, because of the crazy joke Bill told

This type of example shows us two things. First, except for the last clause, *because of the crazy joke Bill told*, the various reorderings attested do not appear to be sensitive to the heaviness of the phrase(s) moved over. This mirrors what we found above with other adverb complement reorderings. Second, V'R has to be reformulated to be able to apply even if the verb had no undischarged internal role.

48. **V' Reanalysis** (Second Revision): Let α be a phrase $[_{V'} \ldots]$. Then α may be reanalyzed as $[_V \ldots]$.

Essentially this is a context free rule reanalyzing V's as Vs.

This formulation of V'R is needed because of the relative freedom of ordering of adverbial expressions in English. If adverbial expressions are to be treated as proposed in Larson (1988, 1990), it seems that the version of V'R stated above is the only one general enough to get the facts.

VP Shell or No VP Shell: Adverb Placement

To understand what must constrain it we must look more carefully at when it does not appear to apply. Leaving aside Larson's problematic double object cases, let us reconsider the restrictions. Recall that V'R feeds LPR. And the combination appears to apply in a wide range of circumstances:

49. [V + PP] over "heavy" NP:
    I gave to John everything that he demanded
50. [V + ADV] over PP:
    Chris walked quickly down the street
51. [V + PP] over PP:
    John talked about Bill to Mary
52. [V + PP] over ADV:
    John buttered the toast, in the bathroom, carefully

The one basic type of complement that can never be moved over is a "light" NP:

53. a. [V + PP] over NP:
    * I gave to John the gift
    b. [V + ADV] over NP:
    * Mikey visited quietly his parents

We have seen many different types of V'R and LPR, but the one thing that is definitely out is movement over an NP.

We might ask whether this restriction is a restriction on the V'R itself or a restriction on the verb movement. As it turns out, there is evidence that this restriction holds of the verb movement. Consider the following examples. (b) is derived from (a):

54. a. Bill e_2 to Mary e_1 about Jan [talks frequently]
    b. Bill [talks frequently] to Mary t_V about Jan t_V

The V' containing [talks frequently] reanalyzes as a V. It is then able to move to e_1 and then on to e_2 deriving the correct order in (b). This example is just to show that it is possible to have V'R, followed by two separate applications of LPR. The first is to e_1, the second to e_2. That this is in fact the correct derivation is suggested by the following example, in which the adverb remains in the position of e_1:

55. Bill talks to Mary [t_V frequently] about Jan t_V

Now consider the following pair:

56. a.   Bill told Mary quietly about Jan
    b. * Bill told quietly Mary about Jan

The derivation of (a) is as follows:

57. a.   Bill e_2 Mary e_1 about Jan told quietly
    b.   Bill told Mary [t_V quietly] about Jan t_V

(56a) is derived by first applying V′R to [told quietly], followed by LPR to e_1. This is exactly the same as the derivation of (55), and the first step of the derivation of (54), above.

Now consider the derivation of the ungrammatical (56b). (56b) is derived by allowing one more application of LPR, exactly analogous to the second step of the derivation of (54):

58. *   Bill [told quietly] Mary t_V about Jan t_V

The only difference between this ungrammatical derivation and the grammatical derivation of (54), above, is the type of element being raised "over"; here it is an NP.

The derivation of (56a) shows us that V′R is quite content to apply whether or not there is an NP in the inevitable path of LPR. What apparently is sensitive to the NP is the rule of LPR itself.

Let us now attempt to state, at least in descriptive terms, the relevant restrictions. First, V′R essentially just reanalyzes any V′ as V. Second, LPR moves a V which was originally a V′ to the next highest V position, unless there is a "light" NP intervening.

This is a bizarre-sounding rule. And as far as I can determine all the parts are needed: it is necessary to state the fact that the verb in question was once a V′, since we see normal verbal head-movement over NPs of

VP Shell or No VP Shell: Adverb Placement 83

all types. However, the most unusual stipulation of the rule is that it can only apply if there is no "light" NP intervening. We cannot just say NP because heavy NPs do not block it. We cannot just say "light" phrase, since we have seen that lots of phrases, many not obviously heavy, can be raised over.

Suppose we conceptualize the "former V'" restriction as the following: a V node dominating lexical material other than V. One characteristic of a verb that is a former V' is that it contains lexical material other than V. Now we can state LPR:

59. **Light Predicate Raising**: If α is of the form $[_V \ldots \beta \ldots]$, where β is lexical and $\beta \neq V$, α cannot move over a "light" NP.

Since move α is a free rule in the grammar, and Vs must move independently, it can be assumed to be able to apply for free. Thus, LPR needs only to state when it cannot apply, because otherwise it is simply standard V movement.

As simplified as the statement of LPR now is, I suggest it is simply missing a generalization. It would be a completely general rule if it did not have to be restricted from moving a V over an NP. So, what it comes down to is an unexplained categorial distinction.

What makes NPs different from other phrases? One obvious answer is that they typically appear in Case positions. Other phrases, PPs, CPs, adverbs, even "heavy" NPs, do not appear (obligatorily) in Case positions. Suppose that the reason the LPR cannot move over a light NP is that the NP is no longer in the path of LPR.

Suppose, as an embellishment of Larson's account, that every NP object, not just those in the double-object construction, moves to a higher position for Case. Suppose, further, that LPR can only apply within a certain domain of VP, the domain containing PPs, CPs, adverbs, etc,:

60. Bill told Mary quietly about Jan

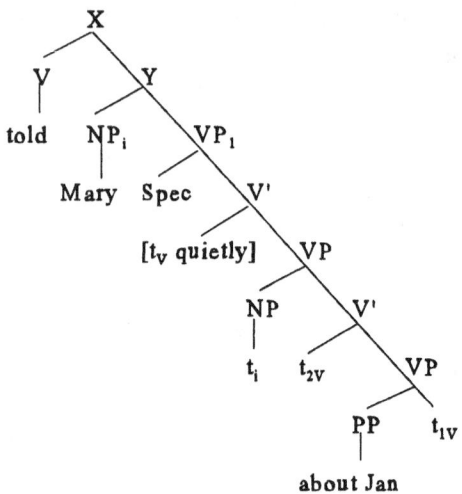

Here is the derivation: the V' [told quietly], originally in the position marked t_{1v}, is reanalyzed as a V. It moves through the position marked t_{2v} and on up to the next V. The object is generated in the position marked t_i but needs to move to a higher position for Case, the specifier of Y. The verb itself moves up to a higher head position under X, leaving the adverb in VP_1.

This alternative to Larson's proposal raises a couple of questions. First, what are the labels X and Y? Second, why can't the light predicate including the adverb also move to X, like the main verb? What determines the point above which a light predicate is no longer welcome? I.e., what makes VP_1 special?

Assuming that a reasonable definition of VP_1 can be given (one that comes to mind is Complete Functional Complex (CFC, Chomsky 1986b), essentially the domain in which a head's θ-roles are all discharged) this proposal removes the possibility of a direct object and LPR from interacting, thus allowing a more general statement of the rule:

61. **Light Predicate Raising** (Revised): If α is of the form $[_V \ldots \beta \ldots]$, where β is lexical and β ≠ V, α is within its CFC.

VP Shell or No VP Shell: Adverb Placement

What this leaves us with is a version of Larson's (1988) VP proposal the "top" part of which is functionally different from the bottom part. The top part (X and Y) contains the position to which only the inflected V can move (not a reanalyzed V'), and to which an NP moves for Case. The bottom part (VP_1) is the domain in which θ-roles are assigned.

For Larson's account of adverb placement, using V' R and LPR, to work, it is necessary to divide the tree into two functionally different domains. This is precisely what my account does. The verb moves to a functional head position (F); and the object moves to a functional specifier position for Case, Spec,AGRo. The VP itself is the lexical domain in which θ-roles are assigned. Consider (62), which represents Larson's adverb analysis embedded within my tree structure:

62. Bill told Mary quietly about Jan

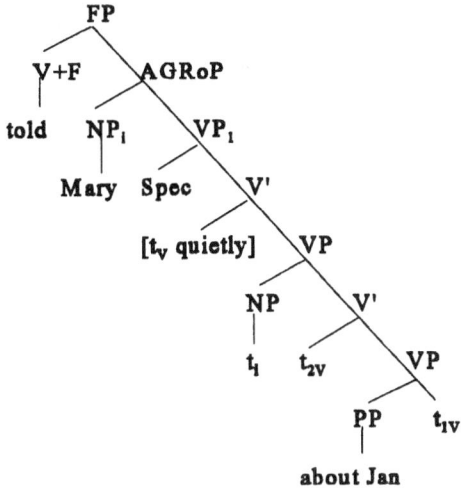

The main difference between this structure and the one I propose is the treatment of VP-internal adverbials. I argued above that they are simply VP/V'-adjoined. I do not assume Larson's view of projecting them from a lower VP-internal position. However, as we have seen, it is possible to maintain such a view of adverbial projection, just in case a tree structure along the lines of (62) is adopted.

I would like to conclude that Larson's account of adverb placement requires him to distinguish functionally the different VP-shells in his structure. By calling them all VP, important differences among them are incorrectly masked.

4.5 CONCLUSION

The previous chapter established a constituent structure that my proposal as well as the VP-shell account of Larson (1988) were consistent with. Exploiting the main difference between the present account and the VP-shell account, that the object resides in the specifier of a projection that is not VP, I showed in this chapter that whether adverbs are placed in a tree by adjoining to projections, as is standard, or are projected in one position and moved around via V' Reanalysis and Light Predicate Raising, it is necessary to distinguish functionally the type of position the object sits in from the type of position other VP elements sit in. The present account does this, while the VP-shell account does not.

CHAPTER 5
ECM as Raising to Object AGR

5.1 INTRODUCTION

The goal of the previous three chapters was to show that in English simple transitive sentences, the direct object has overtly moved from its base VP-internal position to a VP-external Case position: Spec,AGRo. That was then the first step towards showing that objects generally move for Case, analogously to subjects.

This chapter and the next discuss two other types of "object" construction: the ECM construction and the double object construction. The subject of this chapter, ECM, "exceptional Case-marking", refers to the *LGB*-style account of what had once been called "raising to object". The phenomenon involves the subject of an embedded infinitive which in many ways behaves like the object of the matrix clause, and in others behaves like an embedded subject. I will argue that underlyingly it is the subject of the embedded infinitive but it overtly moves to Spec,AGRo, the accusative Case-position external to the matrix VP.

5.2 EXCEPTIONAL CASE MARKING, A.K.A. RAISING TO OBJECT

5.2.1 Introduction

Rosenbaum (1967) argues that in the following example, *John*, the logical subject of the embedded verb *convinced*, has raised to object position of the verb *believe*:

1. I believe John to have convinced Bill

Initial plausibility for this proposal is that if *John* is in pronoun form, accusative, not nominative, is found:

2. I believe him/*he to have convinced Bill

Also, subsequent raising to subject by passive is possible for *John*:

3. John is believed (by me) to have convinced Bill

Further support is lent by the fact that the derived object can be a reflexive. On then standard assumptions, a reflexive was licensed by a clausemate:

4. I believe myself to have convinced Bill

Besides Rosenbaum (1967), early accounts arguing that the embedded subject moved to object position included R. Lakoff (1968), Kiparsky and Kiparsky (1970) and Postal (1974). Bresnan (1972, Chapter 3, Part C) was the first, I believe, to suggest that no such raising takes place. Building on Kiparsky and Kiparsky's (1970) claim that the complement of *believe* in these cases was a bare S, not an S' as was standardly assumed, Bresnan suggested that the facts pointed out above might find another explanation. If passive raises any NP contiguous to V on the right then the subject of the infinitive can raise directly from the infinitive to matrix subject position. If the notion of "clausemate" for reflexives were defined on S' rather than S, then the lower subject would be a clausemate of the matrix subject. She does not address the form of the pronoun: accusative.

Jump forward some years to Chomsky's (1981) *LGB* approach. The θ-Criterion is formulated in such a way as to ensure that a complement position of a head is a thematic position. The Projection Principle requires this to be true at all levels of representation. The result is that movement into a complement position is ruled out by the combination of the two principles. This greatly restricts the application of "move α", but at the same time rules out the possibility of raising to object.

A verb like *believe* takes an S' complement. A rule of S' deletion (with infinitival S) allows the verb to govern S. S' deletion allows the verb *believe* to "exceptionally" govern into the specifier of its complement, thus Case-marking it accusative, as in (2). Passive and reflexives both come under Condition A of the Binding Theory which ensures that the anaphor (the NP trace, or reflexive) is bound by its antecedent within a domain that contains its governor (here *believe*) and either a subject or a tensed INFL. Since their INFL is untensed, the domain for binding is the matrix clause, and thus passive (3) and reflexive (4) anaphors were allowed.

Fast forward another ten years or so to Chomsky (1991). Chomsky proposes that, in general, accusative Case is assigned in a Spec-Head relation between an NP and AGR, the head of a functional projection external to VP. The θ-Criterion/Projection Principle ban on raising the embedded subject to the matrix clause for Case no longer holds. Case positions are specifier positions, just the kind of position an NP would move into. Thus, the possibility for a revived raising to object approach for verbs like *believe* appears.

Lasnik & Saito (1991) in fact propose that what is "exceptional" about exceptional Case-marking verbs is not that they exceptionally govern and assign Case to the subject of the infinitive embedded below them, but rather that it raises to Spec,AGRo in their clause at LF for Case. Lasnik & Saito, following Emonds (1978), Pollock (1989) and Chomsky (1991), assume that the main verb in English remains in VP at S-structure. Thus, their "raising to object" must be covert, otherwise they would derive the wrong surface order: *NP-NP-V-INF. Lasnik (1993) accepts and builds on this conclusion, using it to help argue for LF raising to Spec,AGRo of plain accusative objects.

The previous chapters attempted to show that the raising of objects to Spec,AGRo is the correct account for accusative Case-checking. I went a step further than Chomsky (1993) and Lasnik (1993) would: I tried to show that this movement was in the overt syntax. I showed that the verb and object behave as if they are external to a constituent containing the remainder of the VP complements. I showed that the easiest account of adverb placement is maintained if the object is external to VP at S-structure. Thus, what I will now examine in some detail is the possibility that raising to Spec,AGRo at S-structure is the correct account of "ECM" verbs in English.

I will essentially be comparing three accounts. The account that I will adopt puts the embedded subject in Spec,AGRo of the matrix clause at S-structure. Lasnik & Saito's (1991) and Lasnik's (1993) accounts put it there at LF only. And Chomsky's (1981) account involves no movement but rather exceptional government and Case-marking by *believe*.

I will begin by examining the LF properties of the subjects of the infinitives. How "high" are they at LF? The answer will be, pretty high. The evidence points towards their being in the matrix clause at LF (Lasnik & Saito 1991, Lasnik 1993). This result will remove the *LGB* proposal from the running as it assumes no movement into the matrix clause, ever. Then I will examine the S-structure properties of the structures in question. Two conceptual arguments, based on observed surface word order, will be provided showing that theory-internally overt raising to Spec,AGRo makes more sense. Two arguments will show that the ECM subject is intermingled with matrix material, thus implying it is in the matrix clause. And one argument will provide evidence for the vacated position from which the ECM subject has moved in order to reach Spec,AGRo. I will conclude, contra Lasnik & Saito (1991) and Lasnik (1993), that the embedded subject of the infinitive is indeed in Spec,AGRo at S-structure.

5.2.2 The LF Position of the ECM Subject

This section will examine the evidence for the position of what I will refer to as the ECM subject. The two accounts I will be comparing differ in how high in the tree they place the ECM subject. The standard account (of Chomsky 1981), places the ECM subject in the embedded subject of

ECM as Raising to Object AGR

infinitive position, at S-structure and at LF. The alternative accounts place the ECM subject in the specifier of AGRoP in the matrix clause. The alternative accounts differ on the level at which this occurs: Lasnik & Saito (1991) and Lasnik (1993) argue movement to Spec,AGRo is at LF; I will support the claim that such movement is in the overt syntax. Thus, Lasnik & Saito and Lasnik and I all agree on one thing: the ECM subject is in Spec,AGRo in the matrix clause at LF. I will be comparing roughly two camps in this first part. The "standard" account of ECM, with its ECM subject in the infinitive at LF, and the "raising" account, with its ECM subject in Spec,AGRo at (at least) LF.[12]

5.2.2.1 Two Accounts

Let us consider the relevant structures. One point first: over the years it has been controversial as to whether or not an ECM verb like *believe* selects a CP (formerly S′) or an IP (formerly S). As far as I can tell the arguments in favor of CP are: (1) to generalize to a single one the "types" of clausal complements available to any verb, and (2) to account for the lack of subjacency effects by providing a Spec,CP escape hatch for movement. One fact in favor of IP is that the verb is supposed to exceptionally govern the embedded subject, which the extra CP level makes dubious. I will for now simply assume that the verb selects IP (=AGRsP), following essentially Bresnan (1972). This is most likely necessary due to the claim that ECM is really raising of NP out of "IP" to Spec,AGRo of the main clause. Such movement is presumably not going to be licit over a CP node.

Now, back to the structures. For space reasons I only include the relevant portion of the tree:

5. The Standard Account

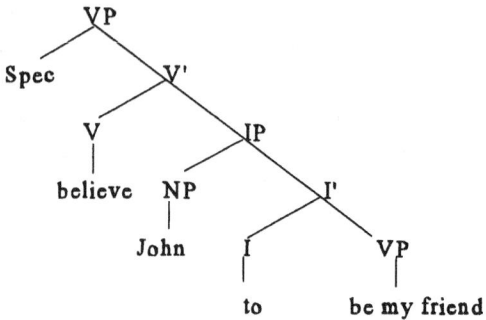

The standard account has the ECM subject in the infinitival Spec,IP at LF (I have placed *to* in I, but nothing hinges on that). The verb *believe* governs and Case-marks *John*.

Now the raising account:

6. The Raising Account

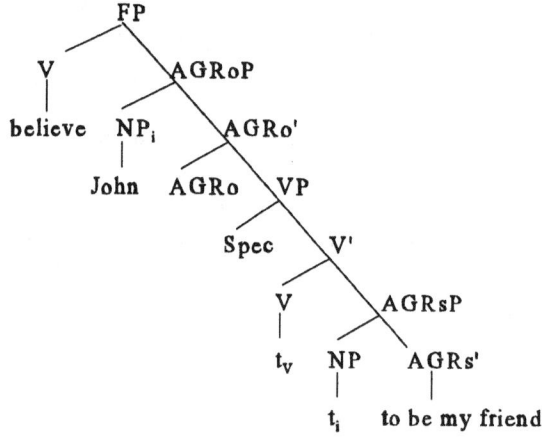

The raising account places the subject of the infinitive in Spec,AGRo. In Spec,AGRo it checks its accusative Case features. As this is the LF representation, the verb is, in fact, likely to be higher, in AGRs. I have abstracted away from that and simply placed it under noncommittal "FP" (see chapter 3).

ECM as Raising to Object AGR

Consider the differing predictions made by these two accounts. The raising account predicts that a noun phrase in the position of *John* should asymmetrically c-command material in or adjoined to the matrix VP. The standard account predicts that a noun phrase in the position of *John* will asymmetrically c-command elements within its own clause, but nothing else, and certainly not material in the matrix VP.

5.2.2.2 The Barss & Lasnik Tests

Recall from Chapter 2 the series of phenomena which arguably show asymmetric c-command, the Barss & Lasnik (1986) tests (B&L tests). To apply these tests to the ECM case we need to construct examples in which a noun phrase appears within or adjoined to the matrix VP headed by the ECM verb. If the ECM subject has this NP in its domain we can conclude that the ECM subject asymmetrically c-commands the NP.

The examples that follow all involve adjoined adverbials like those pointed out in Contreras (1984). As shown there, and in Chapter 2, an NP in Spec,AGRo asymmetrically c-commands NPs embedded within such adverbial phrases. If the ECM subject also does so, this provides strong support for the claim that the ECM subject is in Spec,AGRo at LF. As it is sometimes difficult to distinguish the attachment of the adverbial–as matrix or embedded–I have tried to construct examples in which the embedded infinitive is stative or at least not easily modified by a temporal adverbial adjunct.

Following Lasnik (1993), from whom some of these data were drawn, I will contrast the ECM sentence with its tensed CP counterpart in which there is no doubt that the subject is embedded.

Anaphor Binding. The ECM subject can bind a reciprocal in an adverbial phrase adjoined to (or within) the matrix VP. Note that the judgments are for the matrix attachment of the adverbial. (9) is from Lasnik (1993):

7. a. Cindy believed Bobby and Peter to be guilty only after each other's confessions
   b. * Cindy believed that Bobby and Peter were guilty only after each other's confessions

8. a.　　Marcia expected the two friends to be noncommittal before each other's overt display of loyalty
   b. *　Marcia expected that the two friends would be noncommittal before each other's overt display of loyalty
9. a. ?　The DA proved the defendents to be guilty during each other's trials　[Lasnik 1993]
   b. ?*　The DA proved that the defendents were guilty during each other's trials

QNP-Binding. A quantified ECM subject can bind a variable in a matrix adverbial:[13]

10. a.　　Carol had believed each boy to be innocent until after his confession proved him otherwise
    b. ?　Carol had believed that each boy was innocent until after his confession proved him otherwise
11. a.　　Mike expected every table to be clean before he saw it
    b. ?*　Mike expected that every table would be clean before he saw it
12. a.　　The DA proved every boy to be innocent during his trial
    b. ?*　The DA proved that every boy was innocent during his trial

Each ... the other. An *each* in the ECM subject can be related to a *the other* in a matrix-adjoined adverbial:

13. a.　　Greg believed each of his brothers to be innocent before the other ratted
    b. *　Greg believed that each of his brothers was innocent before the other ratted
14. a.　　Sam expected each leg of lamb to be the worst he'd seen before the other's delivery
    b. *　Sam expected that each leg of lamb was the worst he'd seen before the other's delivery
15. a.　　The DA proved each boy to be innocent during the other's trial
    b. ?*　The DA proved that each boy was innocent during the other's trial

ECM as Raising to Object AGR

Negative Polarity Items. A comment: it is extremely difficult to construct the relevant examples because some of the kinds of temporal adverbials used above to show the object is VP-external independently license NPI so they cannot be used. That limits the kinds of appropriate adverbials. Combining that with the problem of finding an adverbial that nicely modifies *believe* and *expect* leaves very few possible examples. The first example is from Lasnik (1993), with *prove*, which is much easier to modify. The second is mine with *consider*, an ECM verb we have not been considering until now:

16. a. ? The DA proved none of the defendents to be guilty during any of the trials
    b. * The DA proved that none of the defendents were guilty during any of the trials
17. a. Alice considered none of the boys to be innocent during any of the investigations
    b. * Alice considered any of the boys to be innocent during none of the investigations

(17a) is fine on the interpretation in which Alice may have ended up considering some of the boys to be innocent after the investigations, or had considered them to innocent before the investigations.

Generalization: in V NP_1 INF [$_{ADV}$ ... NP_2 ...], NP_1 asymmetrically c-commands NP_2.[14]

The B&L tests, then, seem to support the raising account over the standard account. The standard account, as represented in (5), places the ECM subject in the embedded IP. It is predicted incorrectly not to c-command material adjoined to the matrix VP. The raising account, diagramed in (6), places the ECM subject in the matrix Spec,AGRo, thus correctly predicting it to c-command VP-adjoined material.

Assuming that the B&L tests are a test of LF configurations, we have shown that the raising account is to be preferred to the standard account for the LF representation of an ECM sentence.

5.3 THE SURFACE POSITION OF THE ECM SUBJECT

For the rest of this chapter I will be comparing two accounts. My account, which I will call the "overt raising" account, is that the ECM subject is in the matrix Spec,AGRo at S-structure. Lasnik & Saito's (1991) and Lasnik's (1993) "covert raising" account is that the ECM subject moves to the matrix Spec,AGRo at LF.

5.3.1 "Halfway" Movement

Consider the treatment of objects of transitive verbs by the proponents of the covert raising camp. At S-structure (Spell-Out) the direct object is in VP along with the main verb. At LF both raise out of VP, the object winding up in Spec,AGRo to check its Case and agreement features. The relevant point is that until LF the object remains *in situ*. Consider now the behavior of the ECM subject. The null hypothesis is that it would remain *in situ* until LF at which point it would move to Spec,AGRo to check its features. This is clearly not the case:

18. a.   Laverne believes [$_{AGRsP}$ Shirley$_i$ to have been [$_{VP}$ arrested t$_i$]]
    b. * Laverne believes [$_{AGRsP}$ to have been [$_{VP}$ arrested Shirley]]
19. a.   Richie expects [$_{AGRsP}$ Ralph$_i$ to [$_{VP}$ arrive t$_i$ at nine]]
    b. * Richie expects [$_{AGRsP}$ to [$_{VP}$ arrive Ralph at nine]]

(18) is an example of an embedded passive. (19) contains an embedded unaccusative. On standard assumptions the subjects of such types of embedded clause are base-generated in VP. On the standard account, movement from VP is forced to Spec,AGRsP (or Spec,IP on earlier accounts) because the NP needs Case. This story is no longer available on the covert raising account. Spec,AGRsP is not a Case position. Thus, the covert raising account is left having to explain the overt movement "halfway" to the final Case position.

A potential story might be to invoke the Extended Projection Principle. In the minimalist approach that might mean that AGRs (or T) has a feature that needs checking, even though the clause is non-finite. This could potentially motivate movement to Spec,AGRs. There are a couple of problems with this proposal, though. First, this feature would have to be a "strong" one since it motivates overt (pre-LF) movement. Since this is a nonfinite inflection with no agreement, such a proposal would fly in the face of any attempt at trying to relate strength of features with overt inflectional morphology. Secondly, such a proposal would not be strictly kosher in the minimalist framework since it would violate Greed (Chomsky 1993). Greed essentially blocks NP movement for any other reason except to satisfy the NP's own needs. This case would be movement to satisfy the needs of the head, not the NP, thus would violate Greed. While I do not claim to assume Greed as a principle of grammar, the covert raising account is couched in the minimalist framework and hence would presumably be constrained by such a principle. Short of invoking a minimalist-compatible EPP explanation, the covert raising account is surprised by these data.

On my account the facts above follow straightforwardly. I claim that the ECM subject moves to the matrix Spec,AGRo at S-structure. It does so for Case reasons. This means that movement to the matrix Spec,AGRo for the subject of a passive or unaccusative in an ECM infinitive is exactly analogous to movement to Spec,AGRs for the same type of subject but in a finite clause.

20. a. Laverne believes [$_{AGRoP}$ Shirley$_i$ [$_{AGRsP}$ to have been arrested [$_{VP}$ t$_V$ t$_i$]]]
    b. [$_{AGRsP}$ Shirley$_i$ has been arrested [$_{VP}$ t$_V$ t$_i$]]
21. a. Richie expects [$_{AGRoP}$ Ralph$_i$ [$_{AGRsP}$ to arrive [$_{VP}$ t$_V$ t$_i$]]]
    b. [$_{AGRsP}$ Ralph$_i$ arrived [$_{VP}$ t$_V$ t$_i$]]

There is no "halfway" movement. The NP moves overtly for Case.

5.3.2 Adverbs I

Postal (1974: Ch. 4) uses the fact that the verb and object cannot be separated by an adverb to argue that an ECM subject is in fact a matrix object:

22. a. I believe very strongly that Tony is honest
    b. * I believe very strongly Tony to be honest

These examples illustrate the fact about English discussed in some detail in Chapter 4: an adverb can separate a verb from its non-NP complement but not from its NP complement. I accounted for this generalization by arguing that adverbs could not be adjoined to AGRoP. In (a) the verb *believe* moves out of VP, past the VP adverb, leaving the CP behind. In (b) the verb moves out of VP, past the adverb. However, the embedded subject, in this case, does not move up to Spec,AGRo, resulting in ungrammaticality.

Consider the covert raising account of ECM. At S-structure the ECM subject is still in the embedded infinitive. Then why is (b) ungrammatical? The *LGB* story might have been that *believe* cannot exceptionally Case-mark the embedded subject if an adverb intervenes (see Stowell 1981, Chomsky 1981 on Case-adjacency requirements). This account is no longer available, though an analogous one might be attempted. One might try to argue that in some way the adverb blocks the NP movement required to get *Tony* up into Spec,AGRo at LF. This is an unlikely story given the fact that adverbs do not usually block NP movement as discussed in chapter 4 ((23) from Johnson 1991):

23. a. Gary has probably left
    b. Gary in fact will leave
24. a. Gary has already been arrested
    b. Gary probably arrived on time

On the standard assumption that subjects are base-generated in VP (either as VP-internal "external" arguments, subjects of passives, or subjects of unaccusatives), adverbs do not appear in general to block NP movement to Spec,AGRs at S-structure.

We are left with no obvious way to rule out examples like (22b) on the covert raising approach to ECM. The overt raising approach nicely accounts for the observed contrasts. I take this to be strong evidence in its favor.[15]

5.3.3 Adverbs II

5.3.3.1 Postal's Argument

Postal (1974, Ch. 4) makes another argument relevant to the question of LF or S-structure movement to Spec,AGRo. Before examining his argument let's make some initial observations about adverbial modification. I will start by concentrating on Jackendoff's (1972, Ch. 3) Class I adverbs. These are interesting because they can appear in a variety of positions, with different meanings depending on the position. Consider the following examples, adapted from Postal (1974):

25. a. Incorrectly, Nixon will end the war
    b. Nixon, incorrectly, will end the war
    c. Nixon will incorrectly end the war
    d. Nixon will end the war incorrectly
    e. Nixon will end the war, incorrectly

Examples (a), (b) and (e) are unambiguous, meaning approximately, "it will be incorrect of Nixon to end the war." Following Jackendoff I will refer to this as the S-adverb reading. Examples (c) and (d) are unambiguous as well, meaning however, "the manner in which Nixon will end the war is incorrect." I will call this the manner reading.

What is of interest for us is that an S-adverb reading is available if the adverb is attached to the left of the sentence (a), to the right of the sentence (e), and just after the subject of the sentence (b). I will follow Jackendoff and assume that the intonational break in (e) signals the higher right-attachment of the adverb. The manner adverb reading is available in the VP (d) and just preceding the verb (c). Notice that the adverb, besides modifying the verb in some way, also says something about the subject. This type of adverb is called "subject-oriented". This contrasts with "speaker-oriented" adverbs like *probably, evidently*, etc.

Jackendoff further notes that S-adverbs modify positions which subject NPs have moved through/from. Consider the following:

26. Nixon$_i$ seemed [t$_i$ incorrectly to have ended the war]

In Jackendoff's terminology, S-adverb interpretation proceeded cyclically. On an earlier cycle *Nixon* was in the lower clause, thus allowing the embedded S-adverb to be interpreted with *Nixon*. We can assume that S-adverb interpretation is sensitive to NP traces at LF. Postal's examples involve these adverbs in ECM contexts. Some modified examples follow:

27. a. John expected that Nixon, incorrectly, would end the war
    b. John expected Nixon, incorrectly, to end the war

Postal's point was that in (a) the adverb modifies the embedded clause only, giving an S-adverb reading: "it was incorrect of Nixon to end the war." But the adverb in (b) can be construed as ambiguous. On the one hand, it can modify the embedded clause, giving an S-adverb reading: "it was incorrect of Nixon to end the war." It can also modify the matrix clause, also with an S-adverb reading: "it was incorrect of John to expect Nixon to end the war." It is the second interpretation which interests us.

Let us first consider the interpretation of (a) and the first interpretation of (b). In (a), *incorrectly* is just after the subject. It receives an embedded S-adverb interpretation, as expected. The first interpretation of (b) has *incorrectly* modifying *Nixon*, thus treating it as its subject. For Jackendoff that would mean that on some cycle *Nixon* is the subject of the embedded clause. To us that means that *Nixon* or the trace of *Nixon* is the subject of the embedded clause. This reading is consistent with both the covert and overt raising accounts.

The second reading of (b) is more interesting. On this reading, the matrix subject *John* is understood as the subject which the subject-oriented adverb modifies. According to Jackendoff, as outlined above in (25), the only way an adverb can be interpreted as an S-adverb is by being left-adjoined to S, being just after the subject, or being adjoined on the right, set off by a pause. Clearly the adverb is not to the left of or directly after the subject or a trace of the subject *John*. This leaves only the possibility that the adverb is in fact adjoined on the right to the matrix clause.

If the adverb is adjoined to the right of the matrix sentence, that implies quite clearly that the ECM subject *Nixon* is also part of the matrix clause.

ECM as Raising to Object AGR

On the overt raising account which I am supporting, this state of affairs is predicted straightforwardly. *Nixon* is in the matrix Spec,AGRo at S-structure. The first reading of (b) is available because the adverb is in the embedded clause and takes the trace of *Nixon* in the embedded subject position as its subject, as in (26), above. On the second reading, the adverb is adjoined to the matrix clause on the right periphery, as in (25e). It takes *John*, the subject of that sentence, as its subject. The reason that *Nixon* appears before the adverb is that it is overtly in the matrix clause.

Consider the covert raising account. *Nixon* is in the embedded Spec,AGRs at S-structure. The first reading of (b) is available because the adverb is in the embedded clause and takes the embedded subject as its subject. The second reading of (b) requires the adverb to be adjoined to the matrix clause. If this is the case then what of the embedded subject? It cannot be the case that *Nixon* is in Spec,AGRs and the adverb is in the matrix clause in the same S-structure representation. Recall that (a) shows us that generally an embedded adverb cannot get matrix scope, so an LF movement approach for (b) seems dubious.

This type of example is severely damaging to the covert raising account. It is not clear how that account can reconcile such data. The overt raising account, however, as argued by Postal, elegantly accounts for the facts. We now turn to a potential counterargument to this account. I will show that the counterargument finds an explanation when the nature of ECM verb modification is examined more carefully.

5.3.3.2 Bresnan's Counterarguments and Other Issues

What the order V-NP-ADV-INF actually shows has been called into question in several places. Bresnan (1976) argues it shows nothing about raising and should not be used as an argument for it. I discuss her counterargument and show that a closer look at adverb types explains most of her counterexamples. I show others of her counterexamples themselves to have structures other than those she assigns, removing them as counterexamples. Johnson (1991), accepting Bresnan's claims about at least some of the counterexamples, suggests that the ECP be modified to disallow raising just in case a V'-adjoined adverb intervenes. I show that the most challenging counterexamples he discusses find an alternative explanation thus not requiring an ECP revision. Further, I show that the proposed ECP revision over-restricts movement, thus being dubious independently.

5.3.3.2.1 Bresnan (1976)

Bresnan (1976) discusses the argument of Postal's (1974) reproduced in the previous section and attempts to debunk it. I will now consider her counterarguments. She cites the following examples from Postal (1974), which are similar to those just discussed:

28. a. I can prove that Bob easily outweighed Martha's goat
    b. I can prove Bob easily to have outweighed Martha's goat

Only in (b) can *easily* modify *prove*. She then provides the following pair as a counterexample, where the adverb is meant to modify the matrix verb, not *give*:

29. a. * I expected John quite confidently to give the lecture
    b.   I persuaded John quite easily to give the lecture

She claims that the explanation for (28) would predict (29a) to be acceptable. (29b) is meant to show that a verb that uncontroversially takes an object can easily be modified by an adverb. Thus, the conclusion is not warranted that an object can raise.

In order to address Bresnan's counterarguments we need to examine the types of adverbs available for use with the various types of verbs found in the ECM construction. It turns out that certain adverbs are barred independently from cooccuring with certain ECM verbs, thus accounting for a large portion of Bresnan's examples. This examination is what we turn to now.

First, we need to untangle a couple of things. One more datum is needed for this to make sense. (29a) improves dramatically if *quite confidently* is set off by an intonational break:

30. I expected John, quite confidently, to give the lecture

At this point the sentence is ambiguous, though perhaps leaning towards the lower interpretation, in which *John* is confident. There are ways to disambiguate it, though. If *quite confidently* is placed after the infinitival *to* only the embedded reading is possible with or without intonational breaks:

31. I expected John to (,) quite confidently (,) give the lecture

On the other hand, the matrix reading can be brought out by taking advantage of something discussed by Jackendoff (1972, p. 90). He notes that there cannot be two subject-oriented S-adverbs in one sentence (clause):

32. a.   John quite confidently has been giving the lecture
    b.   John has unfairly been giving the lecture
    c. * John quite confidently has unfairly been giving the lecture

First, a complex tense was required in order to find positions for two S-adverbs. Recall that they can occur just after the subject and just after the first aux. What (c) shows is that, though independently there are slots for two subject-oriented S-adverbs, they cannot co-occur.

Now reconsider our example. If *unfairly* is added to the embedded infinitive, that should force *quite confidently* <u>not</u> to be interpreted as part of the embedded clause, thus favoring the matrix interpretation:

33. I expected John, quite confidently, to unfairly give the lecture

This is indeed the case. What this discussion has shown is that it is possible to get a matrix reading on the adverb in Bresnan's example. If the adverb is set off intonationally, which marks it as an S-adverb in final position (see (25), above), it can receive such an interpretation. If it appears slightly lower (after *to*) only the embedded reading is available, as expected. And if the embedded clause already has a subject-oriented adverb the potentially ambiguous adverb is forced to get the matrix interpretation.

The question is still there: why is (29) not so great? I think that this can be answered if we consider the matrix verb a little more carefully.

Recall that an adverb that directly follows a verb, without an intonational break, is interpreted as a manner adverb, as in (25d), repeated here:

34. Nixon ended the war incorrectly

We see this type of adverb in an ECM sentence in Bresnan's example cited from Postal, repeated here:

35. I can prove Bob easily to have outweighed Martha's goat

This example is fine without any intonational breaks. And it has a manner interpretation. Why can *prove* appear with an adverb without an intonational break, and *expect* cannot?

The answer, I believe, is that *prove* but not *expect* is independently capable of taking a manner adverb. If *prove* can take a manner adverb the example just cited is predicted. If *expect* cannot take a manner adverb then the fact that an adverb following must be an S-adverb, and thus set off by an intonational break, is explained.

Manner adverbs, besides verb phrase finally, can appear before the verb. To properly distinguish them from S-adverbs, an aux or two is necessary since in simple sentences the space between subject and verb can contain either type of interpretation. Consider the following:

36. a. I have been proving Bob to outweigh Martha's goat
    b. I have been easily proving Bob to outweigh Martha's goat
37. a. I have been expecting John to give the lecture
    b. ?* I have been quite confidently expecting John to give the lecture

The (a) examples establish that these verbs are acceptable in the compound verb form required to make the point. The (b) examples place the adverb in a position in which only a manner adverbial interpretation is available. With *prove* the example is fine. With *expect* it is not; the '?' is due to the minute possibility of getting an S-adverb interpretation in this position. A manner reading is clearly out.

What this shows is that *expect* cannot take a manner adverb like *quite confidently*. That means that if an adverb follows it, it must be an S-

ECM as Raising to Object AGR

adverb. As an S-adverb, it must be right-adjoined and hence set off by intonational breaks. Thus, Bresnan's counterexample in fact fits right in with my account.

Many of the acceptable examples involving ECM verbs and adverbs are like (29) above, involving an S-adverb right-adjoined and thus set off by an intonational break. Recall that this type of intonation and interpretation is required in simple sentences, as in (25), above.

A second argument Bresnan (1976) makes suggests that Postal (1974) is confusing parenthetical adverbs with nonparenthetical adverbs and that the distribution of the former is so wide as not to make the point that Postal claims they make. First, it should be pointed out that Jackendoff (1972) argues that parentheticals are simply S-adverbs; he shows their distribution is the same as other S-adverbs and that they obey the same semantic restrictions as other S-adverbs. So, Postal's throwing parenthetical and nonparenthetical adverbs together is not *a priori* a bad plan.

In favor of her claim, Bresnan provides examples like the following:

38. I arranged for my relatives, in spite of protests, to have jobs in our department

The point being made, I believe, is that parenthetical adverbs related to the matrix clause can be interspersed in a blatantly embedded clause such as *for my relatives to have jobs in our department*.

The argument hinges on the claim that the adverbial is sitting in the embedded clause. But to show that, it needs to be shown that *for my relatives to have jobs in our department* is in fact a clause. It might not be. However, consider the possibility that we have a control structure. *For my relatives* is a PP in the matrix clause and PRO is the subject of *to have jobs*:

39. I arranged [$_{VP}$ [$_{PP}$ for my relatives]] (X) [$_{CP}$ PRO to have jobs]

If this structure is possible, then the adverbial would find a place in the position marked (X).

In favor of this structure is the following sentence:

40. I arranged for my relatives [$_{CP}$ for their visas to be ready when they arrived]

The fact that a full CP can be found after the *for my relatives* phrase casts doubt on the claim that *for my relatives to have jobs in our department* is <u>necessarily</u> a single clause.

On the other hand, notice that there is reason to think that it <u>can</u> be a clause. *My relatives* can be replaced by an expletive, which would be inconsistent with the PP/control structure:

41. a. I arranged for it to rain on my birthday
    b. I arranged for there to be a party on my birthday

Taking (40) and (41) together suggests we have two different structures possible. However, only one of them is going to be compatible with a parenthetical adverbial: (39), the control structure. The clear prediction, then, is that an expletive and a parenthetical cannot be possible simultaneously since they each are diagnostic of a different structure. This appears to be born out:

42. a. ?* I arranged for it, in spite of protests, to rain on my birthday.
    b. *   I arranged for there, in spite of protests, to be a party on my birthday

We see that the adverbial is inconsistent with the non-Control structure.

What this means, then, is that the parenthetical adverbial does in fact respect clause boundaries, thus potentially forming the basis for an argument about constituency, as Postal has used it.[16]

Bresnan punctuates her point that nonparentheticals and parentheticals behave differently by observing the following contrast:

43. a.   John irrationally believes pollution to be beneficial
    b. *   John believes pollution irrationally to be beneficial

44. a. John, quite without reason, believes pollution to be beneficial
    b. John believes pollution, quite without reason, to be beneficial

However, as I pointed out above, this contrast means nothing unless it has been established that *believe* can even take a manner adverb like *irrationally*. Recall that Jackendoff's Class I adverbs are ambiguous depending on position. Since the adverb follows the verb directly without any break it must be a manner adverb. If *believe* does not take manner adverbs (or at least this manner adverb) then the ungrammatical example is bad for independent reasons having nothing to do with the question of raising.

First, I should point out that the example improves if *irrationally* is treated as an S-adverb:

45. John believes pollution, irrationally, to be beneficial

Secondly, we can test *believe* for compatibility with a manner reading by placing the adverb just before the verb after several auxiliary verbs (see (25), above):

46. a. John will have believed pollution to be beneficial for five years come November
    b. ?? John will have irrationally believed pollution to be beneficial for five years come November

Example (a) shows that the verb is acceptable in the compound verb form. Example (b) is a bit hard to judge. There appears to be an acceptable reading. However, the reading is compatible with an S-adverb interpretation like (47a), not a manner adverb reading like (47b):

47. a. It is irrational of John to have believed pollution to be beneficial . . .
    b. * The manner in which John will have believed pollution to be beneficial . . . is irrational

This suggests that *believe* is not capable of taking a manner adverb like *irrationally*.

Another piece of evidence pointing in that direction is the behavior of *believe* with a full CP complement:

48. John believes (,) irrationally (,) that pollution is beneficial

In this case, though a strong intonational break is not necessary, there is still a clear feeling that this is an S-adverb, not a manner one. The sentence means, "it is irrational of John to believe that pollution is beneficial." It does not mean, "the manner in which John believes pollution to be beneficial is irrational." This further supports the claim that *believe* does not take a manner adverb like *irrationally*.

Taken together, these facts point to the conclusion that (43b) only shows that *believe* is incompatible with a manner adverb, not that raising has not occurred.

5.3.3.2.2 Other Issues

Johnson (1991) considers more examples like those pointed out by Bresnan (1976). A subset of them appears not to be amenable to the type of account I suggested for Bresnan's counterexamples. That is, there appear to be ECM verbs which can be modified by what appears to be a manner adverb, yet still do not allow that adverb to intervene between the ECM subject and the embedded infinitive. The most intriguing example is the following:[17]

49. * Sam considers Mittie strongly to have been misled

In this example *strongly* is definitely not being interpreted as an S-adverb. To give it Jackendoff's (1972) paraphrase test, the meaning is not, "it is strong of Sam to consider Mittie to have been misled." On the other hand, it does not really mean, "the manner in which Sam considers Mittie to have been misled is strong," either.

ECM as Raising to Object AGR

It does pass one positional test for manner adverbs:

50. Sam has been strongly considering Mittie to have been misled

Again, this is clearly not getting an S-adverb reading. Other ECM verbs are acceptable in principle with *strongly*, though not in the NP-ADV-INF order:

51. a. Cindy strongly believes Buddy to be the murderer
    b. * Cindy believes Buddy strongly to be the murderer
52. a. Marcia strongly suspects Wally to be the murderer
    b. * Marcia suspects Wally strongly to be the murderer

And these also pass that positional test for manner adverbs:

53. Greg has been strongly suspecting/believing Bobby to be the murderer for about five years now

There is one crucial difference between an adverb like *strongly* and manner adverbs. Manner adverbs can follow a normal direct object; *strongly* cannot:

54. a.   Nixon ended the war incorrectly
    b.   John dropped his cup of coffee clumsily
    c.   Bill worded the letter carefully
55. a. * Laverne considered that possibility strongly
         (cf. Laverne strongly considered that possibility)
    b. * Squiggy believed her story strongly
         (cf. Squiggy strongly believed her story)
    c. * Carmine suspected her motive strongly
         (cf. Carmine strongly suspected her motive)

But, if *strongly* cannot follow the direct object of a simple transitive clause, then it is not surprising that it cannot follow the ECM subject in (49). I have no explanation for why an adverb like *strongly* cannot follow the object, but I assume that whatever it is, it will equally account for the ECM example above.

I would like to take a moment to consider Johnson's (1991) account of the ungrammatical (49) as well as a variety of examples superficially like it. He assumes that manner adverbs (he considers *strongly* a manner adverb) to be adjoined to a V' projection in the VP. He then amends the ECP so that the additional V' level creates a barrier for antecedent government. Since the ECM subject moves directly from the infinitival subject position, a non-theta-governed position, it must antecedent govern its trace. The extra V' blocks such government.

I think that this amendment of the ECP, unfortunately, will over-restrict NP movement. Specifically, I believe it predicts that a manner adverb in the matrix VP will also block movement from the embedded infinitive in the case of passive. Consider the following examples:

56. a. Wally$_i$ is strongly suspected [t$_i$ to be the murderer]
    b. Wally$_i$ is suspected strongly [t$_i$ to be the murderer]
57. a. Buddy$_i$ is strongly considered [t$_i$ to be the most likely candidate]
    b. Buddy$_i$ is considered strongly [t$_i$ to be the most likely candidate]
58. a. Eddie$_i$ is strongly believed [t$_i$ to be the murderer]
    b. Eddie$_i$ is believed strongly [t$_i$ to be the murderer]

The (a) examples, with the adverb preceding the verb may or may not be adjoined to an X' and thus may or may not be causing a problem for antecedent government. However, the (b) examples have the adverb in the same VP-internal V'-adjoined position as the ungrammatical example (49). While the (a) examples are somewhat more natural, any contrast between the (a) and (b) examples is nowhere near the expected ECP strength. On the other hand, whatever constraint blocks *strongly* from being separated from the verb, leading to the ungrammatical case of (49), above, is satisfied in these examples, thus leading to their grammaticality.

5.3.3.3 Summary

The surface order V-NP-ADV-INF in which NP is an ECM subject and ADV is an adverb interpreted as part of the matrix clause provides a real challenge to the covert raising account of ECM. The overt raising account derives the order straightforwardly.

5.3.4 Floating Quantifiers

5.3.4.1 Introduction

Consider the following examples:

59. a. The boys will have been all eating cake for three hours
    b. The boys will have all been eating cake for three hours
    c. The boys will all have been eating cake for three hours
    d. The boys all will have been eating cake for three hours

Sportiche (1988) suggested that quantifiers like *all*, which can appear in various locations between the surface subject position and VP, rather than having been "floated" away from the subject, are in fact "stranded" behind by the subject on its way to Spec,AGRs. On the assumption that the subject starts out in the VP and moves to Spec,AGRs for Case, the floating quantifiers can be seen as marking the path the subject potentially took:

60 [$_{AGRsP}$ the boys$_i$ [t$_i$ will [t$_i$ have [t$_i$ been [t$_i$ eating cake for three hours]

We will assume that this basic idea is correct. After looking a little more closely at the exact positions such quantifiers can sit in, we will turn to the ECM contexts and examine their behavior there. Since the covert and overt raising accounts differ on whether there is movement to Spec,AGRo in the matrix clause in the overt syntax, only the overt movement account predicts the embedded Spec,AGRs to be empty at that level. This empty position, in turn, provides a possible stranding site for a floated quantifier. Such a prediction is not made by the covert raising account. We now turn to a careful examination of the relevant facts.[18]

5.3.4.2 A Closer Look

Let's examine the distribution of *all* a little more carefully. As (d) in the above examples shows, *all* is acceptable directly after the subject before *will*. The same is true before the modals like *might*, *can* and *should*:

61. a. The boys all might leave after the movie
    b. The boys all can leave for all I care
    c. The boys all should leave before it's too late

However, I find that *all* is quite uncomfortable before inflected *be*:

62. a. ?* The boys all are leaving now
    b. ?* The boys all are my friends

Switching the order of *all* and *be* leads to perfection:

63. a. The boys are all leaving now
    b. The boys are all my friends

Why would such a contrast obtain? If we take seriously the claim that *all* marks a position through which the subject has moved, these data could be interpreted to show that there is a specifier position between the modals and the subject in which *all* can sit. No such specifier position is available between the inflected *be* and the subject.

Let us consider the possibility that the modals and inflected *be* sit in different positions at S-structure. Suppose that *be* is in AGRs and the modals sit in a functional head position just below AGRs, call it X. Then, *all* can sit in the Spec,XP:

64. a. The Position of *all* and Inflected *be*

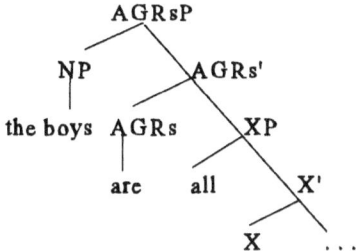

b. The Position of *all* and Modals

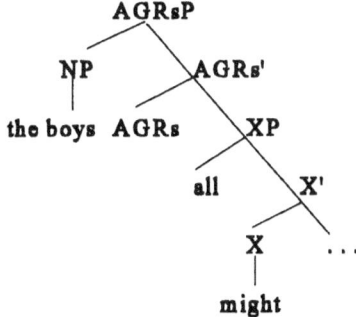

The orders *are-all* but not ?*all-are are then expected, as is the order *all-might*.

Notice, of course, that the order *might-all* is possible:

65. a. The boys might all leave after the movie
    b. The boys can all leave for all I care
    c. The boys should all leave before it's too late

This is accounted for under the present hypothesis as well. Since the subject moves through any number of specifiers on its way to Spec,AGRs–cf. the examples in the introduction to this section–, it can pass through Spec,XP as in the above examples, as well as through the specifier of whatever projection is just below XP, deriving the order found in these examples.[19]

Now, consider the placement of the S-adverb *probably*. It can sit comfortably between the subject and a modal:

66. a. The boys probably will leave after the movie
    b. The boys probably should leave at 10
    c. The boys probably can leave anytime

Interestingly, a similar restriction appears with inflected *be*. The adverb is less likely to come between the subject and *be*:

67. a. ?? The boys probably are leaving now
    b. ?? The boys probably are my friends

And again, the inverted order is perfect:

68. a. The boys are probably leaving now
    b. The boys are probably my friends

Let us try to assimilate this to what we noticed above. Suppose that *probably* adjoins only to maximal projections. If this is correct, then we derive the contrast just pointed out. There is a maximal projection between the modal and the subject in Spec,AGRs to which the adverb can adjoin: XP. There is no maximal projection between the inflected *be* and the subject, thus no adverb:

ECM as Raising to Object AGR

69. a. The Position of *probably* and Inflected *be*

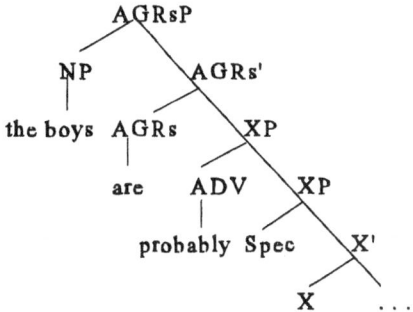

b. The Position of *probably* and Modals

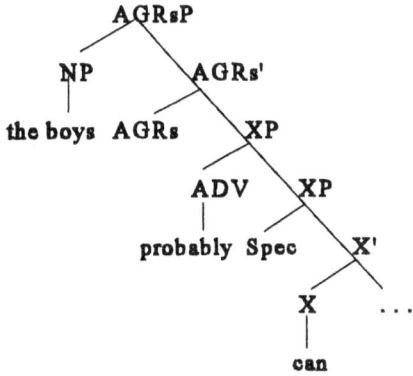

We are now ready to ask what happens when there are a floating quantifier and an adverb together. Consider the prediction. I predict that, since the adverb can adjoin to XP, and the quantifier can sit in Spec,XP, the order *probably-all* should be found. And this pair will be able to intervene between the subject and modals, but will follow the inflected *be*.

I will start with the modals. Indeed, the order *probably-all* is found, and it can intervene between the subject and the modal (a). The reverse order in that position is not as good (b):

70. a.   The boys probably all will leave after the movie
    b. ?*   The boys all probably will leave after the movie

This is what we expect. *Probably* is adjoined to XP, *all* is in Spec,XP, and *will* is in X. It is impossible to get *all* and *probably* in the reverse order before *will*.

Now consider inflected *be*. Again the order *probably-will* is found. The pair cannot intervene between the subject and the inflected *be*, in either order (b), but rather follows *be* (a):

71. a.   The boys are probably all leaving now
    b. ?* The boys probably all are leaving now
    c. ?* The boys all probably are leaving now

In the good example *be* is in AGRs. *Probably* is adjoined to XP, and *all* is in Spec,XP.

ECM as Raising to Object AGR

Let us examine the trees:

72. a. The Position of *probably, all* and Inflected *be*

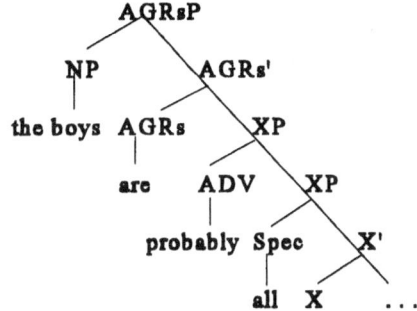

b. The Position of *probably, all* and Modals

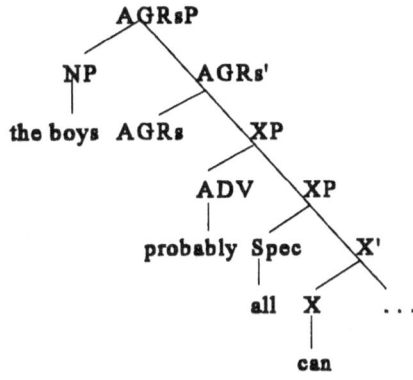

Now let us examine the behavior of these items in nonfinite clauses. Consider the following data:

73. a.   It would worry Martha for [the boys all to leave]
    b. ?   It would worry Martha for [the boys probably to leave]
74. a. ?   It would worry Martha for [the boys probably all to leave]
    b. *   It would worry Martha for [the boys all probably to leave]

First, a comment: *probably* is not perfect in an infinitive so it is the contrast I am focusing on. What this contrast appears to show is the same order restriction on *probably* and *all* as we saw above. Between the subject and *to* the order *probably-all* is acceptable, but the reverse order *all-probably* is out.

If we assume that *to* sits in X, like the modals do in the finite clause, the data fall out. In the better example, *the boys* is in Spec,AGRs, *probably* is adjoined to XP, *all* is in Spec,XP and *to* is in X. This gets us just the right, and only, order (before *to*). Let's look at the tree:

75. The Position of *probably*, *all* and *to*

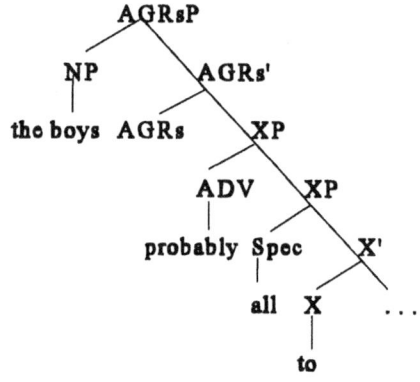

Consider the alternatives. If *to* sat in AGRs, we would have no explanation for why *probably* and *all* can intervene between the subject and *to*. If *to* were in a lower functional projection, we would have no explanation for why the order *all-probably* is so bad, since *all* could be in Spec,XP and *probably* could be adjoined to the maximal projection of whatever *to* sits in. The most likely account puts *to* in the same position held by the modals in finite clauses, what I am noncommittally calling X. This suggestion could possibly explain the ungrammaticality of modals in nonfinite contexts:

76. a.   *   It would worry Martha for the boys to can leave
    b.   *   It would worry Martha for the boys to might leave
    c.   *   It would worry Martha for the boys to will leave

5.3.4.3 Floating Quantifiers in ECM Sentences

The account just proposed makes predictions with respect to the question of the surface position of an ECM subject. A nonfinite clause has *to* in X. That leaves space above *to* for *probably* and *all*: *all* can sit in Spec,XP, and *probably* can be adjoined to XP. The subject, if it is present, will sit in Spec,AGRs above *probably-all*.

The covert raising account, which has the ECM subject in the embedded Spec,AGRs at S-structure predicts that the order found should be subject-*probably-all-to*, as in the above examples. Crucially, if what I have said is on the right track, the following order should not be found: *subject-*all-probably-to*, again corresponding to the ungrammatical example above.

The overt raising account, which puts the ECM subject in Spec,AGRo at S-structure makes a different prediction. Specifically, it predicts that the following order should be possible: subject-*all-probably-to*. This is precisely the order that the covert account rules out. Why does the overt account rule it in? Because the ECM subject vacates Spec,AGRs at S-structure, leaving another specifier position open for *all* to appear in. The prediction of the overt raising account is born out:

77. John expects the boys all probably to have left

Consider the relevant part of the tree:

78. ECM with *all* and *probably*

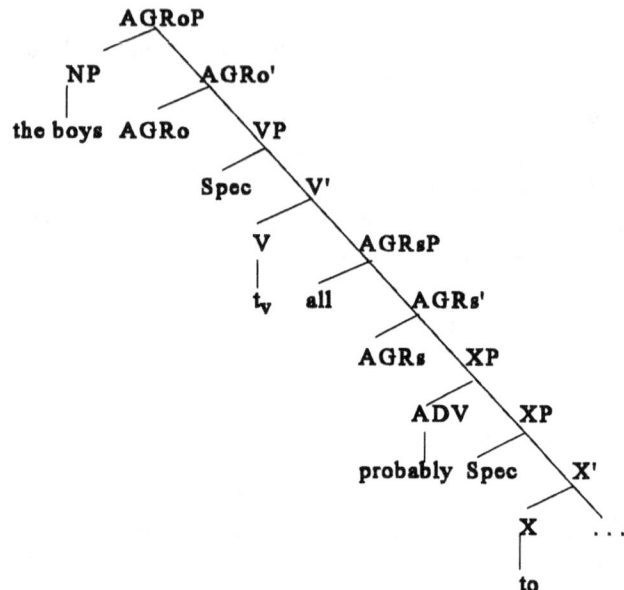

As in the other examples, *to* is in X and *probably* is adjoined to XP. The difference here is that since the NP has moved from Spec,AGRs to Spec,AGRo, the vacated position becomes a position for *all*. This fact is completely mysterious on the covert raising account, since there is no obvious difference between the two types of infinitive. The overt raising account, then, makes the correct prediction.

5.3.5 Particle Verbs

Our last argument in favor of overt vs. covert movement of the ECM subject to Spec,AGRo, comes from particle verbs. The argument will be made here without delving too deeply into the details of the construction.

Johnson devotes a great deal of his (1991) article to particle verbs. The "characteristic paradigm" is replicated here (p. 593):

ECM as Raising to Object AGR

79. a. Mikey looked the reference up
　　b. Mikey looked up the reference
　　c. Betsy threw the bicycle out
　　d. Betsy threw out the bicycle
　　e. Brent dusted the counter off
　　f. Brent dusted off the counter

These examples illustrate what is interesting about particle verbs. The object of the particle verb can show up before the particle or after it. If the object is a weak pronoun it must precede the particle (p. 594):[20]

80. a.　　Mikey looked it up
　　b. *　Mikey looked up it
　　c.　　Betsy threw it out
　　d. *　Betsy threw out it
　　e.　　Brent dusted it off
　　f. *　Brent dusted off it

As Johnson points out the alternation displayed above is restricted to NPs. Other types of arguments and non-arguments of the particle verb follow the particle (p. 594-5):

81. a.　　Mikey teamed up with the women
　　b. *　Mikey teamed with the women up
　　c.　　Betsy narrowed in on the problem
　　d. *　Betsy narrowed on the problem in
82. a.　　Mikey pointed out that Gary had left
　　b. *　Mikey pointed that Gary had left out
　　c.　　Betsy tried out loudly singing the national anthem
　　d. *　Betsy tried loudly singing the national anthem out
83. a.　　Mikey slips up all the time
　　b. *　Mikey slips all the time up
　　c.　　Betsy figured out the problem carefully
　　d. *　Betsy figured carefully out the problem
　　e.　　Brent pushed down the pin with a hammer
　　f. *　Brent pushed with a hammer down the pin

Thus, in general the verb and its particle are contiguous. The only time this is not the case is if the particle verb takes an NP object, in which case the object may come between the verb and particle. Johnson summarizes the situation (p.595):

84. Noun Phrases dependent on the particle verb for accusative Case may appear on either side of the particle, unless the Noun Phrase is a simple pronoun, in which case it must appear preceding the particle.

Johnson argues that direct objects move to a high VP-internal position for Case. This is very similar to the account I have been arguing for, the details of Case-assignment being one of the biggest differences. On Johnson's account of the particle verb, the verb + particle are generated as a single verbal head within VP. In general two possibilities are available: (1) the verb + particle can head-move as a unit upwards past the object, deriving the order V-Prt-NP; or (2) the verb can head-move alone (excorporating from the complex head à la Roberts 1991), stranding the particle behind, deriving the order V-NP-Prt.

I will tentatively adopt this account. The only difference is that the object is in Spec,AGRo. The two options outlined above remain essentially the same: (1) the verb + particle head-move upwards out of VP past the object; or (2) the verb alone head-moves upwards and out, like a regular non-particle verb, stranding the particle in the VP. (1) and (2) correspond to (a) and (b), respectively:

85. a. Mikey looked up the reference
        Mikey$_i$ [[looked-up][$_{AGRoP}$ the reference$_j$ [$_{VP}$ t$_i$ t$_V$ t$_j$]]]

    b. Mikey looked the reference up
        Mikey$_i$ [[looked][$_{AGRoP}$ the reference$_j$ [$_{VP}$ t$_i$ [t$_V$ up] t$_j$]]]

What is relevant for the present argument is that there are a few ECM particle verbs. These are verbs which occur with a particle, but also have the subject of the embedded infinitive dependent on them for Case.

Consider the predictions of the two accounts of ECM. The covert raising account, which moves the ECM subject to the matrix Spec,AGRo at LF, predicts that the order V-Prt-NP should always obtain. This is

ECM as Raising to Object AGR

because NP would be in the embedded infinitive until LF at which point it would move to Spec,AGRo. Thus, the order V-NP-Prt would be unexpected.

The overt raising account, which moves the ECM subject to the matrix Spec,AGRo at S-structure, predicts that, like regular objects of a particle verb, it should be able to appear between the verb and the particle, deriving the order V-NP-Prt. Alternatively, if the ECM subject is in Spec,AGRo and the V+Prt have head-moved together, the order V-Prt-NP is predicted.

Once again, the overt raising account makes the right prediction (Johnson 1991, p. 595):

86. a. Mikey made out George to be a liar
    Mikey$_i$ [[made-out][$_{AGRoP}$ George$_j$ [$_{VP}$ t$_i$ t$_V$ [$_{AGRsP}$ t$_j$]]]]

    b. Mikey made George out to be a liar
    Mikey$_i$ [[made][$_{AGRoP}$ George$_j$ [$_{VP}$ t$_i$ [t$_V$ out] [$_{AGRsP}$ t$_j$]]]]

Example (b) is the interesting example. We have a noun phrase from the embedded clause overtly interpolated among matrix elements. This provides the final, and quite strong, argument in favor of overt raising of the ECM subject.

5.4 CONCLUSION

This chapter has presented five arguments in favor of the overt raising account. The first two were conceptual, based on assumptions about motivations for movement. These showed that the covert raising account required special assumptions just in ECM contexts which, on the overt raising account, were unnecessary. Two others concentrated on cases in which clearly matrix material and alleged embedded material are interpolated leading to the conclusion that the embedded material is actually matrix material. The fifth argument, based on the placement of floating quantifiers, tried to show that besides the evidence for the ECM subject being in the matrix clause at S-structure, there is evidence for the empty position it vacated in the embedded infinitive.

CHAPTER 6
The Double Object Construction

6.1 INTRODUCTION

Sentences like the following have raised many interesting questions about English phrase structure:

1. a. Jan showed Greg Marcia's diary
   b. Cindy gave Bobby Kitty Karryall
   c. Mike sent Bibi Galini the plans

Among the issues raised by sentences like these are: (1) how are the two NPs licensed in the structure, i.e. how is Case assigned to both NPs?; and (2) what is the syntactic/structural relationship between the two objects at the different levels of representation?

I will begin by briefly reviewing the original Barss & Lasnik (1986) observations about the double object construction. What they showed was that the second object is in the domain of the first with respect to a number of phenomena. I argued, following Larson (1988, 1990), in Chapter 2 that this shows the first NP to asymmetrically c-command the second by at least LF. I established that the first NP was in fact external to VP and asymmetrically c-commanded not only the second object but other VP-internal and VP-adjoined material.

After this review we will examine more closely the behavior of the second object in the double object construction with respect to the B&L tests. We will see that it has other VP-internal and VP-adjoined material within its c-command domain, suggesting that at least at LF, it too is VP-external.

I will then outline my proposal for the surface and LF representations for the double object construction in English. I will argue that there are two AGRoP projections in the functional array of the double object predicate. The projections provide specifier positions to which the two objects of the construction move at S-structure for Case. In English, these two Cases are not distinguished morphologically. In other languages, e.g. German (see Brugger & Poletto 1993, Sabel 1994, Haiden 1995), the two AGR heads check off two verbal Cases whose morphological instantiations differ: dative and accusative. I assume that the ability of a verb to license two Case features via AGR checking is a property of a verb with two internal arguments.

I will then argue for the surface representation that I assign. I begin by showing that, first, the verb and the first object are external to a constituent containing the second object and VP elements: the lower AGRoP. Second, I show that the verb and both objects are external to a constituent containing the remainder of the VP material: VP.

We will then examine adverb placement. This will show that the assumptions we have in place about adverb distribution immediately predict the adverb facts in the double object construction, as viewed here.

Having discussed the LF and surface configurations of the double object construction, some time is spent studying the underlying structure. Two types of account are discussed. First, Larson's (1988) proposal, which was touched on in Chapter 2, will be reviewed. I will discuss three ways in which it is inadequate: constituency, adverb placement, and (LF and underlying) hierarchical relations. Second, the "clausal DP" proposal advanced in Johnson (1991) will be examined. I will support such a proposal, arguing for a somewhat different structure, and differing radically on the surface instantiations and Case-assignment properties I assume for it.

Three arguments are presented favoring my interpretation of the clausal DP proposal: floating quantifier positions, scope freezing and passive in the double object construction. A look at the relation between LF position and NP interpretation (from Diesing 1992) shows that the clausal DP proposal makes two further types of prediction: that extraction out of NP_1 is impossible, and that NP_1's specificity is directly dependent

The Double Object Construction

on the specificity of NP_2 (the latter prediction is, as far as I know, not made by any other account). Some remaining issues show that my interpretation of the clausal DP proposal finds indirect support in the way its behavior parallels other better understood movement phenomena: (overt and covert) wh movement and QR.

6.2 THE OBJECTS AT LF

6.2.1 The Barss & Lasnik Tests

Barss & Lasnik (1986) observed that in the double object construction the first NP has the second NP in its domain. The following "tests" are meant to show this. The first battery is reproduced from Chapter 2, to remind the reader of the tests and their results for the two objects of the double object construction.
   Binding Principles. NP_2 can be a reflexive or reciprocal and be bound by NP_1, satisfying Condition A of the binding theory. Note that NP_2 does not bind NP_1 or Condition C/B would be violated in (a). If NP_1 is an anaphor, it cannot be bound by NP_2 (b):

2. a.   I showed John/him himself (in the mirror)
    b. * I showed himself John (in the mirror)
3. a.   I showed the professors each other's students
    b. * I showed each other's students the professors

Quantifier Binding. NP_1 as a quantified NP can bind a bound variable pronoun in NP_2 (a), but not vice versa (b):

4. a.   I denied each worker his paycheck
    b. * I denied its owner each paycheck
5. a.   I showed every friend of mine his photograph
    b. * I showed its trainer every lion

Weak Crossover. NP_1 can be wh-moved and still bind a pronoun in NP_2 (a), but the reverse is impossible (b):

6. a. Which worker did you deny his paycheck?
   b. * Which paycheck did you deny its owner?
7. a. Who did you show his reflection in the mirror?
   b. * Which lion did you show its owner?

Superiority. If both NPs are wh-words, NP_1 can be moved leaving NP_2 in situ, but not vice versa:

8. a. Who did you give which book?   ["awkward"–B&L]
   b. * Which book did you give who?

Each . . . the other. As (a) shows, NP_1 headed by *each* licenses *the other* in NP_2. If NP_2 contains *each* it does not license *the other* in NP_1 (b):

9. a. I have each man the other's watch
   b. * I gave the other's trainer each lion

Negative Polarity Items. A negated NP_1 licenses a polarity item in NP_2, as in (a). The reverse is impossible (b):

10. a. I gave no one anything
    b. * I gave anyone nothing

Generalization: in V NP_1 NP_2, NP_2 is in the domain of NP_1.

Thus, the conclusion of these tests, as Larson (1988) argued (and see Chapter 2), is that the first object in the double object construction asymmetrically c-commands the second. That result is consistent with a number of proposals. These tests conclude, following my claim from Chapter 2, that the first object is in Spec,AGRo, and the second object could be in a VP-internal position, like other verbal complements. Alternatively, the second object could also be VP-external, in a position asymmetrically c-commanded by the first object, but which asymmetrically c-commands VP and its contents.

To discover which of these possibilities is correct we need to check the second object to find out its "domain", that is, what is asymmetrically

The Double Object Construction 129

c-commanded by it? Let us consider, then, the behavior of NP$_2$ with respect to the B&L tests.

Binding Principles.

11. a. ? Marcia showed Cindy the two boys during each other's performance
    b. * Marcia showed Cindy each other during the two boys' performance
12. a. * Mike gave Carol the fucker after the letter's unwanted arrival
    b.   Mike gave Carol the letter after the fucker's unwanted arrival

Quantifier Binding.

13. a.   Peter gave Bobby each candy bar only after its/the fucker's expiration date had passed
    b. * Peter gave Bobby the fucker only after each expiration date had passed
14. a.   Harvey sent Marcia every invitation on its/the fucker's own letterhead
    b. * Harvey sent Marcia the fucker on every invitation's letterhead

Weak Crossover.

15. a. ? Whose money did you give the women at his house?
    b. * Which house did you give its owner the money at?
       * At which house did you give its owner the money?

Superiority.

16. a.   Which gifts did you give John at which house?
    b. ?* Which house did you give John which gifts at?
       ?* At which house did you give John which gifts?

Each . . . the other.

17. a.   Alice gave Sam each dog on the other's leash
    b. * Alice gave Sam the other dog on each's leash
18. a.   John sent Bill each check after the other expired
    b. * John sent Bill the other check after each expired

Negative Polarity Items.

19. a.   Laverne gave Shirley nothing at any of the events
    b. * Laverne gave Shirley anything during none of the events
20. a.   Richie showed Fonzie none of the pictures during any of the exhibitions
    b. * Richie showed Fonzie any of the pictures during none of the exhibitions

Generalization: in V NP_1 NP_2 [. . . NP_3 . . .], NP_3 is in the domain of NP_2.

The B&L tests seem to support the claim that NP_2 asymmetrically c-commands other NPs in VP or adjoined to VP (continuing to assume that these adverbial clauses are adjoined to VP). This suggests that at least by LF, NP_2 is external to VP. Also, from the original B&L tests, we know that NP_1 asymmetrically c-commands NP_2 at LF. That implies, then, that NP_2 is between NP_1 and VP at LF.

6.2.2 The Proposal

The proposal I will make, and support below, is the following. Both objects in the double object construction move to specifier positions of AGRo projections external to VP. This movement is Case-driven, and is overt. That is, at S-structure, NP_1 is in Spec,$AGRo_1$ and NP_2 is in Spec,$AGRo_2$ (the indices 1 and 2 on the AGRo projections have no significance and are added only for ease of reference):

The Double Object Construction

21. Proposed Double Object Structure (S-structure and LF)

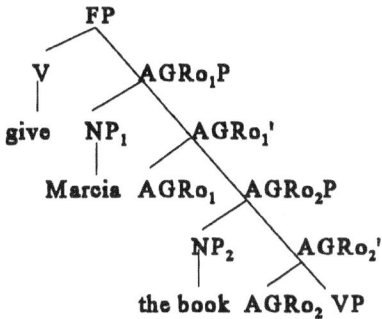

This structure represents what I will be arguing for the next few sections. Once we look a little more carefully at the underlying relations we can explicate the VP part of the structure. For now, what I have to say is consistent with this structure or the one we will come up with in later sections.

The representation encodes what we have discovered so far: NP_1 and NP_2 both asymmetrically c-command the VP and its contents; and NP_1 asymmetrically c-commands NP_2. Assuming the B&L tests to probe for LF structure, the current structure is consistent with the LF facts we have discovered. In the next section I will argue that this structure is correct for S-structure as well.

6.3 THE SURFACE CONFIGURATION OF THE DOUBLE OBJECT CONSTRUCTION

6.3.1 Introduction

The representation in (21), if it is to hold of S-structure as well as LF, makes several predictions about constituency that we will now test. In particular, first it claims that the verb and the first object are external to a constituent containing the second object and other VP elements: $AGRo_2P$. Secondly, it predicts that the objects of the double object construction should be external to a constituent containing the remaining VP complements and adjuncts: VP. Thirdly, it predicts that the adverbs which occur freely within VP, as discussed in Chapter 4, will continue to do so, not interacting with either object. If my claim that adverbs cannot adjoin to AGRoP is correct, then the fact that no adverb can intervene among the string V-NP-NP follows naturally from my proposal. These predictions are what we turn to now.

6.3.2 V and NP_1 are External to VP at S-Structure

The structure in (21), which places NP_1 in Spec,$AGRo_1$ and NP_2 in Spec,$AGRo_2$, predicts that the verb and NP_1 should be external to a constituent containing NP_2 and other verbal complements and adjuncts. This is correct as the following constituency tests suggest.

Coordination. Consider the following examples:

22. a. I gave John [the book in the morning] and [the magazine in the evening]
    b. Rachel sent Marcia [a telegram at her office] and [a box of roses at her apartment]
    c. I showed Sam [my gardenias after breakfast] and [my daffodils after lunch]

What we see, then, is a constituent containing the second object and a verbal adjunct being coordinated independently of the first object and the verb. We have something like the following:

23 I_i gave John$_j$ [$_{AGRo2P}$ the book [$_{VP}$ t_i t_V t_j in the morning]] & [$_{AGRo2P}$ the magazine [$_{VP}$ t_i t_V t_j in the evening]]

Right Node Raising. Similar examples involving right node raising can be constructed:

24. a. I have given John and Sam has given Bill a pewter mug for Christmas
    b. I showed Sam and once even showed Peter the tattoo on my leg in the shower

The Double Object Construction

The RNR examples are difficult because, as Abbott (1976) argued, one might suggest that the PP allegedly in the RNR'd VP, is really a single PP external to VP, modifying both VPs independently. I have tried to construct examples where the PP is understood twice, once for each RNR'd VP. So, in (b), the two events of being in the shower are different for each VP. I assume that this means that PP is in VP, not in the higher IP modifying the whole sentence.

In any event, assuming this to be on the right track, what we have RNR'ing is the lower AGRoP:

25. [$_{AGRo2P}$ a pewter mug [$_{VP}$ t t$_V$ t [for Christmas]]]

6.3.3 Both Objects are External to VP at S-Structure

A second claim made by the structure in (21) is that both NP$_1$ and NP$_2$ are external to VP at S-structure. Constituency tests confirm this to be correct.

Coordination. If the two objects are external to VP then coordination of VP should coordinate the remainder of VP's contents minus the verb, and two objects:

26. a. I gave Greg a gift on purpose last Christmas but only reluctantly this year
    b. I sent Sam a telegram quickly yesterday but less hurriedly today
    c. I sent Tom a letter at home this morning and at his office this afternoon

These examples are a bit awkward but I think point in the right direction. The coordinated VP would look like the following:

27. [$_{VP}$ [... at home] this morning]

Right Node Raising. A similar point can in theory be made with RNR, though, again the examples become difficult to construct:

28. a. I've given Bill a pewter mug and Sam has given Peter a toaster without regrets for Christmas.
    b. I've sent Tom a letter and John has sent Bill a telegram from home in the morning

For example, I believe (b) can be understood to be talking about different homes and mornings, suggesting the PPs are in the RNR'd VP:

29. [$_{VP}$ [. . . from home] in the morning]

Summary: though the coordination and RNR examples can take some work to construct, I think they point to the conclusion that the two objects of the double object construction are external to a constituent which contains the remaining VP material: VP. This then supports the claim that they have moved to VP-external Case positions: the specifiers of two AGRo phrases.

6.3.4 Adverb Placement

Recall our examination of the placement of Jackendoff's (1972) Class II adverbs in Chapter 4. A verb with one PP complement can have the adverb on either side of the PP:

30. a. Chris walked down the street quickly
    b. Chris walked quickly down the street

A verb with two PP complements can have an adverb before or after either PP:

31. a. Sam talked to Carol about Oliver quietly
    b. Sam talked to Carol quietly about Oliver
    c. Sam talked quietly to Carol about Oliver

The same is true of a verb taking a NP and PP complement; that is, an adverb can appear on either side of the PP:

The Double Object Construction

32. a. Cindy showed her book to the boys quietly
    b. Cindy showed her book quietly to the boys

I suggested that these adverbs can adjoin to any projection of V, thus intermingling freely with VP complements:

33. Sam talked [$_{VP}$ (ADV) to Carol (ADV) about Oliver (ADV)]

If these adverbs appear outside of VP, their distribution is more constrained (recall these examples from Chapter 4):

34. a. (Quietly) Mikey (*quietly) has (*quietly) not (?quietly) been (quietly) visiting (*quietly) his parents (quietly)
    b. (Loudly) Betsy (*loudly) has (*loudly) not (?loudly) been (loudly) singing (*loudly) the anthem (loudly)
    c. (Quickly) Chris (*quickly) has (*quickly) not (?quickly) been (quickly) hitting (*quickly) the dog (quickly)

In Chapter 4, the distribution of Class II adverbs was described as follows:

35. Adjunction status (with reference to example (34a)):

- AGRsP = okay (before *Mikey*)
- AGRs' = * (before *has*)
- NegP = * (before *not*)
- TP = ? (before *been*)
- FP = okay (before *visiting*)
- AGRoP = * (before *his parents*)

The point of these examples was that in the functional area of the tree Class II adverb placement is highly constrained. Reference to particular functional heads/projections seems necessary to adequately constrain adverb distribution.

What is relevant for our purposes is the fact that an adverb cannot precede an NP object. I took this to mean that adjunction to AGRoP is impossible. I assume, then, that this is one of the restrictions, among several, on the distribution of these adverbs among the functional categories.

Having said that, we can go back and look at the data involving the double object construction. On a more standard view, that the second object is in VP, we would predict, if our simple statement of VP adverb placement is correct, that a VP adverb can appear on either side of the second object. In other words, the order V NP_1 ADV NP_2 should be acceptable. On the other hand, on my account, in which NP_2 is in Spec,AGRo at S-structure, we predict that it can only be <u>followed by</u> an adverb, since to precede the NP an adverb would have to adjoin to AGRoP, which we have ruled out. So, the order V NP_1 ADV NP_2 is predicted to be ungrammatical. This is the case as the following illustrate:

36. a. * Cindy showed the boys quietly her book
    b. * John sent Mary quickly a letter
    c. * Greg gave Jan slowly the present

6.3.5 Summary

This section has examined constituency and adverb placement in the double object construction. The results point in the direction of the structure in (21), in which both the first object and the second object are in the specifier positions of AGRo phrases.

6.4 THE UNDERLYING STRUCTURE OF THE DOUBLE OBJECT CONSTRUCTION

6.4.1 Introduction

In this section I will discuss two promising views of the underlying and surface structures of the double object construction, those of Larson (1988) and Johnson (1991). Starting with Larson's account I will point out that it makes the wrong predictions in two ways: in the surface constituency and in the adverb placement facts. It also assigns an underlying structure that, on Larson's own view of Binding Theory, predicts unattested connectivity effects in the double object construction.

I will then move on to examine the "clausal DP" proposal of Johnson (1991). On this proposal, the two objects underlyingly form a DP small clause constituent, in which the first is the "subject" of the second. A

The Double Object Construction

number of factors point towards the likelihood of this account, which will be reviewed below.

Ultimately, I will follow the spirit of the clausal DP hypothesis, though adjusting it to account for the findings already pointed out above about the double object construction: that the two objects are both in Spec,AGRo positions at S-structure. The interpretation of the clausal DP proposal that I assume has a number of interesting consequences and makes several correct predictions, reviewed in what follows.

6.4.2 Larson's (1988) Account

6.4.2.1 Review

Recall Larson's account of the double object VP. The first object is in a higher VP-shell, leaving a trace in V'. The second object is right-adjoined to V'. Let us recall the tree:

37. Cindy showed the boys her book

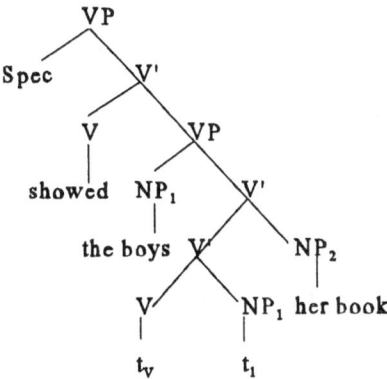

6.4.2.2 Constituency

The first hint that Larson's (1988) structure in (37) is on the wrong track comes from the constituency tests pointed out above. There I showed that in V NP$_1$ NP$_2$ [$_{VP}$X Y], X and Y appear to form a constituent excluding the two objects of the double object construction. This followed on my account since the two objects are external to VP, allowing VP to provide the constituent containing X and Y.

A quick look at (37) suggests that this is not, at least obviously, predicted on Larson's account. Recall the way Larson generates adverbial material. The lower on the thematic hierarchy an element is, the lower in the VP it is generated. So, less argumental material will be generated further down in lower VP-shells. This worked well with regular non-double object VPs: the NP, PPs and other complements appeared to the left, in higher positions, and the adverbial material appeared to the right, in lower positions. However, the double object construction has one odd property that makes this impossible: the second object is base-generated on the <u>right</u> of V' predicting it to be the last element in the VP. If adverbial clauses and such are generated in VP, they should precede the second object:

38. a. * Beaver gave Wally in the morning the quarter
    b. * June showed Ward during his explanation the photos

Therefore, on the simplest interpretation of the Larson account, we find it to predict the incorrect order of adverbials and second object.

Besides predicting the wrong order, this structure does not give us the correct constituency. We know that NP$_1$ and NP$_2$ can be separate from other VP material. Thus, to give Larson a chance, we must assume that something can be done, further than (37). There are two clear possibilities, each of which can handle some of the facts but not all: (1) assume that adverbials can be right-adjoined *outside* of the second object, at least deriving the correct order; or (2) assume the second object moves leftward to the left of the adverbs and other VP elements. Let us consider these options in turn.

Assuming VP adverbials either to be optionally base-generated on the right, or to move there, automatically gives the correct order:

39. a. Beaver gave Wally the quarter [in the morning]
    b. June showed Ward the photos [during his explanation]

The Double Object Construction

Let us start with the possibility that they are base-generated there. The biggest obstacle for this view is the results of the B&L tests which show that NP_2 asymmetrically c-commands into these adverbials. If they are base-generated to the right of the second object, they will be higher than it in the structure. So base-generating them on the right makes the wrong predictions for hierarchy. It also does not allow the correct constituency, since the adverbials would still not be contiguous to other VP material, like argument PPs and such which will still be on the left of NP_2.

Consider then the possibility that the adverbials are base-generated as described by Larson, but then move rightward outside of the second object. For constituency this might have a better chance since at least underlyingly they form a constituent with other VP material not including either of the two objects. What about the B&L tests? The problem was that the overt order NP ADV was found in the cases tested, suggesting that the B&L tests are passed with the rightward-moved adverbial. Once again, however, the rightward-moved adverbial should now be higher than NP_2 in the structure, predicting no asymmetric c-command.

Perhaps the adverbial optionally can lower at LF to its base position in order to satisfy the B&L tests, thus allowing for asymmetric c-command by NP_2 at LF. This encounters problems with the Condition C effects though:

40. * Mike gave Carol the fucker after the letter's unwanted arrival

The S-structure configuration would put the adverbial higher than the second object. If LF lowering to the base position were optional the adverbial should be able to opt not to do it, thus avoiding Condition C effects. The fact that they are unavoidable seems to suggest that the lowering would be obligatory. This is odd.

Let us agree that the rightward movement/generation approach to the adverbials with respect to NP_2 leads to wrong or at least bizarre conclusions. Let us now turn to the other possibility: that NP_2 moves leftward to a position to the left of the lower adverbials.

Taking another look at (37) there is no obvious position to which NP_2 can move. Our constraints are that NP_2 follow NP_1 and precede VP adverbials. Without saying anything else, that would imply that NP_2 must move to left-adjoin to V'. A second possibility would be to posit the existence of an extra VP-shell, the specifier position of which is empty, allowing NP_2 to move into it, perhaps for Case. These two possibilities are outlined below:

41. Revised Larsonian Double Object Structure

    a. NP_2 left-adjoins to V'

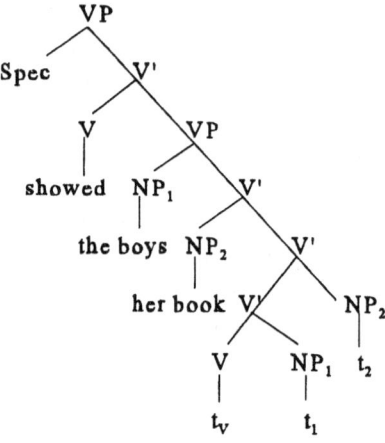

b. NP_2 moves to the specifier of extra VP-shell

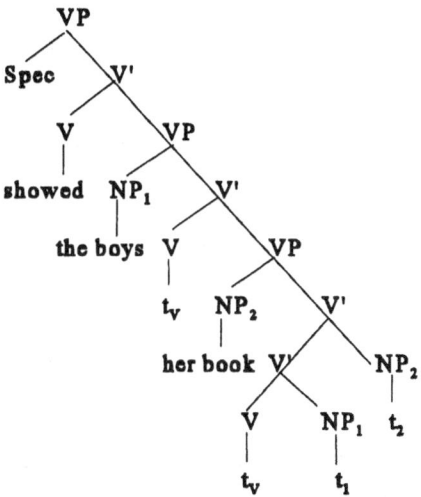

These structures both satisfy what we know about the double object construction: (1) that the adverbial phrase is asymmetrically c-commanded by NP_2; (2) that the adverbial phrase follows NP_2; and (3) that the adverbial phrase, along with other VP material, can form a constituent excluding the two NPs, here one of the lower V's.

In fact these structures are quite similar to the one I propose. They are so close that it might be difficult to distinguish them on purely empirical grounds. Thus, we must look for conceptual grounds on which to choose between the Revised Larsonian structure and my proposal. I turn to this in the next section.

6.4.2.3 Adverb Placement

Recall that one of the advantages my account has over accounts which do not remove NPs from VP is the simple statement of the distribution of VP adverbs: they can adjoin to any projection of V, intermingling with verbal complements. This is illustrated schematically by the following (repeated from above):

42. Sam talked [$_{VP}$ (ADV) to Carol (ADV) about Oliver (ADV)]

The Revised Larsonian structure in (41), in order to account for the distribution of these adverbs, will have to have some way of distinguishing the "top" part of the VP, where the NPs are, from the "bottom" part, where the non-NPs are. This is in order to avoid the following ungrammatical examples:

43. a. * Greg gave lovingly Harvey the CD
    b. * Greg gave Harvey lovingly the CD

There are at least two methods the Larsonian might employ. First, one could try to maintain that adverb generation proceeded as Larson first described, contra the results of Chapter 4, where we were unable to make it generate all and only the correct examples. The adverb is generated in a lower VP position, like other less argumental elements. Then by the rules of V' Reanalysis (V'R) and Light Predicate Raising (LPR), as revised in Chapter 4, we could essentially move the adverbs to various positions in the tree. What we need to do is make sure they do not end up too high, among the NPs. As I suggested, we could limit LPR to applying only within the CFC of the VP. That is, LPR can only apply within the domain in which the theta positions of the main verb are discharged. That limits adverb movement to the lower V' containing the traces of the arguments in (41).

This would correctly block LPR into the NP area of the tree. But conceptually what is this restriction? It is essentially saying that there is some tangible difference between the lower "thematic" part of the VP and the higher "Case-position" part of the tree. The labels V, V' and VP mask this difference, suggesting that all parts of VP are equal. Again, the adverb placement facts, if dealt with in Larson's way, show that we need to be able to distinguish the two quite different areas of VP.

But this is precisely what the proposal I am making does: the VP is the "thematic" part of the tree, the domain in which theta roles are assigned and in which the adverbs can freely be generated; the functional area of the tree is the "Case-position" part (and other functions) of the tree. By assigning different labels with different functions the behavior of something like adverb placement is not as surprising, conceptually.

The Double Object Construction

If Larson's original method of adverb generation is abandoned and adverbs are allowed to be generated in various locations, and are not restricted by LPR, the same problem arises. We still need to allow the adverbs to be generated anywhere within the lower "thematic" part of the VP, and be restricted in the higher "Case-position" part of the tree. Again, this kind of bifurcation in the tree is exactly what is provided by an account which distinguishes more carefully the thematic part of the tree from the functional part.

I conclude, then, that while the Revised Larsonian double object structure in (41) accounts nicely for the empirical facts concerning constituency and hierarchy, it fails on conceptual grounds when the details of adverb placement are examined. My structurally quite similar proposal makes all the right empirical predictions as well as distinguishing conceptually two parts of the tree which need to be distinguished, as we have seen.

The previous two subsections, looking at Larson's account with respect to constituency, hierarchy and adverb placement, only touch on the question of the underlying structure of the double object construction. There is one strong argument against the actual underlying configuration encoded in both Larson's original structure, (37), and the revised structure, (41). I turn to this argument in the next subsection.

6.4.2.4 Lack of Connectivity in the Double Object Construction

Recall Larson's original structure for the double object construction, repeated from above for ease of reference:

44. Cindy showed the boys her book

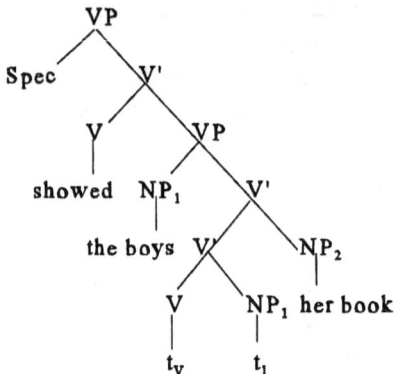

What is of interest is the pre-S-structure representation assumed for this structure. Underlyingly, NP_1 is in the position of t_1. This means that at some point in the derivation NP_2 c-commands NP_1. This is interesting because it is well-known that there are often connectivity effects for Condition A of the binding theory. This fact has been expressed by e.g. Belletti & Rizzi (1988) by considering Condition A to be an "anywhere" rule. This means that if there is ever a point in the derivation at which Condition A can be satisfied, it is satisfied.

Belletti & Rizzi (1988) use this to explain examples like the following:

45. a. Pictures of himself worry Max
    b. [e [$_{VP}$ [$_{V'}$ [worry pictures of himself] Max]   [D-structure]

If verbs like *worry* have two internal arguments, and the lower one moves to subject position at S-structure, the connectivity effects can be explained. At D-structure the surface subject is an object, c-commanded by the higher experiencer object.

Interestingly Larson (1988) uses Belletti & Rizzi's results and accepts the "anywhere" version of Condition A (p. 368). He does this to argue for something unrelated to the present discussion. What he seems not to notice is that acceptance of Condition A as an anywhere condition leads his structure to predict that there should be such connectivity effects in the

The Double Object Construction

double object construction. The second object should be able to bind the first. This is not the case, as Barss & Lasnik (1986) showed:

46. a.   I showed Bill and Tom each other's friends
    b. * I showed each other's friends Bill and Tom

This suggests, then, that, not only is the surface representation proposed by Larson (1988) insufficient to account for the various surface facts, but the underlying representation makes the wrong predictions. Thus, whatever underlying representation I propose will have to have NP_1 asymmetrically c-commanding NP_2 at all points in the derivation.

6.4.2.5 Summary

This section has concentrated on the Larsonian account of the double object construction. It was shown that as a surface representation it cannot, as is, account for the constituency and B&L facts, observed above. Revising it to do so, and then facing the adverb placement facts shows it to be compatible with the facts if two functionally distinct "parts" of the VP are recognized: the lower thematic part, and the upper Case-assignment part. I argued that dividing the VP up this way was unnecessary and conceptually odd. The proposal I made divides the tree up in just the right way: the upper functional part is where the NPs are, having moved there for Case; and the lower thematic part is the VP, where theta roles are assigned and unmoved verbal complements sit. Finally, examining the underlying structure of Larson's VP shows it to incorrectly predict connectivity effects. I now return to looking for an underlying structure which will allow the surface representation successfully argued for so far, without predicting incorrect connectivity effects. I turn now to the account proposed in Johnson (1991), a version of which I believe will fare better in these respects.

6.4.3 Johnson's (1991) "Clausal DP"

6.4.3.1 The Proposal

Johnson (1991) tentatively proposes the following structure for the double object construction (p. 618):

47. Johnson's Clausal DP

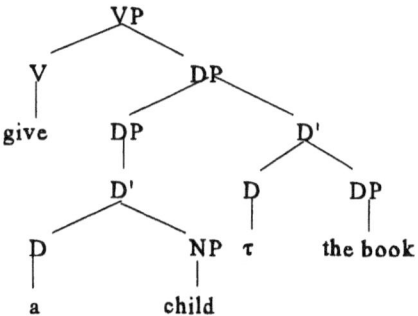

The basic idea, originally due to Kayne (1984), is that the double object verb takes a small clause in the form of a DP. The head of the DP is τ, its complement is the second NP (DP) in the double object construction, and its specifier holds the first.

6.4.3.2 Initial Motivation

Let me review some of the motivation from Kayne (1984) and other sources for this clause-type structure, outlined in Johnson (1991). First, Kayne (1984) points out that the small clause approach perhaps explains why nominalized double object verbs do not have the same argument structure as their verbal counterparts. The same is true of other verbs taking small clauses (Johnson 1991, p. 615):

48. a. * the gift of Gary (of) the book
    b. * Gary's gift (of) the book

The Double Object Construction

49. a. * envy of Sam (of) his job
    b. * Sam's envy (of) his job (with relevant meaning)
50. a. * the belief of Mittie intelligent
    b. * Mary's belief intelligent
51. a. * a consideration of Chris unhappy
    b. * Chris's consideration unhappy

Second, Johnson points out (p. 616) that in some languages whose anaphors show a subject orientation, the first object of the double object construction behaves like a subject. Thus, the following contrast from Danish (from Herslund 1986, p. 135):

52. a. * Jeg fortalte drengen$_i$ om sin$_i$ bamse
       I told boy-the about self's teddybear
    b. ? De gav ham$_i$ sin$_i$ bekomst
       They gave him self's what-he-deserved

Third, the two objects of the double object construction can move together as a unit for object shift in Danish (Vikner 1990, section 4.3):

53. Peter viste [hende den] jo
    Peter showed her it indeed

Johnson further points out that the first object can move independently, but the second cannot (p. 616; examples from Vikner 1990):

54. a.   Peter viste hende jo bogen
         Peter showed her indeed book-the
    b. * Peter viste den jo Marie
         Peter showed it indeed Marie

These facts point to the conclusion that the small clause in the double object construction is in fact a DP, and not some verbal type of clause. Since object shift in Scandinavian targets NPs and not other complements, and it can move the small clause of the double object construction as a unit, it leads to the conclusion that the small clause is nominal.

The fourth type of evidence in favor of the clausal DP proposal targets its DP-hood. Johnson (1991, p. 616-618) discusses an observation of Green's (1974) that a constant element to the meaning of the double object construction in English is a sort of possession relation that holds between the first and second NP. This relation is also what is found between a genitive NP and the NP it is contained in.

For example, (a) does not entail that Gary learned a lesson, where (b) does:

55. a. Mittie taught a lesson to Gary
    b. Mittie taught Gary a lesson

The following pairs illustrate that *New York* and *first base* are incapable of having the relevant possession relation:

56. a. Sam sent a telegram to Gary/New York
    b. Sam sent Gary/*New York a telegram
57. a. Betsy threw a ball to Gary/first base
    b. Betsy threw Gary/*first base a ball

The same sort of restrictions hold between a genitive NP and the remainder of the NP:

58. a.   Gary's lesson
    b.   Gary's telegram
    c. * New York's telegram
    d.   Gary's ball
    e. * first base's ball

The claim then is that if the two objects in a double object construction make up a big NP (DP) the fact that they have similar restrictions on them as do other members of NP would follow.

6.5 CONSIDERATIONS AND REVISIONS

Johnson (1991) argues that the specifier of the clausal DP is not a Case-position. That is, the first object must move elsewhere for Case. As discussed briefly above (in Chapter 5), Johnson assumes the specifier of VP to be an accusative Case position (as well as a higher specifier, but for the present purposes Spec,VP will do), so NP_1 moves to Spec,VP for Case. He also assumes that the clausal DP needs Case. He suggests that this occurs via incorporation into the verb of the head of D: τ.[21]

Johnson's account, as it stands, is going to have trouble with three facts about the double object construction that we have observed: (1) the second object asymmetrically c-commands other material in or adjoined to VP; (2) the two objects are both external to a constituent containing the remainder of the verbal material; and (3) no adverb can intervene between the two NPs at S-structure. On the other hand, his account deals straightforwardly with the connectivity issue pointed out above. Since the first object is underlyingly in the specifier of the DP that the second object is a complement of, and at S-structure moves to a higher Case position, the first object always c-commands the second. No connectivity effects are predicted, or observed.

With respect to (1) and (2), I do not believe Johnson addresses this issue. He does address (3). He proposes (p. 631) to revise the ECP so that X' projections can count as potential barriers to antecedent government. Thus, if an adverb is V'-adjoined and the NP in Spec,DP, a non-theta-governed position, tries to move to Spec,VP, it will not be able to antecedent-govern its trace. This requires that no adverb appear between the two objects.

However, recall from chapter 5 that this proposal was also meant to cover the ungrammatical ECM cases in which an adverb like *strongly*, intervened between the ECM subject and the verb. Johnson's ECP ruled that out. I showed that *strongly,* independently of ECM constructions cannot appear after a verb, so the ECP revision was not needed. I went on to show that in fact the ECP revision ended up blocking acceptable movement:

59. a.   *   I believe John strongly [t to be the murderer]
    b.   John was believed strongly [t to be the murderer]

The revised ECP is meant to block (a), but will also block the much better (b). Not only is the revised ECP not needed for these examples, it appears to over-restrict movement. I conclude that as it stands, Johnson's account predicts that adverbs should intervene between the two objects of the double object construction.

I think that the Kayne-Johnson small clause proposal, assumed as the underlying structure, is an interesting one with some independent motivation. So let us incorporate it into the account and try to make sense of it with relation to the other facts about the double object construction as pointed out in (1) through (3) above.

We will start with (2), the observation that the two objects are external to a projection containing the remainder of the verbal complements. It seems that this could be accommodated in one of two ways. First, we could assume that the whole clausal DP moves to Spec,AGRo. This would get us the two objects external to VP, and in the right order. A question arises as to how the NP in Spec,DP gets Case, since presumably AGRo will not case mark an NP in an NP's specifier. A second possibility would first be to move the NP_1 to a higher Case position, as on Johnson's account. Then we could follow that by moving the whole clausal DP, which as Johnson argues presumably needs Case as well. This would be closer to the proposal I have been supporting all along: each object of the double object construction moves to its own Spec,AGRo for Case. Let us assume that something like that is correct.

Now what about (1), the observation that the second object asymmetrically c-commands other VP internal and adjoined material? We are halfway there since we at least have the second object above VP. However, taking Johnson's proposal at face value, c-command out of the clausal DP does not obtain. We assume the first object is in the higher Spec,AGRo, and the second object <u>embedded in the clausal DP</u> is in the second Spec,AGRo:

The Double Object Construction

60.

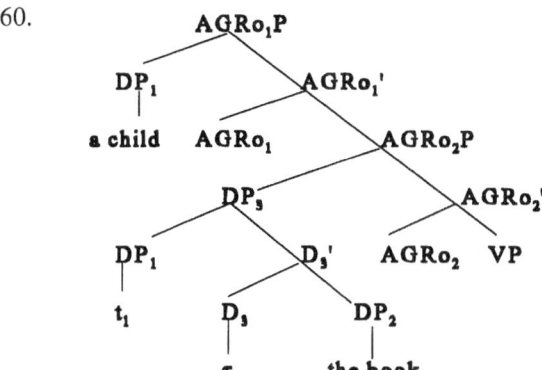

I have labeled the clausal DP, DP_3 for convenience. DP_3 successfully c-commands VP and its contents. But the second object, DP_2 does not. There is too much structure.

I would like to amend Johnson's proposal in a way that will allow the second object to c-command VP but will not, as far as I can tell, affect any of the other claims of the clausal DP proposal. First, the question arises as to exactly what τ is. Recall it had some function on Johnson's account, since it incorporated into V, thus licensing the clause like Case. Besides that, as far as I can tell it has no function. Suppose it is not there. After all we do not need it for its one function since the clausal DP is in fact in a Case position at S-structure: Spec,$AGRo_2$. Suppose on the other hand that the second object is the clausal DP. That is, the head of the second object is the head of the clausal DP, and the first object is base-generated in the specifier of that DP:

61. Revised Clausal DP

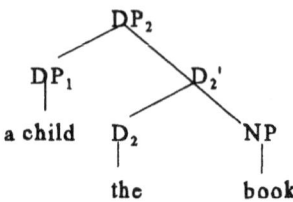

On this revised proposal, underlyingly the first object of the double object construction is actually contained within the second object. Thus, underlyingly, the parallelism between the double object DP and a regular genitive DP is even greater. One difference is the choice of head. The head of *a child's book* is the *'s* (Abney 1987) while the head of the DP in *give a child the book* is *the*. The *'s* has Case-assigning properties and so the NP in the specifier does not need to vacate it in search of Case. The *the*, however, does not assign Case. The NP in its specifier has to find Case elsewhere.

Let us examine the structure of the double object construction with the revised clausal DP:

62.
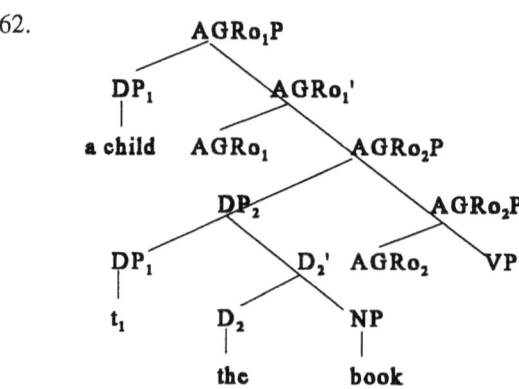

DP_1 is in Spec,$AGRo_1$, where it checks its Case. DP_2 is in Spec,$AGRo_2$, where it checks its Case. DP_2 is external to VP and can c-command it and its contents. And now the adverb facts fall together as well. Since adverbs

The Double Object Construction

cannot adjoin to AGRoP, no possibility of an adverb intervening between the two objects arises.

6.6 SOME CONSEQUENCES AND FURTHER MOTIVATIONS

The revised clausal DP proposal has some interesting consequences which suggest it may be on the right track. The following few subsections catalog these.

6.6.1 Floating Quantifiers

Consider the following examples, adapted from Maling (1976):

63. a. I gave the kids both a quarter
    b. I gave the kids all some candy to keep them quiet
    c. Dad bought the twins both bicycles for Christmas

Continuing to assume that floating quantifiers are really stranded quantifiers marking positions in which an NP has been, these examples are puzzling on a view not incorporating a clausal DP.

On a view that accepts the conclusions of this section–that both objects are VP-external–but does not accept the clausal DP approach, these appear to lead to one conclusion: there is a third NP position available in the double object construction. One is Spec,AGRo$_2$, where NP$_2$ sits. Another is the position held by NP$_1$. The third is that held by the stranded quantifier, stranded by NP$_1$'s movement to its final position:

64. I gave [the kids]$_1$ [each t$_1$] [a quarter]$_2$ [$_{VP}$ ...]

This third position surprises us. Why should it be there? What position is NP$_1$ actually in?

However, on the clausal DP hypothesis we already expect a position to appear between the two NPs: it is the position out of which NP$_1$ moved, the specifier of NP$_2$:

65. I gave [the kids]₁ [$_{DP2}$ [each t₁] a quarter] [$_{VP}$ ...]

So, our assumed approach to floating quantifiers combined with the present clausal DP hypothesis explains this otherwise puzzling fact.

6.6.2 Scope Freezing

Another fact about the double object construction that has been puzzling is that as far as scope relations go the first object always has the second in its scope (examples from Larson 1990).

66. a. The teacher assigned some student every problem
    b. The teacher assigned every problem to some student

Every problem cannot have scope over *some student* in (a), unlike (b).

One might think that perhaps the second object in the double object construction simply cannot get scope outside its S-structure position. This is not the case. It can get wider scope than other material, but if it does get wider scope, the first object must also have wider scope.

Larson (1990) points out (p. 605, fn. 10) that the second object can show a de dicto/de re ambiguity with respect to a higher predicate. So in the following example *every apartment in the building* is ambiguous between being read opaquely and being read transparently with respect to *promise*. Interestingly, if *every apartment in the building* is de re, *someone* must be de re as well:

67. I promised to rent someone every apartment in the building

As Larson points out, a de re reading for *every apartment in the building* requires it to be assigned scope beyond *promise*. And if this is done, obligatorily the same scope is required for *someone* giving it the de re reading.

These observations follow straightforwardly on the clausal DP approach. The second object contains a trace of the first object. If the second object undergoes QR for scope assignment, the first must have

The Double Object Construction 155

done so as well. Why? Because the second object contains a trace of the first:

68. a.   promise [someone]$_1$ [t$_1$ every apartment]$_2$
   b.   [someone]$_1$ [t$_1$ every apartment]$_2$ promise ... t$_1$ t$_2$
   c. * [t$_1$ every apartment]$_2$ promise [someone]$_1$ t$_2$
69. a.   assign [some student]$_1$ [t$_1$ every problem]$_2$
   b. * assign [t$_1$ every problem]$_2$ [some student]$_1$ t$_2$

NP$_1$ must c-command NP$_2$ at LF in order to satisfy the ECP. On an account of the double object construction which does not have any relationship between the two objects, this restriction is mysterious.

6.6.3 Passive

It is well known that in standard varieties of American English, passive in the double object construction moves the first object to subject position, but not the second (see Perlmutter & Postal 1983). Consider the following examples:

70. a.   Cindy sent Buddy the letter
   b.   Buddy$_1$ was sent t$_1$ the letter
   c. * The letter$_2$ was sent Buddy t$_2$

A number of accounts for this have been proposed. On the standard assumption that in passive somehow the accusative Case feature of the verb is absorbed, one account of this paradigm argues that *the letter* in (a) is inherently Case-marked by the verb so that passive does not effect its Case.[22]

That account is dubious for one good reason. As I think I have shown, the second object, like the first, is VP-external arguably because it has moved for structural Case in Spec,AGRo. This means, on the one hand, that the NP is not in its D-structure inherent Case-marked position as claimed by the inherent Case approach (or put another way: the NP moved–why?). On the other hand, the NP appears to be able to get structural Case, casting doubt on the necessity of an inherent Case account altogether.

Let us re-think passive for a moment. The Case assignment approach I have been taking, following essentially Chomsky (1993), is that the verb itself has Case features that it checks off in AGRo. If the verb has one internal argument, it has one Case feature. If it has two internal arguments, it has two Case features. The fact that a verb has Case features to check implies that the functional array of the tree had better have the correct number of AGRo projections. If the verb has one Case feature, one AGRoP is needed. If the verb has two Case features, two AGRoP's are needed. The functional projection AGR does not itself have Case features; it simply mediates between the DP and the verb. And, following Chomsky, I assume that every AGR is the same. It is just a functional element mediating Case checking.

If this is on the right track, then passive of a double object verb absorbs one of the two Case features the verb has to check. With only one Case feature left, only one AGRoP is needed in the functional array. Let us assume, for the argument, that we have the S-structure account of the double object construction I argued for above except without the clausal DP idea. That is, underlyingly the two arguments are generated in VP independently. If the double object verb is passivized, then one Spec,AGRo is licensed to mediate Case-assignment. Thus, one of the two arguments can move to Spec,AGRo. The other can go to Spec,AGRs (since alongside losing accusative Case, the verb loses its external argument). On the hypothesis that we do not have a clausal DP, how is it to be determined which DP moves to Spec,AGRs and which to Spec,AGRo? Without some extra machinery, ungrammatical (c) is as likely to be derived as grammatical (b).[23]

On the other hand, if the clausal DP approach is adopted, only one of the two DPs could possibly move to Spec,AGRs: the DP which is underlyingly in the specifier of the clausal DP. Why? Because if the clausal DP itself moved to Spec,AGRs the trace of the other DP within it would not satisfy the ECP:

71. a.   Buddy$_1$ was sent t$_1$ [t$_1$ the letter]$_2$
    b. * [t$_1$ the letter]$_2$ was sent Buddy$_1$

6.6.4 Position and Interpretation

A well-known correlation between the interpretation of an NP and whether it can be extracted out of, and a little-known effect partially correlating the interpretation of the first object in a double object construction with the interpretation of the second, lead us to look a little more closely at NP interpretation and LF positions of objects. I will essentially follow Diesing's (1992) Mapping Hypothesis (with the caveat that much more careful attention is paid to it and its effects in the following chapter) and assume that objects appearing in VP at LF (e.g. by "lowering" there) are interpreted as nonspecific/existential. Those which remain in Spec,AGRo are interpreted as specific/quantificational/etc. Our account of the double object construction, which puts a close relationship between the two objects–the first binding a trace in the second–constrains their LF configurational possibilities. We see more evidence for this when we observe the facts about extraction out of the objects in the double object construction, as well as the interpretations possible for the two objects.

6.6.4.1 A Prediction: Extraction out of NP_1

Diesing (1992) discusses the well known observation that extraction out of NP is sensitive to the interpretation of the NP. Consider the following contrasts (taken from Diesing 1992, 97):

72. a.   Who did you see pictures of?
    b.   Who did you see a picture of?
    c.   Who did you see many pictures of?
    d.   Who did you see several pictures of?
    e.   Who did you see some pictures of?
73. a. *? Who did you see the picture of?
    b. *? Who did you see every picture of?
    c. *? Who did you see most pictures of?
    d. *? Who did you see each picture of?
    e. ?? Who did you see the pictures of?

The NPs in (72) all are interpreted as existential or nonspecific NPs; the NPs in (73), however, are quantificational or presuppositional. According to Diesing, interpretation is guided by the Mapping Hypothesis, which determines which part of the syntactic tree maps onto which part of the semantic (DRT) representation:[24]

74. *Mapping Hypothesis*: Material from VP is mapped into the nuclear scope. Material from IP is mapped into the restrictive clause.

What this means for us is that if a phrase is presuppositional or quantificational, such as a definite NP or specific indefinite NP, it must be VP-external at LF in order to map onto the restrictive clause. If a phrase is existential, nonpresuppositional, etc., such as a nonspecific indefinite NP, it must be VP-internal at LF to map onto the nuclear scope of the representation.

Diesing argues then that the link between interpretation and grammatical extraction out of NP is only indirect. The grammatical extraction examples all involve extraction out of an NP which is in VP at LF; the ungrammatical examples involve extraction out of an NP external to VP at LF. She argues that the extraction is sensitive to the position, not the interpretation, of the NP.

To make this proposal more concrete I will abstract away from the details of Diesing's analysis, since she assumes objects to be in VP at S-structure, and implement her idea in my framework. On my account, objects are VP-external–in Spec,AGRo–at S-structure. That implies that at LF, they either remain there, and get interpreted as quantificational (being mapped onto the restrictive clause), or they lower to their VP-internal base position, and get interpreted as existential (mapped onto the nuclear scope). (Chapter 7 discusses LF "lowering" in detail.)

What about extraction? Diesing attributes the ungrammaticality of (73) to the ECP. Intuitively, looking at the LF representations, we can describe the generalization as the following: an LF complement of V is not a barrier to extraction; and an LF non-complement is a barrier to extraction. Assuming barrierhood is defined to include a statement about theta government, essentially the contrast boils down to the question of whether NP is theta governed at LF. For concreteness we will assume the

The Double Object Construction

following definitions (essentially Chomsky 1986a, adapted from Johnson 1991, but amended so XP, but not X', is a blocking category):

75. **Empty Category Principle**: A non-pronominal empty category must be properly governed.

76. α properly governs β iff:
    a. α theta governs β, or
    b. α antecedent governs β.
        i) α theta governs β iff α theta marks and governs β.
        ii) α antecedent governs β iff α and β are coindexed and no barrier for β excludes α.

77. **Barriers**
    α, a maximal projection, is a blocking category for τ iff α includes τ and is not theta governed. Φ is a barrier for τ iff Φ includes τ and:
    a. is a blocking category for τ, or
    b. Φ immediately dominates a blocking category for τ

Now consider the LFs of acceptable and unacceptable extractions out of DP:

160   Noun Phrase Licensing

78. Extraction out of DP

a. Who did you see a picture of   [LF]

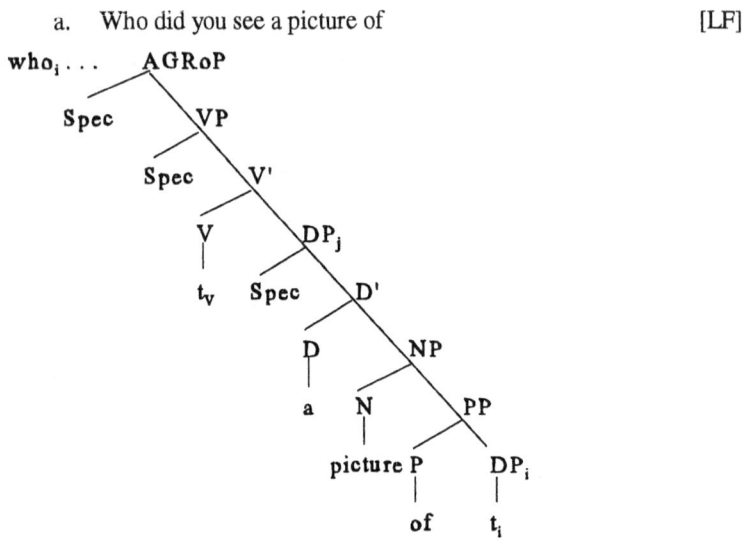

b. *   Who did you see the picture of?   [LF]

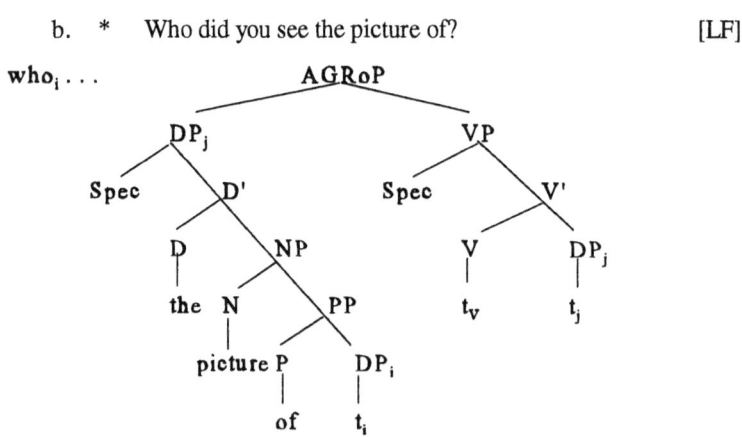

In the grammatical example, (78a), since DP_j is to be interpreted as existential it has "lowered" to VP at LF. Diesing (1992) assumes syntactic lowering; I will exploit the copy and delete strategy in chapter 7. Whatever

The Double Object Construction

the mechanics of it, the phrase appears in VP at LF. DP_j, then, is theta governed by the trace of V at LF. Thus, DP_j is not a barrier for extraction of DP_i. In the ungrammatical example, (78b), DP_j is in Spec,AGRo at LF. This is because it is meant to obtain a nonexistential reading. Being nonexistential it must be VP-external at LF. Since it is not in VP, it is not theta governed by anything at LF. Thus, DP_j is a barrier for the extraction of DP_i, hence the ungrammaticality.

Now, let us turn to the double object construction. Not surprisingly, extraction out of the second object is fine:

79. a. Who did you say Cindy sent Bobby a picture of t?
    b. What did Mary tell you John bought Shirley a box of t?
    c. Who did Ron say Kim sent me a story about t?

These examples are all acceptable assuming a nonspecific interpretation of the second object. If the account outlined above is on the right track, that implies that the second object can appear in a theta governed position at LF.

Before turning to the structure, let us consider the behavior of the first object. Perhaps surprisingly, extraction out of the first object is significantly worse:

80. a. * Who did you say Cindy sent a friend of t a picture?
    b. * What did Mary tell you John bought friends of t a book?
    c. * Who did Ron say Kim sent an acquaintance of t a threatening letter?

To avoid the specificity effect, to be discussed in the next section, the second object must be nonspecific in order to allow the first also to be nonspecific. Even with this, though, the examples are bad. This, then, implies that the first object in the double object construction cannot be in a theta governed position at LF.

Now, let us consider the account of double objects I have proposed. Underlyingly, the two objects form one clausal DP in VP. At S-structure each object moves to its own Case position external to VP. In order to receive nonspecific interpretations the objects can lower to VP, following the Mapping Hypothesis. However, in VP, only the second object, the clausal DP itself, is theta governed. The second object's DP will not be a barrier to extraction. On the other hand, the first object, in the specifier position of the clausal DP, is not theta governed. Thus, it's DP will be a barrier to extraction.

Consider the structures:

81. Extraction out of the Objects in the Double Object Construction

    a. Who did you say Cindy sent Bobby a photo of t? [LF]

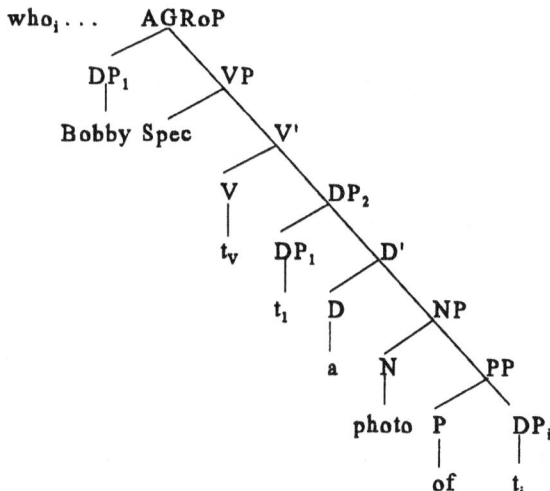

The Double Object Construction

b. * Who did you say Cindy sent a friend of t a picture? [LF]

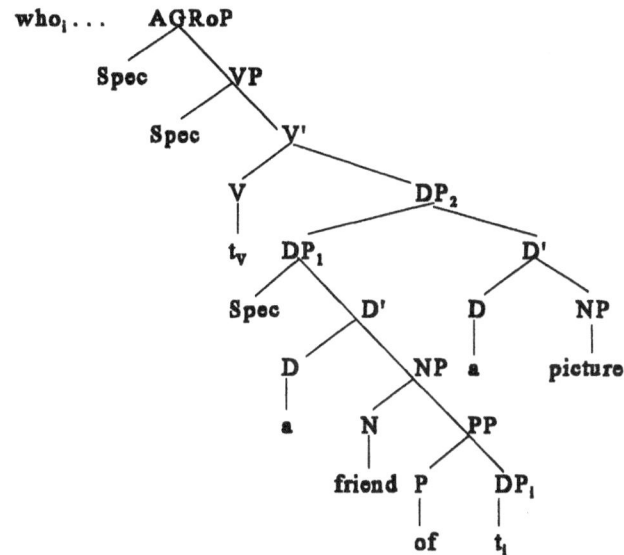

In (81a), in which DP_2 is interpreted as existential, it "lowers" to VP at LF. DP_2 is, therefore, theta governed by the trace of V. Thus, DP is not a barrier to extraction. Now consider (81b). DP_1 is in Spec,DP_2. While DP_2 is theta governed, DP_1 is not. Hence, DP_1 is a barrier to extraction.

The intuition behind this analysis is that extraction is impossible out of any LF specifier. But it is acceptable out of an LF complement. Since the DP_1 is a specifier throughout the derivation it has no chance of not being a barrier to extraction. Since DP_2 can lower to its base VP complement position, it can avoid being a barrier at LF.

This account makes a prediction about the behavior of subjects. A subject which can lower to a VP complement position should be able to be extracted out of. One that was generated in a specifier position and moved to a specifier should always be a barrier. Though (a) is not absolutely perfect, it contrasts with (b):

82. a. ? Who did you say [some friends of t] were found dead in the cemetery?
  b. * Who did you say [some friends of t] saw John on TV?

If the passive subject in (a) can lower to its base V complement position at LF, it need not be a barrier for extraction. In (b) which has a transitive subject, the assumption is that it is always in a specifier position, thus unavoidably a barrier to extraction.[25]

A second prediction it makes is that the ECM subject should be able to be extracted out of just in case it can lower to a V complement position at LF. Assuming, again, that passive subjects have such a base position as opposed to transitive ones, consider the following contrast:[26]

83. a. ? Who did you say John expects [friends of t] to be arrested?
  b. * Who did you say John expects [friends of t] to call Mary?

Again, the (a) example is not perfect, but a contrast is felt.[27]

This type of analysis is available not only to the clausal DP proponents. It is also follows on an account of double objects in which the first object is base-generated in a VP-internal, but not theta-governed position. As long as the first object cannot end up in a complement position, the contrasts will follow. An account which base generates the first object as a complement, on the other hand, predicts it should not be a barrier for extraction. Let us now turn to such an account and see what happens.

Larson's (1988) account of the double object construction places the first object as complement of V at D-structure. The second object is adjoined to V'. At S-structure the first object is in Spec,VP:

The Double Object Construction

84. Cindy showed the boys her book

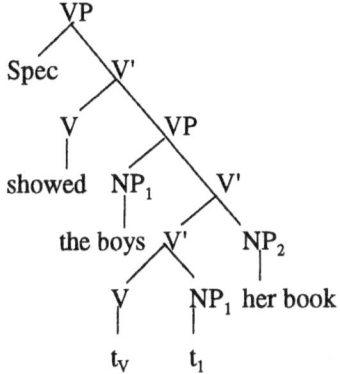

Taking Larson's structure at face value and applying my account of extraction out of object it appears that the wrong predictions are made. NP_1 is a D-structure complement and thus should be able to lower to that position, be theta governed, and not be a barrier. NP_2 is adjoined to V', but its V' sister, according to Larson (1988), reanalyzes as V to assign inherent Case, so perhaps it also theta governs in that configuration.

Thus, the problem is NP_1. Larson is of course not obligated to follow my analysis so let us consider other accounts consistent with his structure. He could claim that the ECP must be satisfied at S-structure. At S-structure NP_1 is in a specifier and thus is a barrier.

However, recall that extraction out of regular objects is acceptable, if they are nonspecific. On Larson's account a transitive object is base generated as a sister to V if there are no lower arguments. If there are lower arguments, the NP is base generated as a specifier:

85. a. [$_{IP}$ e [$_{VP}$ John [$_{V'}$ saw Mary]]]
    b. [$_{IP}$ e [$_{VP}$ John [$_{V'}$ e [$_{VP}$ Mary [$_{V'}$ saw in the park]]]]]

In (a), the object *Mary* is generated as a sister to V. In (b), the PP *in the park* is generated as sister to V. *Mary* is generated in Spec,VP, as is *John*. Ultimately NP movement of the subject in both examples and verb movement in (b) derive the correct surface orders.

What this means is that sometimes an object is a complement and sometimes it is a specifier. Does this affect extraction possibilities?

Extraction out of an object which is a specifier (b) is just as acceptable as extraction out an object which is a complement (a):

86. a. Who did you say you saw t?
    b. Who did you say you saw t in the park?

Larson's account, then, cannot try to link extraction (im)possibilities to specifier vs. complement position. It is not clear to me what other syntactic differences there could be between a regular direct object and NP_1 in the double object construction.

Summary: the clausal DP proposal can plausibly account for the fact that the first NP in a double object construction cannot be extracted out of. The account generalizes nicely to cover extraction out of all LF specifiers. Larson's (1988) account, which treats the first NP in the double object construction on a par with a normal transitive object does not predict the extraction contrasts found.

6.6.4.2 The Specificity Effect

Having touched on the relationship between position and interpretation, let me mention a curious generalization appearing to hold for the double object construction in English (pointed out to me by Janina Radó and Kyle Johnson, p.c.). If the second object is definite or specific, the first must be as well. That is, if a potentially nonspecific indefinite object is NP_1, it must be given its specific interpretion if NP_2 is definite or also specific. The effect is more obvious when compared to the non-double object alternants:

87. a. I sent a doctor the letter
    b. I sent the letter to a doctor

The effect is subtle and difficult to nail down. Comparing (a) and (b), (b) can mean that I sent some letter under discussion to some doctor or other. It seems to be unimportant to me or the hearer who the doctor is. On the other hand, (a) implies that there is a specific doctor that I have in mind and that, though this doctor is not already salient in the discourse (hence the use of the indefinite), the hearer should take it to mean that I didn't just

The Double Object Construction 167

send the letter to any old doctor. While (b) can be the answer to the question, "What did you do with the letter?", (a) does not seem an appropriate answer to this question.

This effect does not appear to be present when both objects are potentially nonspecific indefinites:

88. a. I sent a doctor a letter
    b. I sent a letter to a doctor

I think for (a) and (b) both indefinites can get a nonspecific interpretation. This means that I am saying that I sent some doctor some letter and that the hearer need not be concerned with which doctor or letter. These can both be an answer to the question, "What did you just do?"

I will not give a full analysis of this phenomenon but will point in the direction of an answer (and see Chapter 7 for more discussion). Diesing (1992), as discussed above, argued that the LF position of an indefinite determines its interpretation. A VP-internal indefinite is interpreted as an existential/non-specific indefinite. A VP-external indefinite and definite gets a presuppositional/specific interpretation; this is essentially her Mapping Hypothesis. Without going into the motivation for Diesing's hypothesis let us consider what it predicts for the cases at hand.

If nonspecific indefinites must be in VP at LF, then the mapping from S-structure to LF will have to involve lowering nonspecific subjects and objects back into their VP-internal base positions (again see the discussion in Chapter 7). On the other hand, if specific indefinites and definites must be VP-external at LF to get the appropriate interpretation, they can remain in their S-structure, VP-external, positions for the mapping to LF.

Consider now the examples showing our specificity effect. The second object is specific/definite. It must be VP-external at LF. If the first object <u>wants</u> to be nonspecific it must lower to VP at LF. However, if the first object lowers to VP, it will not be able to bind its trace in the second object at LF, violating the ECP:

89. a.   I sent [a doctor]$_1$ [t$_1$ the letter]$_2$ [$_{VP}$ ...]   [LF]
    b. *   I sent [t$_1$ the letter]$_2$ [$_{VP}$ ... [a doctor]$_1$ ...]   [LF]

In (a), both objects are VP-external at LF, being interpreted as specific, and the ECP is satisfied. In (b) the second object is VP-external and thus specific, but the first object has lowered back into VP for a non-specific interpretation. However, doing so it has left its trace in NP_2 ungoverned thus violating the ECP at LF.

An alternative explanation would be that unless NP_2 lowers to VP, NP_1 has no VP-internal base position. Recall that NP_1 is base generated as the specifier of NP_2. If NP_2 remains in Spec,AGRo, so does the base position of NP_1, thus ruling out lowering for NP_1.

Either explanation, though, has at its root the clausal DP hypothesis and the claim that NP_1 is underlyingly part of NP_2.

6.7 REMAINING ISSUES

The clausal DP proposal, which places the trace of NP_1 in the specifier of NP_2, appears to make the wrong predictions in one domain. Consider the following examples:

90. a. What did you give John t?
    b. Which letters will you send Marcia t?
    c. How many calendars did you show Shirley t?

What is unusual about these cases is that we have overt wh movement of NP_2, the phrase containing the trace of NP_1. A couple of questions are raised: (1) what is the internal structure of a wh phrase containing the trace of another argument?; and (2) how does that trace satisfy the ECP?

Question (1) leads to a broader question: what is the internal structure of any phrase normally thought to be an entire DP, when it contains the trace of another argument? So, besides the wh phrases above, we have examples like the following:

91. a. I gave him it
    b. I showed him Mary

The Double Object Construction

Standardly, pronouns and names are thought to be entire DPs, incapable of having material in their specifiers, if they even have specifiers. The clausal DP proposal would place NP_1 in the specifier of these phrases.

Whatever the answer to this question is, it is not an isolated problem for just the clausal DP proposal. The same question arises for other small clauses. For example, (a) arguably has the structure in (b):

92. a. I consider John a good friend
    b. I consider [John$_i$ [t$_i$ [a good friend]]]

In favor of this is the possibility of leaving a floating quantifier in the position of t:

93. a. I consider the boys each a good friend
    b. I consider [the boys$_i$ [each t$_i$ [a good friend]]]

Given this, the following duplicates the problem pointed out above:

94. Q: Do you consider John your best friend?
    Do you consider [John$_i$ [t$_i$ [your best friend]]]
    A: Yes, I would consider him/John that
    I would consider [him$_i$ [t$_i$ that]], or
    I would consider [him$_i$ [that]]

In the answer, the pronominal *that* refers to the predicate *your best friend*. Each of the two structures leaves us with questions. The first one again is, how can a pronoun have a trace in its DP? The second one is, if the pronoun does not have a trace in its DP, where did *him* come from?

In favor of the first structure are examples like the following:

95. Q: Do you consider Mark and Robbie your best friends?
    A: Yes, I consider them/the boys each that, and more
    I consider [them$_i$ [each t$_i$ [that]]]

Also, it is possible to passivize *consider* completely removing its subject, uncontroversially leaving a trace:

96. Q: Has John always been considered your best friend?
    A: Yes, he's always been considered [t₁ [that]]

On the assumption that *consider* takes a DP, not larger, small clause complement, it must be admitted that the pronoun *that* can replace the small clause while allowing the trace of the subject in its specifier:

97. [_DP_ t₁ [that]]

Let us assume, then, that in principle it is possible for a pronoun to contain a trace in its specifier. Having decided that, we can simply extend that to the case of names and wh phrases. That answers question (1). The wh phrase can have a trace in its specifier position:

98. what: [_DP2_ t₁ [what]]

Now, question (2) concerned how NP₁ binds its trace if the wh phrase containing the trace is moved overtly:

99. [_DP_ t₁ [what]]₂ did you give John₁ t₂

To satisfy the ECP, *John* must c-command t₁ at LF. What we want at LF is for at least some of the moved phrase containing t₁ to be in the position of t₂. Notice that this problem is duplicated for other small clauses:

100. Q: What do you consider John?
     [_DP_ t₁ [what]]₂ do you consider John₁ t₂
     A: I consider John a good friend

And passive can blatantly move the small clause subject uncontroversially leaving a trace in the moved wh phrase:

101. Q: What has John always been considered?
     [_DP_ t₁ [what]]₂ has John₁ always been considered t₂
     A: He's always been considered t a very close friend
        He₁'s always been considered [_DP_ t₁ [a very close friend]]

The Double Object Construction 171

Notice that if the small clause is indeed a DP, an alternative analysis which might claim that only *a very close friend* is what *what* questions cannot be correct. The reason is that *a very close friend* is only a D', and it is a fairly common assumption that wh movement moves full DPs not D's.

To address question (2) let us develop a suggestion of Chomsky's (1993, p. 49). Chomsky was accounting for reconstruction effects like the following, which are quite parallel to our trace-in-DP examples. Compare (a) and (b):

102. a. [Which pictures of himself$_1$]$_2$ did Mary think John$_1$ bought t$_2$
     b. [t$_1$ [what]]$_2$ did you give John$_1$ t$_2$

In both examples we have a moved wh phrase containing an anaphor, in (a) a reflexive, in (b) an NP trace.

Chomsky's proposal is that A'-movement uses the copy and delete strategy. That is, A'-movement leaves a full copy instead of a trace. Then, at some level we have the following for the double object example:

103. [$_{DP}$ t$_1$ [what]]$_2$ did you give John$_1$ [$_{DP}$ t$_1$ [what]]$_2$

To get from this to the properly interpretable LF representation Chomsky (p. 50) assumes that another operation, akin to QR, applies moving the wh word out of the wh phrase, leaving something like this:

104. [what] [$_{DP}$ t$_1$ [t]]$_2$ did you give John$_1$ [what] [$_{DP}$ t$_1$ [t]]$_2$

He suggests that we need to get from this kind of structure to the appropriate operator-variable structure. So, in the operator position (Spec,CP), everything but the operator must delete; in the trace position, the copy of the operator material deletes. This would leave us at LF the following representation:

105. [what] did you give John$_1$ [$_{DP}$ t$_1$ [t]]$_2$

Many question are left open by this proposal. For example, what is this step– "akin to QR"?, what ensures the correct deletion?, etc. However, it does leave us with exactly the LF representation we need. *John* c-commands t_1 at LF and thus satisfies the ECP as desired. I will then leave this problem as potentially solvable.

A second question arises once that first one is solved. If it is possible to "reconstruct" the DP containing the trace of NP_1 at LF, thus allowing NP_1 to bind t_1, why is the same sort of operation not available for QR? Recall the scope freezing phenomenon found in the double object construction (from §6.6.2):

106. The teacher assigned some student every problem

This can have only the interpretation in which NP_1 has scope over NP_2. I suggested that this followed from the clausal DP proposal since NP_2 contains the trace of NP_1:

107. a. [some student]$_1$ [t_1 every problem]$_2$
     b. * [t_1 every problem]$_2$ [some student]$_1$ t_2

Interestingly the same facts hold for QR of expressions containing overt anaphors. Consider the following:

108. Mary thought that some boy bought every picture of himself
     a. [some boy]$_1$ [every picture of [himself]$_1$]$_2$
     b. * [every picture of [himself]$_1$]$_2$ [some boy]$_1$ t_2

This can only be interpreted with *some boy* having scope over *every picture of himself* as in (a), not the reverse, as in (b). This restriction is quite plausibly analyzed as a binding problem: the anaphor needs to be bound by its antecedent. Once again this is quite parallel to our trace-in-DP example: we have a quantified expression containing an anaphor, this time NP trace. If the quantified expression QRs over the antecedent of the anaphor, the trace is not bound at LF.

With overt wh movement, we found reconstruction was possible. With covert QR, reconstruction apparently is not possible. Recall that the copy and delete strategy for A'-movement was how we derived the reconstruction effects for wh movement. There are two possible directions to look for an answer. One is to question whether the copy and delete strategy for movement is available to all A'-movement. The dichotomy

The Double Object Construction

might be covert vs. overt movement with the latter following the copy and delete strategy and the former not. A second possibility is to assume both types of movement follow the copy and delete strategy but what differs is what deletes where. Let us consider these possibilities in turn.

Possibility one is that the copy and delete strategy is available for only overt movement. Covert movement like QR moves the phrase leaving a trace/variable, not a copy. This dichotomy is disconfirmed by the following. Covert wh movement can exhibit reconstruction effects, suggesting that the copy and delete strategy is available for it:

109. Q: Who thinks that John bought which pictures of himself?
      A: Marcia thinks he bought the nude
      Greg thinks he bought the one in the clown outfit
      Cindy thinks he bought the one with the green frame

LF wh movement of the wh phrase in situ is assumed to account for the readings observed. What is important for us is that this reading is available even with the binding of *himself* by *John*. This suggests that an LF like the following is available:

110. which$_j$ who thinks John$_1$ bought t$_j$ pictures of [himself$_1$]

This is predicted on the copy and delete strategy for A'-movement.

Let us consider a second version of possibility one: QR does not use the copy and delete strategy while all other A'-movement operations do. This would account for the binding differences we have noted:

111. a. * [every picture of [himself$_1$]]$_2$ [some boy]$_1$ bought t$_2$
     b.   [which] ... John$_1$ bought t picture of himself$_1$

The same LF representations could be derived if we explore the second possibility: all A'-movement uses the copy and delete strategy but what deletes differs. Specifically, if (a) and (b) are the final LF representations we want, the difference between a true quantified expression like *every picture* and a wh phrase operator-variable construction like *which picture* is where the restriction on the operator appears in the representation. With a true quantified expression the restrictor must apparently remain closer to the quantifier itself, as in (a), while with a wh phrase operator, the restrictor can be in the embedded position, as in (b). Thus, after copy movement, the choice of what deletes would differ. If the restrictor is on a quantifier, the "downstairs" copy of the restrictor deletes. If the restrictor is on a wh phrase, the "upstairs" copy deletes.

Either the second version of the first possibility (that QR does not exploit the copy and delete strategy) or the second possibility (that restrictors delete differently depending on what they restrict) seems plausible. Surely other considerations can help us choose the correct approach but for now I will simply assume that one is workable. In chapter 7 a principled distinction is drawn between "overt" copy and delete movement and "covert" QR-type movement which will account for the above contrasts.

What this means, then, is that my account of the scope freezing above is right in line with whatever account one has for other scope freezing phenomena, as with embedded anaphors. As well, my account of the wh movement possibilities of the second object of the double object construction is parallel to the account of similar phenomena with overt anaphors.

In fact, that such parallels are found between the double object construction with its hidden anaphor in NP_2 and other constructions with overt anaphors serves to independently support the kind of account I have proposed.

6.8 CONCLUSION

I have proposed an account of the double object construction which is consistent with all of the properties we have discovered: the two objects are external to VP at S-structure and potentially at LF; and, the underlying relationship between the two places the second within the scope of the first. The particular version of the clausal DP proposal I adopt has a number of interesting consequences which ultimately support it: the placement of floating quantifiers, scope freezing phenomena, passive, extraction out of NP, and the specificity effect.

CHAPTER 7
LF Noun Phrase Positions

7.1 INTRODUCTION

The previous chapters of this thesis have concentrated on the distribution of noun phrases in the overt syntax. Specifically, I argued that subject and object NPs appear in the specifiers of AGR phrases at S-structure. Most of the arguments presented relied on data involving definite NPs. This chapter will begin by showing that the same sorts of arguments suggest that indefinite NPs behave like definite ones in the overt syntax. This needs to be established because then I turn to their behavior at LF. While definite NPs appear in Spec,AGR at LF, indefinite NPs vary in their LF positions: they can appear in Spec,AGR or in their base VP-internal positions. My goal will be to provide a syntactic analysis which can account for this.

Since at S-structure definite and indefinite NPs alike are in Spec,AGR, yet at LF some of the indefinite NPs are in VP, we must tackle the question of what LF "lowering" is. I argue that employing the copy and delete strategy for A-movement, as suggested by Chomsky (1993), allows a neat account of the observed PF/LF mismatches. However, the copy and delete strategy opens up new questions about the nature of copying and the constraints on deletion. These questions are probed and potential answers are provided.

Ultimately, two interesting claims are made by the analysis. First, if A-movement is copy and delete movement and a suggestion by Marantz (1994) is correct, it must occur prior to the split to PF and LF. In fact, all copy and delete movement must apply before the split to PF/LF. This is a welcome result because it provides a principled account for the differences between LF movement and overt movement. The latter but not the former (e.g. QR) shows reconstruction effects, a hallmark of copy and delete movement.

A second claim made by the analysis is that certain positions must be filled at PF. It is shown that this cannot follow from a simple feature strength account (cf. Chomsky 1993) since that is only meant to motivate overt movement, not constrain deletion. I suggest that certain specifier positions must be filled at PF because their projections are licensed at that level. A licensed head requires a filled specifier. This approach is meant to capture extended projection principle effects as well as force objects to appear overtly in Spec,AGRo.

7.2 THE SURFACE POSITION OF INDEFINITE OBJECTS

Previous chapters tried to establish that definite direct objects are in Spec,AGRo, a functional position dominating VP, at S-structure. I will begin this chapter by first showing that some of the same arguments can be made suggesting that indefinite direct objects also overtly reside in this position. The types of indefinite NPs I will focus on are those discussed in e.g. Diesing (1992): NPs headed by the indefinite determiner *a(n)*; NPs headed by the so-called weak determiners like *some*, *many*, and the cardinal determiners, *one*, *two*, etc. (Milsark 1977); and bare plural (determinerless) NPs.

7.2.1 Adverb Placement

Indefinite objects, like definite ones, appear adjacent to the verb. No adverb can intervene:

1. a. * Mikey visited quietly his parents
   b. * Mikey visited quietly a good friend/friends/some friends
2. a. * Betsy sung loudly the anthem
   b. * Betsy sung loudly an anthem/anthems/some anthems

LF Noun Phrase Positions

3. a. * Chris hit quickly the dog
   b. * Chris hit quickly a dog/dogs/some dogs
4. a. Mikey visited his parents quietly
   b. Mikey visited a friend/friends/some friends quietly
5. a. Betsy sung the anthem loudly
   b. Betsy sung an anthem/anthems/some anthems loudly
6. a. Chris hit the dog quickly
   b. Chris hit a dog/dogs/some dogs quickly

A VP-internal subcategorized PP and an object (definite or indefinite) can however be separated from the verb by an adverb (the (c) examples, which are pretty good, are supposed to show that the PP isn't extraposed):

7. a. Cindy put her books quietly into her backpack
   b. Cindy put a book/books/some books quietly into her backpack.
   c. What did Cindy put her books quietly into t?
8. a. Peter showed the pictures quietly to his sisters
   b. Peter showed a picture/pictures/some pictures quietly to his sisters
   c. Who did Peter show the pictures quietly to t?
9. a. Geordi explained the problem loudly to Data
   b. Geordi explained a problem/problems/some problems loudly to Data
   c. Who did Geordi explain the problem loudly to t?

The generalization seems to be that indefinite and definite objects have the same distribution with respect to this type of adverb.

In Chapter 4 I argued that these facts could best be explained if the adverbs in question are adjoined to projections of V or specific functional projections in the inflectional domain of the tree. The examples in (1)-(3) are ungrammatical because the adverb has illicitly adjoined to AGRoP, not a possible adjunction site for these adverbs. Since the object (definite or indefinite) appears in Spec,AGRo overtly, the order V-ADV-OBJ is not possible. The grammatical examples above have the adverb adjoined within VP, thus leading to their grammaticality. The point of this paradigm is that indefinite NPs appear to show the same restriction as definite NPs, which was explained above placing the NPs in a particular position at S-structure.

7.2.2 Right Node Raising

Indefinites, like definites, can be stranded while VP is RNR'd:

10. Mary told a story, and Sam explained a problem, to Bill after dinner
11. I showed an office, and Mary showed a computer lab, to the prospective students during their interview
12. Ginger saw a bird, and Thurston saw a weasel, in the park after dinner

I argued in Chapter 3 that the definite objects in this type of sentence are in Spec,AGRo and what is "raised" is VP. These facts suggest the same is true for indefinite objects:

13. Mary told [$_{AGRo}$ a story [e]] and Sam explained [$_{AGRo}$ a problem [e]] [[$_{VP}$ t$_V$ t$_{NP}$ to Bill] after dinner]

Whatever the exact nature of this process, it appears to be able to target VP minus direct object as a constituent. If the object–definite or indefinite–moves to a VP-external position as in the diagram, this is expected.

7.2.3 VP Coordination

An indefinite, like a definite, can be stranded in VP-coordination:

14. Mary told a story [t to Bill after breakfast] and [t to Sam after dinner]
15. I showed an office [t to the prospective students during their interviews] and [to the faculty after our meeting]
16. I shared a cup of coffee [t with John during his visit] and [t with Mary after her accident]
17. I had a piece of pizza [t at home during Star Trek] and [t at Cindy's after work]

18. Ginger saw a bird [t in the park after dinner] and [t at the dock at sunset]

In Chapter 3 I used this type of coordination to argue that a definite object was in a VP-external position, Spec,AGRo, at S-structure and what is coordinating is VP. These examples, with indefinite NPs, suggest the same account is available for indefinites:

19. Mary told [$_{AGRoP}$ a story [[$_{VP}$ t to Bill after breakfast] and [$_{VP}$ t to Sam after dinner]]]

7.2.4 Particle Verbs

Particle verbs were discussed in chapter 5. As the following paradigm (adapted from Johnson 1991) shows, indefinite and definite objects behave the same in the particle verb construction:

20. a. Mikey looked the reference up
    b. Mikey looked a/some reference(s) up
21. a. Mikey looked up the reference
    b. Mikey looked up a/some reference(s)
22. a. Betsy threw the bicycle out
    b. Betsy threw a/some bicycle(s) out
23. a. Betsy threw out the bicycle
    b. Betsy threw out a/some bicycle(s)
24. a. Brent dusted the counter off
    b. Brent dusted a/some counter(s) off
25. a. Brent dusted off the counter
    b. Brent dusted off a/some counter(s)

I followed Johnson (1991) and argued that the order V-NP-PRT is derived if both the verb and the object have moved from their base positions to higher positions, leaving the particle behind. I argued that the verb moves to a functional head position (F) and that the object moves to Spec,AGRo. What is important about this paradigm is that definiteness appears to make no difference; both types of object undergo this movement.

To summarize: what the above considerations show is that definite and indefinite objects behave alike at S-structure: they are in a VP-external position, Spec,AGRo.

7.3 THE LF POSITION(S) OF NOUN PHRASES

We have seen above that both definite and indefinite objects are in Spec,AGRo at S-structure. This section will argue that there are good reasons to believe that indefinites do not always appear in their S-structure positions at LF. In particular, indefinites which are interpreted existentially appear in their base VP-internal positions at LF. This section outlines the evidence for such a claim. The following section reviews Diesing's (1992) mapping hypothesis, which is meant to explain this distribution. And the subsequent sections discuss the syntax of the apparent lowering operation needed to derive such LF representations.

7.3.1 Antecedent Contained Deletion

Lasnik (1993) and Hornstein (1994) provide an account of Antecedent Contained Deletion (ACD) which crucially relies on the account of direct objects we have been developing here. That is, they show that ACD can be treated rather elegantly if we assume that objects move to Spec,AGRo by LF.[28]

If ACD involves copying VP into the position of *do*, the problem of infinite regress arises (from May 1985):

26. a. Dulles suspected everyone Angleton did
    b. Dulles [$_{VP}$ suspected everyone Angleton did [$_{VP}$ e]]
    c. e = [$_{VP}$ suspected everyone Angleton did [$_{VP}$ e]]

Lasnik and Hornstein, following May (1985), argue that the problem of infinite regress disappears on the assumption that objects move out of VP by LF. They differ from May in arguing that this movement is to Spec,AGRo:

27. Dulles suspected [$_{AGRo}$ everyone Angleton did [$_{VP}$ e]][$_{VP}$ t$_V$ t$_{DO}$]]

This construction, then, can be used as a probe for LF position. If an NP is in Spec,AGRo at LF it should allow ACD, if it is in VP the problem of infinite regress reappears and ACD should be blocked.

Diesing (1992) shows that ACD is in fact restricted to certain types of NP. Like May she argues that ACD is fed by QR so only NPs which QR should license ACD. She provides examples like the following:

28. a. I read every book that you did
    b. I read each book that you did
    c. I read most books that you did

The objects here are all "quantificational" and thus QR at LF allowing for ACD. Milsark's (1977) potentially ambiguous indefinites license ACD, but only on the proportional reading. Diesing argues that the proportional reading is "quantificational" and is derived by QR, thus again licensing ACD:

29. a. I read many (of the) books that you did
    b. I read few (of the) books that you did
    c. I read two (of the) books that you did

However, besides uncontroversially quantificational NPs like those above, two other classes of NP license ACD, definite NPs and names:

30. a.   I read the books that you did
    b. ?   Dulles suspected Philby, who Angleton did as well[29]
                                              [Wyngaerd & Zwart 1991]

If Diesing (and May) are correct it must be assumed that not only quantificational NPs but also definite NPs and names QR at LF in order to license ACD; this is a rather disparate class. On the other hand, if in general NP objects are in Spec,AGRo for independent Case reasons, then the fact that quantificational as well as definite and name NPs all license

ACD is expected. Then the focus instead is on the class of NPs which do not license ACD. It appears that this class is simply the "cardinal" indefinites of Milsark (1977). These NPs are also known as "existential", which is how I will refer to them.

The following paradigm is from Diesing (1992). These ACD examples are all ungrammatical unless interpreted as proportional:

31. a. *? I read many books that you did
    b. *   I read few books that you did
    c. *   I read two books that you did
    d. *   I read books that you did

As opposed to quantificational, name and definite NPs, if we assume existential indefinites reside in VP at LF then the fact that they do not license ACD would be accounted for. ACD would then result in infinite regress. This is the first argument that we might want existential indefinites in VP at LF.[30]

7.3.2 Existential Subjects

We just saw one argument that existential indefinite objects are in VP at LF. I will continue by outlining some arguments that existential indefinites, generally, are in VP at LF.

Kratzer (1989) and Diesing (1992), on whose work this section is based, argued that the subjects of different types of predicates have different interpretations and that these interpretations are dependent on the position of the subject at LF. Consider the following examples:

32. a. Firefighters are available
    b. Firefighters are intelligent

Example (a) has (at least) two readings: an existential reading, which means roughly that at some point in time there are firefighters available; and a generic reading, which means roughly that firefighters generally have the property of being available. In (b) there is only one reading: the generic one. Example (b) is a statement about firefighters, that they are generally intelligent. It does not have an existential reading, which would mean roughly that at some point in time there are intelligent firefighters. Predicates like *available* are termed stage-level predicates and those like *intelligent* are individual-level predicates (Carlson 1977). Stage-level predicates tend to be ambiguous between allowing a bare plural subject to have an existential and generic reading, while individual-level predicates have unambiguous generic bare plural subjects.

Kratzer and Diesing, following Heim (1982), argue that an indefinite NP, like the bare plural *firefighters*, introduces a variable into the logical representation. This variable needs to get bound by something, and that something is what will give the existential vs. generic force of the bare plural. Initial evidence in favor of treating bare plurals as variables comes from their behavior around adverbs of quantification:

33. a. Firefighters are always/seldom/never intelligent
    b. All/few/no firefighters are intelligent

The adverbs of quantification in (a) seem to give the same force to the bare plural subject as the overt determiner-type quantifiers in (b). If adverbs of quantification bind variables (Lewis 1975) thus giving them their quantificational force, then the bare plural subject in (a) seems to provide a variable.

The claim that Kratzer and Diesing make about the generic reading of a bare plural subject follows work by Wilkinson (1986) and Krifka (1988). Their claim is that a null generic operator binds the variable in the case of a sentence like (32b), repeated here:

34. a. Firefighters are intelligent
    b. GEN_x firefighter$_x$ are intelligent
    c. =firefighters are generally intelligent

The same would hold of the generic reading of the bare plural subject of a stage-level predicate like *available*.

That's the generic reading. What about the existential reading? What is special about this reading is that it is not available for the subject of an individual-level predicate. Following Heim (1982), Kratzer and Diesing argue that an existential quantifier is inserted into the representation to bind the leftover variables not bound already by other operators. The specific claim that Diesing makes, and Kratzer supports, is that the domain of the existential quantifier is the VP. Thus, only a variable that's in VP and has not been bound by some other binder can be bound by the existential quantifier deriving the existential interpretation.

The difference, then, between a stage-level predicate and an individual-level predicate will be the availability of a VP-internal position in which a variable can be bound by the existential quantifier. Stage-level predicates have such a position; individual-level predicates do not. Kratzer and Diesing derive this difference by suggesting that stage-level predicates have a VP-internal as well as VP-external subject position; the existential reading is derived by lowering the subject back into its base VP-internal position. There it is bound by the existential quantifier over VP. If the NP does not lower it is interpreted in Spec,IP which is within the domain of the generic operator. The following LFs represent the spirit of the Kratzer/Diesing proposal, though not the actual structures they give:

35. Firefighters are available [S-S]

36. a. GEN_x [$_{IP}$ firefighters$_x$ are [$_{VP}$ x available]] [LF_1]
    b. [e are $\exists_x$ [$_{VP}$ firefighters$_x$ available]] [LF_2]

Kratzer and Diesing differ on their treatment of individual-level predicates. Kratzer argues that individual-level predicates, as opposed to stage-level predicates, only have the VP-external subject position; lowering is not possible because they have no VP-internal base position to lower to:

37. a. Firefighters are intelligent [S-S]
    b. GEN_x [$_{IP}$ firefighters$_x$ are [$_{VP}$ intelligent]] [LF]

Thus, with no VP-internal position, no existential reading is possible, only a generic reading, as observed.

Diesing differs somewhat from Kratzer here. She suggests that in fact both types of predicate have a VP-internal as well as a VP-external subject position, but that the difference between the two types of predicate is in the relationship between the two positions. For Diesing, the copula itself

LF Noun Phrase Positions

is what is structurally ambiguous: the copula associated with a stage-level predicate is a "raising" copula; that associated with an individual-level predicate is a "control" copula. That means that with a stage-level predicate the two subject positions are related by movement, and only one θ-role is involved. Individual-level predicate subject positions are related by control; a PRO subject is in the VP, receiving a second θ-role.

38. GEN_x [$_{IP}$ firefighters$_x$ are [$_{VP}$ PRO available]]   [LF]

The existential reading would be derived by lowering the subject to the VP; if there is no open position to lower the subject to, no existential reading is available. Thus, both Kratzer and Diesing assume that lowering the subject into VP under the scope of an existential quantifier is how an existential reading is derived.

In favor of the lowering analysis for the existential reading are examples like the following (Diesing 1992, 25):

39. a. Firemen$_i$ seem to their$_i$ employers to be available
    b. Gila monsters$_i$ seem to their$_i$ predators to be visible

What is relevant about these examples is that on the bound variable reading of the pronoun, only the generic reading of the bare plural subject is available. On the Kratzer/Diesing proposal, the existential reading would require lowering to the base position of the subject; but such a movement destroys the c-command relationship between the subject and the variable pronoun it binds:

40. * e_i seem to their$_i$ employers [to be [firemen$_i$ available]]

As Diesing points out these sentences contrast with similar sentences without a bound variable pronoun. In this case both readings of the subject are possible:

41. a. Firemen seem to the mayor to be available
    b. Gila monsters seem to the coyotes to be visible

Thus, the claim made by Kratzer and Diesing is that noun phrases which are existentially interpreted must appear in the VP at LF. This claim accords with the results on ACD, that existential objects do not license ACD, apparently because they are obligatorily within VP.

One indication that the Kratzer/Diesing approach is on the right track is the behavior of *there* sentences in English. Milsark (1974, 1977) was the first to point out that *there* sentences in English with *be* are possible only with stage-level predicates. If the claim that individual-level predicates project their external argument into Spec,IP is correct, then it is clear why such predicates are not available in *there* sentences. The expletive and the subject of the predicate would be competing for the same position:

42. a. Linguists are boring
    b. [$_{IP}$ linguists are [$_{VP}$ (PRO) boring]]
    c. * [$_{IP}$ there are [$_{VP}$ linguists/PRO boring]]

The stage-level predicate, which only has an internal argument, leaves Spec,IP open available for the expletive:

43. a. Linguists are available
    b. [$_{IP}$ linguists$_i$ are [$_{VP}$ t$_i$ available]]
    c. There are linguists available
    d. [$_{IP}$ there are [$_{VP}$ linguists available]]

The availability of an existential interpretation is also expected on the Kratzer and Diesing approach. When *there* sits in Spec,IP, the NP is forced essentially to remain in VP, and since the VP is where an indefinite receives an existential interpretation, as opposed to other possible interpretations, we expect correctly a *there* sentence to have an existential reading of an indefinite.[31]

7.3.3 Summary

The previous sections have suggested that while at S-structure direct objects as well as subjects are in Spec,AGR, the LF position is related to

LF Noun Phrase Positions

the interpretation of the noun phrase. Indefinite NPs appear in VP to receive an existential interpretation.

7.4 THE MAPPING HYPOTHESIS

I will not devote a great deal of time to the question of exactly *why* existential NPs should appear in VP while NPs of other semantic types should appear in Spec,AGR at LF. What I will take as my primary concern is an account of the syntax that allows such possibilities.

To ground the discussion slightly I will outline Diesing's (1992) mapping hypothesis, which negotiates the relationship between LF syntactic structures and the semantic representation. I will assume that the mapping hypothesis, or something like it, is what is responsible for *why* NPs of certain semantic types are required to appear in syntactic positions of a certain type.

Diesing (1992) argues that the syntactic LF representation of a sentence is split and mapped onto separate parts of the "tripartite" semantic representation (in the sense of Heim 1982 and Kamp 1981):

44. *The Mapping Hypothesis*
    VP maps into the Nuclear Scope
    IP maps into the Restriction

Thus a sentence like (a), with the LF like (b), gets mapped onto a semantic representation roughly like (c):

45. a. Every fish swam home
    b. [$_{IP}$[every fish]$_i$ [$_{VP}$ t$_i$ swam home]]
    c. [every$_x$]$_{OP}$ [fish$_x$]$_{Restr}$ [x swam home]$_{NS}$

Diesing, following Heim (1982), argues that indefinite noun phrases are variables and need to be bound in one way or another. Where a noun phrase appears at LF will determine in part what the noun phrase can be bound by. One way an indefinite can be bound is by an adverb of quantification. In order to be bound by such an operator the indefinite must appear external to VP at LF in order to map onto the restriction of the operator. So, an indefinite bound by an adverb of quantification in a sentence like (a), will have an LF like (b), which will get mapped onto a semantic representation like (c):

46. a. A fish always swims home
    b. [$_{IP}$[a fish]$_i$ always [$_{VP}$ t$_i$ swims home]]
    c. [always$_x$] [fish$_x$] [x swims home]

A second way an indefinite noun phrase can be bound is by not appearing in Spec,IP at LF; in this case it appears in its VP-internal position and gets bound by a default existential operator. This process is called "existential closure". So, a sentence with an existentially interpreted indefinite subject like (a), will have an LF like (b), and a semantic representation roughly like (c). Note that (c) no longer has three parts; everything (VP) maps onto the nuclear scope alone:

47. a. A firefighter is available
    b. [$_{IP}$ is [$_{VP}$[a firefighter] available]]
    c. $\exists_x$ [firefighter(x) & available(x)]

The LF position of the indefinite NP is crucial to its interpretation. If it is VP-external it can get bound by VP-external operators (such as an adverb of quantification, or a generic operator); if it is VP-internal it gets bound by an existential operator. Another type of indefinite is the specific indefinite and the proportional indefinite. Diesing's treatment of these is that they are inherently quantificational and thus move out of VP to form a tripartite structure like those above.

Strong quantifiers, on Diesing's (1992) view, need to form tripartite structures also because they are inherently quantificational. Thus, they must move out of VP by LF in order to be mapped correctly onto the semantic representation following the mapping hypothesis. On Diesing & Jelinek's (1995) view, the rationale is slightly different but the result is the same. They argue that strong quantifiers are of a semantic type which causes a type mismatch when they attempt to combine with the verb. This forces them out of VP at LF in order to resolve the type mismatch. The result is that strong quantifiers are not in VP at LF.

LF Noun Phrase Positions

So far, we have seen how the mapping hypothesis accounts for why existential indefinites are in VP at LF: to receive their existential interpretation they must appear in the domain of existential closure, which semantically is the nuclear scope, and syntactically is VP. We have also seen why indefinites which are bound by adverbs of quantification (or a generic operator) are VP-external at LF: to be mapped onto the restriction of their relevant operator. Specific and proportional indefinites, and strong quantifiers are all inherently quantificational and thus must form tripartite structures. To do this they must appear outside of VP to map correctly onto the semantic representation (or, in Diesing & Jelinek's view, they are VP-external for type reasons). As we saw above, the evidence from ACD and from the interpretation of subjects of various sorts of predicates accords with Diesing's account. There are two classes left to account for, however: definite noun phrases and names. According to the ACD results, both of these classes are VP-external at LF. While the conceptual motivation for why these NPs should appear in the restriction, rather than the nuclear scope, is a bit unclear, Diesing essentially assumes, following Berman (1991), that all "presuppositional" material appears in the restriction. Since definite NPs and names are presuppositional, they must appear in the restriction, and hence must be external to VP at LF.

What our syntactic account has provided so far is that at S-structure all subject and object NPs are in specifiers of AGR phrases, where they check their Case features. These Spec,AGR positions are external to VP. This predicts that unless something else happens, all subjects and objects will map onto the restriction and be interpreted non-existentially. This, of course, is not correct. As pointed out above, Diesing (1992), like Kratzer (1989), assumes a rule of syntactic lowering, which places NPs appearing overtly in Case positions back down into their VP-internal base positions at LF for interpretational purposes. I will, then, take as my primary concern the question of the nature of this "lowering" operation. This is what we turn to next.

7.5 HOW TO GET THERE

We have seen that Kratzer (1989) and Diesing (1992) suggest that the existential interpretation of an indefinite or bare plural subject is derived by lowering the NP from its S-structure Spec,IP position back down into its base VP-internal position at LF. That NP movement can be "undone" at LF was suggested by May (1977) based on examples like the following:

48. [A unicorn]$_i$ seems [t$_i$ to be in the yard]

In this example *a unicorn* can have scope wider or narrower than the verb *seem*. Thus, what is needed at LF is two possible structures representing the two readings, like the following:

49. a. [a unicorn] seems to be in the yard [LF$_1$]
    b. e seems [a unicorn] to be in the yard [LF$_2$]

Example (a) represents the wide scope reading of *a unicorn*, and (b) represents the narrow scope reading.

Having shown that indefinite objects are in Spec,AGRo at S-structure, and that according to the ACD test existential objects are in VP at LF, a similar lowering operation seems to be needed for objects as well.

The next section will examine lowering, pointing out that while it is empirically well-motivated, a number of theory-internal questions arise if such an operation is allowed. I will argue that there is no such operation and that the effects of lowering follow if we assume a copy and delete theory of A-movement.

7.5.1 On Lowering

The problem we face is that an NP in a certain surface position might be associated with two different LF representations: an LF in which it is in its overt position, and an LF in which it is in its base position. The question is how this one surface NP is associated with the two LF positions. The standard approach, as outlined above, is to assume that an NP can move at LF. This seems right in the case of upward movement, as in the case of e.g. QR. We see many examples of overt upward movement in the syntax so the idea of upward movement in the covert syntax is not particularly surprising. However, the kind of movement we need here would be lowering, downward movement. Since we need the NP to get from its

LF Noun Phrase Positions

surface Spec,AGR position into VP it must move downward to do so. This is suspicious since we do not seem to find such movement in the overt syntax. A proposal which relies on an LF operation such as a type of movement we do not observe in the domain of the overt syntax is *a priori* dubious.

A second theoretical problem faced by the lowering proposal is a type of economy consideration. Chomsky (1991) has argued for the claim that NP movement obeys a sort of "last resort" constraint. NP can move to check its Case but it does not continue to move gratuitously once it is Case-checked, unless it has some other syntactic requirement it needs to satisfy (such as e.g. a wh feature needing to be checked in Spec,CP). Essentially, NP only undergoes syntactic movement if it has syntactic needs left to satisfy. The type of lowering we seem to require has a different sort of motivation. It certainly is not needed to satisfy the syntactic requirements of the NP. It seems that it is in fact needed in order to put the NP in the right position to satisfy semantic needs. Lowering, then, appears to be motivated by semantic, and not syntactic, needs. This clearly violates Chomsky's notion of "last resort" movement, and thus should not be a viable syntactic operation.

A third consideration comes from looking more carefully at the operation itself. If lowering is simply a type of movement, except downward instead of upward, one wonders why it is allowed into a theta position. In the case of e.g. object lowering, the object will have to be assumed to move from Spec,AGRo to complement of V. Certainly upward movement of this sort would be ruled out by the Theta Criterion. The main difference between upward movement and this lowering movement is that lowering moves into a position held by the trace of the NP itself. So, lowering apparently would be allowed into a complement position, but only if the NP moves into the position of its trace. This raises the question of exactly what a trace is. If a trace is an actual syntactic element, but one without phonetic content, why is it possible to move into a position held by one? Even if the NP and the trace are coindexed, why should the NP be able to move into the position held by the trace?

To reiterate, lowering appears to be empirically well motivated, as we saw above in the discussion of ACD and predicate-types. However, conceptually it is at odds with our view of what kinds of syntactic movement should be available in principle. An operation that derived the

192   *Noun Phrase Licensing*

results of lowering while avoiding the conceptual drawbacks, then, would be welcome. Such an operation will be discussed in the following section.

7.5.2 Copy Movement

To deal with standard reconstruction effects like those in (50), Chomsky (1991) proposes that A'-movement leaves a full copy of the moved element which can be present at LF but absent at PF. (50a) is ambiguous; the anaphor can refer to John or Bill. The relevant LFs are those in (b) and (c), respectively (p.49):

50. a. John wondered which picture of himself Bill saw
    b. John$_i$ wondered [which picture of himself$_j$]$_j$ Bill saw t$_j$
    c. John wondered [which e] Bill$_i$ saw [e pictures of himself$_i$]

On the copy theory of movement, there is an intermediate stage at which both copies are present; PF and LF well-formedness (some version of Full Interpretation) requires that only one copy remain. Thus, (b) and (c), above, are derived from the following by deleting the downstairs copy and (parts of) the upstairs copy, respectively:

51. John wondered [which picture of himself] Bill saw [which picture of himself]

While many of the details about what deletes when are left open, the null hypothesis would be that Full Interpretation is obeyed at PF and LF (only one copy can be present at each of those levels), and that deletion should be free up to the point of violating independent requirements on those levels.

Chomsky's claim was that copy and deletion were properties of A'-movement. However, Lasnik (1993), considering reconstruction for binding examples, proposes to extend the theory to A-movement. Consider the following:

LF Noun Phrase Positions

52. a. Pictures of himself seem to Tom to be ugly
    b. [pictures of himself] seem to Tom [[pictures of himself] to be ugly]

Example (a), which involves A-movement, not A'-movement, shows the same sort of reconstruction effect for Condition A as the wh-movement examples above. Though some interesting questions arise with respect to Condition C and also with respect to bare anaphors, Lasnik takes this type of example to favor the extension of the copy and delete strategy to A-movement.

Adger (1994), who was also concerned with NP interpretation as well as object shift operations, also proposed to extend the copy and delete account to A-movement. This is what I will do as well. In the standard cases of A-movement, for example of a definite NP, the NP moves to Spec,AGR. On the copy theory of movement, such movement will leave behind a copy of the moved phrase. At PF and LF only one copy can remain; in this case the lower copy is the one deleted, resulting in PF and LF representations containing an NP in Spec,AGR. This follows from the mapping hypothesis, which requires a definite NP to be VP-external at LF. However, if the NP copied is indefinite, two possibilities seem to arise. In both cases, the PF representation is the same: the lower copy of movement deletes. At LF, though, either copy can delete. If the lower copy deletes, the indefinite is interpreted in Spec,AGR; if the upper copy deletes, the indefinite is interpreted in VP, receiving an existential reading.

Let's work through some examples:

53. a. Firefighters are available
    b. John is available

The underlying structures, following Stowell (1978), have the subjects in their predicate-internal positions (I simplify here by leaving out irrelevant phrases, e.g. TP):

54. a. [$_{AGRsP}$ e [be [$_{AP}$ firefighters available]]]
    b. [$_{AGRsP}$ e [be [$_{AP}$ John available]]]

The first step for both examples is for the subject to move to Spec,AGRs in order to check its Φ features–the A chain gets nominative Case-checked and the copula has its subject agreement checked. A copy of the moved phrase is left in its base position:

55. a. [$_{AGRsP}$ firefighters$_i$ [are [$_{AP}$ firefighters$_i$ available]]]
    b. [$_{AGRsP}$ John$_i$ [is [$_{AP}$ John$_i$ available]]]   [Pre-SPLIT]

This is the representation before the PF/LF split. I would like to claim that at this point the A-chain has been licensed officially in the representation: the chain has been Case-checked. That means that if the Visibility Condition is something that applies at LF, it will see an NP with Case. What will turn out to be important later is that the Φ features of this A-chain have been checked before LF. In fact, generally, all A-movement for feature checking can be assumed to apply before the PF/LF split. This is important because it implies that no such movement is necessary at LF (see section 7.5.3 for discussion). At PF and LF, all that is needed is to decide which extra copies delete. At those levels we will want only one copy of each NP. My claim is that in general the choice of which NP deletes should be free, up to violation of some PF or LF constraint (what those constraints might be will be examined below).

We know what the PF representation looks like; at PF the downstairs copy of the NP apparently always deletes (though see section 7.6.2):

56. a. [$_{AGRs}$ firefighters$_i$ [are [$_{AP}$ e$_i$ available]]]
    b. [$_{AGRs}$ John$_i$ [is [$_{AP}$ e$_i$ available]]]   [PF]

However, at LF (a) has two possibilities: *firefighters* can be in Spec,AGRs, to receive a generic interpretation, or it can be in the AP, to receive an existential interpretation. These two possibilities correspond to deleting the downstairs and upstairs copy, respectively, as illustrated in (57). The (b) example apparently only allows the downstairs copy to be deleted, as in (58):

57. a. [$_{AGRs}$ firefighters$_i$ [are [$_{AP}$ e$_i$ available]]]   [LF$_1$]
    b. [$_{AGRs}$ e [are [$_{AP}$ firefighters available]]]   [LF$_2$]
58. [$_{AGRs}$ John$_i$ [is [$_{AP}$ e$_i$ available]]]   [only LF]

LF Noun Phrase Positions

The copy theory of movement, then, quite nicely provides the relevant PFs and LFs needed independently. However, what constrains the deletions? This question will be the focus of the next section. First, I would like to turn to the question of the nature of copy movement itself.

7.5.3 The Nature of Copying

Thus far I have discussed copy movement as if what happens, technically, is that the phrase to move somehow duplicates itself and places the duplicate in the movement target position. I would like to explore an alternative view espoused in Marantz (1994), which I believe provides both a conceptual handle to the question of copy movement as well as making an interesting empirical prediction.

Marantz (1994) interprets the copy theory of movement in the following way. The lexicon is like a worktable. On it one can build from the lexical items bits of phrases. Those phrases can be inserted (via generalized transformations) into each other building larger phrases. But copy movement, rather than taking a phrase, magically duplicating it, and putting the duplicate in a movement target position, actually takes a second identical phrase from the worktable, and places it in the movement target position. That is, copying is really just building a duplicate phrase of the one you have, from the parts provided you by the lexicon.

This is conceptually appealing because we are not left wondering how the copy process "magically" occurs. It is not copying per se, but rather the building of an identical phrase, and placing it in the tree. The identical phrases (say, one in Spec,AGRs and one in VP) will have to form a chain; and presumably constraints on chain links will force the duplicates to be absolutely identical and to bear the same index.

Empirically, this makes an interesting prediction. If we combine Marantz's interpretation of copying with Chomsky's (1993) claim that access to the lexicon is denied after the split to PF and LF. First, any movement at LF and PF will not be able to employ the copy and delete strategy. Why? Because access to the lexicon is denied beyond the split to PF and LF. This does not necessarily mean that there is no movement of phrases at these levels, but it does mean that such movement will be a different sort of process from the normal "overt" movement.

I believe this is correct. Recall in chapter 6 in discussing the double object construction we notice that standard wh-movement showed reconstruction effects, which I, following Chomsky (1993), suggested were due to the copy and delete strategy for movement. What was interesting was that QR does not show reconstruction effects. If QR is in fact movement at LF, it cannot be movement involving the copy and delete strategy. This is because access to the lexicon is barred to LF. Copying (or building a duplicate) is not possible at LF. This suggests that any LF movement should not show reconstruction effects. And this is what is found with QR.

Interestingly, however, we also noticed that wh- in situ in English does show reconstruction effects. If Marantz is correct, then the movement associated with wh- in situ is not LF movement, but rather "overt" movement. But how can this be? Actually, the copy and delete strategy provides just the mechanism. Wh movement can occur in the overt syntax, employing the copy and delete strategy. But then the question arises of which copies to delete. In the normal case the bottom copy (or copies) is deleted, leaving the top copy to appear at PF. But wh- in situ can be analyzed as a case where instead of deleting the bottom copy, the top copy of the wh phrase is deleted, leaving only the base one to appear at PF. In other words, this view of movement allows two kinds of "covert" movement: pre-SPLIT movement, employing copy and delete; and LF movement, which does not employ the copy and delete strategy. In principle it should be possible to distinguish the two. As we have seen, reconstruction effects are one way to do so.

A second empirical claim made by Marantz's approach is that if A-movement (movement for Case-checking) is understood as described above, as involving the copy and delete strategy, it cannot apply at LF. This claim is intriguing because it contradicts Chomsky's (1993) approach to object movement in English, which he assumes to apply at LF. However, it is consistent with my account of object movement in English: it applies in the overt syntax, employing the copy and delete strategy for movement.

If Marantz is correct then all A-movement is part of the overt syntax, not the syntax of LF. One of the goals of this thesis has been to provide an account of English objects which maintains this claim.

LF Noun Phrase Positions

Having discussed a bit of the conceptual and empirical motivation for the copy and delete approach, as well as having delved into the mechanism behind the copying part, I now turn to the question of deletion. What deletes where?

7.6 CONSTRAINTS ON DELETION

The main claim of the previous chapters was that objects move to Spec,AGRo overtly. What that means, now, under the copy and delete view of movement, is that at PF ("overtly") objects are in Spec,AGRo. Thus, we must ensure that the upstairs, and not the downstairs, copy of the NP remains at PF. The same can essentially be said for subjects. At PF, the downstairs copy of NP movement deletes (but some illuminating cases where this is not so will be discussed below in section 7.6.2).

What the start of this chapter showed was that while it is the case that NPs are in Spec,AGR "overtly" (at PF), their LF position can differ depending on interpretation. If an NP is understood as existential, it is the VP-internal copy of movement which must remain at LF, requiring deletion of the upstairs copy. If an NP is understood nonexistentially, it is the Spec,AGR copy which remains at LF. It still remains to be determined exactly what constrains the deletions.

The following sections will deal with these questions. I begin by taking up the second question, that of LF deletions. Then the subsequent section discusses the question of PF deletions.

7.6.1 LF Deletion

Let us begin by considering the types of structure needed at LF. I have spoken rather loosely about deleting copies without stating precisely what it means to delete a copy. I will now consider some possibilities.

Abstractly, at a point before the split to PF and LF but after movement, we have a representation containing NP copies in the VP-internal base position and the Spec,AGR Case position:

59. $[_{AGRP} NP_i [_{VP} \ldots NP_i \ldots]]$ [Pre-SPLIT]

NP is in Spec,AGR and can successfully check its Φ features. This checking licenses the whole NP_i chain for the Case Filter/Visibility Condition. Independently of deletions, NP_i has its features checked. Even if the CF/VIS applies at LF, the NP appearing there will have its features checked thus satisfying the filter.

At LF there are two different possibilities wanted. One is that NP_i is in Spec,AGR. The other is that NP_i is in VP. These results come about by deleting the downstairs (a) or upstairs (b) copy, respectively:

60. a. $[_{AGRP} NP_i [_{VP} \ldots e \ldots]]$ [LF_1]
   b. $[_{AGRP} e [_{VP} \ldots NP_i \ldots]]$ [LF_2]

One question that needs to be addressed is the nature of the empty categories marked by 'e' in (a) and (b). The nature of the 'e' is going to end up being dependent on the relationship between the NP and 'e'. Consider (a), where 'e' is in the base position of the NP. This is the position to which NP's theta role is assigned. If 'e' is actually completely empty and there is no connection between the position of 'e' and NP, then NP will end up without a theta role at LF. On the other hand, if 'e' and NP are coindexed so that 'e' is much like a trace, then they form a chain and NP can get its theta role from the chain $[NP_i, e_i]$. Thus, I will assume (a') instead of (a):

a'. $[_{AGRP} NP_i [_{VP} \ldots e_i \ldots]]$ [LF_1]

What about (b)? Things are different in this case. NP sits in its theta position, so theta considerations play no role. Also, as pointed out above, NP has had its Φ features checked. This means that NP has no need to have any relation to 'e' in Spec,AGR. I assume, then, that 'e' in this case does not represent a syntactic element and the position is empty. Rather than marking it with 'e' I will not mark it at all. Thus, I will assume (b') instead of (b):

b'. $[_{AGRP} [_{VP} \ldots NP_i \ldots]]$ [LF_2]

Now let us turn to reconsidering Diesing's (1992) mapping hypothesis and how it interacts with LF deletion.

LF Noun Phrase Positions

The mapping hypothesis states that if a noun phrase is in Spec,AGR at LF it will map onto the restriction and will have a non-existential interpretation. This means that the copy that remains at LF in this case will be the upstairs one, as in (a') above. An NP which ends up in a structure like (b') will be interpreted existentially because it is in VP at LF and will be mapped onto the nuclear scope.

The view I take here of the syntax is that deletion is completely free at LF, subject to recoverability. What that means in this case is that the deletion operation itself does not care if NP is definite, indefinite, quantificational, etc. This means that deletion can target the upstairs copy of a definite NP chain, deriving something like (b') above. However, this LF, while syntactically well-formed, will be uninterpretable semantically, because it will have an e.g. definite NP mapping onto the nuclear scope. I do not believe it is the job of the syntax to make sure this does not occur. The fact that a definite NP must be interpreted as non-existential is a matter for the semantic, not syntactic, representation. My concern, then, is to provide the relevant LFs from which the semantics can choose the interpretable ones. Deletion is just a dumb syntactic operation. At the interface with the semantic representation, only the acceptable, interpretable LFs will be interpreted.

Thus, there are no constraints on deletion at LF. What constraints appear to exist are imposed by the interface with the interpretative component. At the interface the mapping hypothesis regulates syntactic elements in syntactic positions ensuring that only the right combinations get incorporated into the semantic representation.

7.6.2 PF Deletion

7.6.2.1 Introduction

PF deletion in English appears at first blush not to be as unconstrained in contrast to LF deletion. However, the constraints can be identified, and I will try to do so now. I begin by trying to establish empirically what the range of deletions actually is. Then I move on to examining a potential account to derive these facts.

Let us begin by concentrating on NP subjects in Spec,AGRs. Before the split to PF and LF we have the following intermediate representation:

61. [$_{AGRsP}$ NP$_i$ ... [$_{VP}$ NP$_i$ ...]]

The PF representation we want in general will look roughly like the following (I put the 'e' in as in the examples above, but probably this empty category will not be present on the PF side):

62. [$_{AGRsP}$ NP$_i$ ... [$_{VP}$ e$_i$ ...]] [PF]

What seems to be required is that the downstairs copy of NP delete, leaving the upstairs copy present at PF.

An initial hypothesis about PF deletion might be that the top copy of NP always remains at PF. However, while this is often true, enough examples like the following exist to suggest that it is not that simple:

63. a. There are three firefighters available
    b. Into the room walked John
    c. In front of her sat her mother

(63a) is a typical *there* sentence. (b) and (c) are examples of directional and locative inversion, respectively (from Rochemont & Culicover 1990). The *there* sentence is assumed, rather uncontroversially, to have the expletive in Spec,AGRs at PF. The inversion examples, according to Rochemont & Culicover (1990), involve a topicalization process to a pre-IP position. I will argue in the following chapter that the preverbal phrases in (b) and (c) are also in Spec,AGRs. For now, let us assume this and continue.

I would like to suggest that these examples all come under a sort of Extended Projection Principle holding at PF. What we see here are cases in which the subject NP appears in a position other than Spec,AGRs and that something else appears in Spec,AGRs. This tells us two things. First, that it is not the case that the top copy of NP is the one that always remains at PF; secondly, that something else other than the subject NP can (in fact, must) appear in Spec,AGRs at PF.

LF Noun Phrase Positions

On the PF side of things these three examples are roughly analogous. We start out with representations like the following, after movement but before the split to PF/LF:

64. a. [$_{AGRsP}$ [3 firefighters]$_i$ are [$_{VP}$ [3 firefighters]$_i$ available]]
    b. [$_{AGRsP}$ [John]$_i$ walked [$_{VP}$ [John]$_i$ [into the room]]
    c. [$_{AGRsP}$ [her mother]$_i$ sat [$_{VP}$ [her mother]$_i$ [in front of her]]]

At this point in the derivation the NP's Φ features are checked. Note the verb agreement with the NP.

If the top copy were what obligatorily had to remain at PF, we would end up with the following acceptable examples, only:

65. a. Three firefighters are available
    b. John walked into the room
    c. Her mother sat in front of her

These are grammatical, so we want this possibility to be available. But these are not the examples pointed out above.

On the other hand, suppose the top copy did delete on the way to PF. We would have an intermediate representation like the following:

66. a. [$_{AGRsP}$ e are [$_{VP}$ [three firefighters] available]]
    b. [$_{AGRsP}$ e walked [$_{VP}$ [John] [into the room]]
    c. [$_{AGRsP}$ e sat [$_{VP}$ [her mother] [in front of her]]]

As these stand they do not represent grammatical sentences in English:

67. a. * Are three firefighters available
    b. * Walked John into the room
    c. * Sat her mother in front of her

However, comparing this set with the ones we started out with, an account presents itself.

Recall that at the point of movement to Spec,AGR, the NP checks its Φ features and is licensed, or Case-marked. I assume that AGR, having checked its features, becomes inert functionally. That is, while it is still present as a node in the tree, it no longer functions as AGR; it simply remains present with an empty specifier position. The empty position in Spec,AGR vacated by the deleted subject NP is truly empty. The fact that we have grammatical examples like (63) and (65) and ungrammatical examples like (67) combined suggest that a completely empty Spec,AGRs is not acceptable at PF. Thus, to get from unacceptable (67) to acceptable (63) I suggest we fill Spec,AGRs.

This filling can occur in a couple of different ways. For (a), an expletive *there* is inserted in Spec,AGRs. For (b) and (c), a prepositional phrase from within VP is moved to Spec,AGRs:

68. a. [$_{AGRsP}$ there are [$_{VP}$ [three firefighters] available]]
    b. [$_{AGRsP}$ [into the room] walked [$_{VP}$ John e]]
    c. [$_{AGRsP}$ [in front of her] sat [$_{VP}$ her mother e]]

Each of these constructions has a number of interesting properties (to be discussed in more detail in chapter 8). The point I want to make is that first, the copy and delete strategy for movement allows a straightforward derivation for these examples; second, it's not the case that the top copy of NP always remains at PF; but third, it does seem to be the case that the PF requires something to appear in Spec,AGRs.

That this is a PF requirement and not an LF requirement is shown by the many examples we saw above in which a subject appeared in VP to be interpreted existentially and nothing appeared in Spec,AGRs. The empty Spec,AGRs at LF appeared to be acceptable. The problem arises when the NP in Spec,AGRs is deleted at PF. Then it must be replaced somehow.

We have, then, identified one apparent constraint on PF which affects deletion indirectly. We can state it and turn to deriving it in a later section:

69. Spec,AGRs must be filled at PF.

Stating it this way allows deletion to be free. However, if PF ends up with nothing in Spec,AGRs, the derivation violates the constraint.

7.6.2.2 Feature Strength

Notice that a story involving feature strength (cf. Chomksy 1993) will not help. This is because of the copy and delete account of movement being considered here. The feature story might say that AGR has strong N features in English so they must be checked before PF, otherwise they will crash at PF. Strong features are assumed to be visible and hence disruptive at PF so they must be checked before PF. This drives overt movement. However, it says nothing about deletion. Feature strength could conceivably get the NP into Spec,AGR in the overt syntax but it is not clear how it will ensure that Spec,AGR be filled at PF. The requirement seems to be that Spec,AGR be filled at PF and a feature strength account, at least as outlined in Chomsky's work, will not help us.

Proposals have been made to derive the overt movement of the subject in English to Spec,AGRs by assuming that some feature in T is strong and must be checked before PF (e.g. Groat 1995). Once again, this suggestion might drive the overt movement of the subject (or perhaps the *there* or inverted phrase in (63) above), but it will not ensure that these phrases are present in Spec,AGRs at PF. If deletion is free, and nothing else is said, there is no reason why the top copy of NP (or XP) cannot delete at PF, deriving the ungrammatical examples in (67) where Spec,AGRs is empty at PF.

What is needed is some way to ensure that Spec,AGRs *remains* filled at PF. It is not just enough to get a phrase into Spec,AGRs in the overt syntax: we have to keep it there. It is not clear how a feature strength account can do this.

7.6.2.3 Spec,AGRo at PF

We have seen that Spec,AGRs must be filled at PF. Deletion of subject NP copies is unconstrained at that level; all that matters is that at PF something must finally sit in Spec,AGRs. What about AGRo? In previous chapters I established that object NPs move overtly to Spec,AGRo. What this means on the copy and delete account of movement is that at PF the top copy of the object always remains. The VP-internal copy deletes.

We could consider the possibility that Spec,AGRo has the same restriction on it that Spec,AGRs has: it must be filled at PF. This appears to be correct. However, there is one crucial difference between the filling of Spec,AGRs and the filling of Spec,AGRo. Spec,AGRo must be filled by the object NP itself. Spec,AGRs can be filled by the subject NP, or if the top copy of movement has deleted, something else like an expletive or VP-internal phrase can appear there. We do not find examples like *there* sentences, and direction/locative inversion with Spec,AGRo:

70. a. * I saw there a man
    b. * I saw in the yard a man
    c. * I called from the room John

If Spec,AGRo has a requirement that it simply be filled at PF why do we not find such examples? We expect this requirement to be satisfied by various strategies, among them movement of something other than the original object into Spec,AGRo.[32]

Let's consider the possibility that the above ungrammatical examples are ruled out for independent reasons. Suppose, then, that Spec,AGRo (if it is present) must be filled at PF. This will ensure that the top copy of an object NP chain will remain and the bottom copy delete, at PF. Why is it not possible to satisfy this restriction with anything other than the object NP itself?

One difference between the ungrammatical *there*/inversion examples and the grammatical ones is that the ungrammatical ones involve movement into a position in the middle of the syntactic tree, while the acceptable ones involve movement into the top position in the tree. This has the feeling of a strict cycle condition phenomenon. If the strict cycle condition were to rule these examples out independently then we could say that Spec,AGRs and Spec,AGRo observe the same constraint, and then move on to trying to derive it.

The strict cycle condition, as interpreted in Chomsky (1993), states that movement must always in some way extend the tree. It has been used to ensure that languages which overtly move the subject and the object both to Spec,AGR positions must move the object first, extending the tree by generating and filling Spec,AGRo, move the subject, extending the tree by generating and filling Spec,AGRs. Intuitively this seems to be the type

LF Noun Phrase Positions

of restriction we see. Suppose that after deletion of the upstairs copy of NP the specifier position is not just empty, but rather, it deletes. Combine this claim with the requirement that Spec,AGR must be filled at PF. This means that if the specifier has been deleted, it must be regenerated and filled at PF. If this AGRP is at the top of the tree then regenerating and filling Spec,AGR extends the tree; it makes it bigger:[33]

71. a. [$_{AGRsP}$ NP$_i$ [$_{AGRs'}$[AGRs] ... [$_{VP}$ NP$_i$ PP]]   [deletion →]
    b. [$_{AGRsP}$[AGRs] ... [$_{VP}$ NP$_i$ PP]]   [regenerate & fill →]
    c. [$_{AGRsP}$ PP [$_{AGRs'}$ [AGRs] ... [$_{VP}$ NP$_i$ e]]

However, an analogous deletion, regeneration and filling operation is not possible for Spec,AGRo. This is because such a process would not extend the tree:

72. a. [$_{AGRsP}$ ... [$_{AGRoP}$ NP$_i$ [$_{AGRo'}$[AGRo] ... [$_{VP}$ NP$_i$ PP]]   [deletion →]
    b. [$_{AGRsP}$ ... [$_{AGRoP}$[AGRo] ... [$_{VP}$ NP$_i$ PP]]   [regenerate & fill →]
    c. [$_{AGRsP}$ ... [$_{AGRoP}$ PP [$_{AGRo'}$ [AGRo] ... [$_{VP}$ NP$_i$ e]]

The strict cycle condition appears to provide an independent way to rule out the ungrammatical *there*/inversion examples while allowing us to state a simple constraint on PF positions:

73. Spec,AGR must be filled at PF.

I will devote the next section to trying to derive this constraint.

7.6.2.4 Filled Positions

By examining Spec,AGRs and Spec,AGRo at PF we have found what appears to be a constraint on that level: these specifiers must be filled. We now want to ask why this is the case.

I have considered so far movement to Spec,AGRs and to Spec,AGRo and noticed that at PF these positions always appear filled. There is, however, one more potential deletion target to consider. In Chapter 2, I interpreted the minimalist approach to structural Case checking to imply that the object of a preposition also appears in Spec,AGR to check its Case features. Recall that I suggested that a PP is embedded within AGRP (called AGRpP). The complement of P moves to Spec,AGRp to check its Φ features.

In Chapter 2, I assumed without comment that the movement of NP to Spec,AGRpP was part of the covert syntax of LF. However, if, as discussed above, Marantz's (1994) view of copy movement is correct, the movement of the object of P to Spec,AGRpP cannot occur at LF. It must occur in the overt syntax. Consider an intermediate pre-SPLIT representation:

74. [$_{AGRpP}$ NP$_i$ [$_{PP}$ P NP$_i$]] [pre-SPLIT]

At this point NP checks its Φ features and is Case-licensed.

The only thing that is special about the NP in Spec,AGRpP is that at PF it's the top copy that deletes, unlike with AGRs and AGRo:

75. [$_{AGRpP}$ [$_{PP}$ P NP$_i$]] [PF]

Notice, however, that no LF A-movement was required. All movement for checking precedes the split to PF and LF.

AGRpP seems to have the opposite restriction on it from AGRoP and AGRsP. It cannot be filled at PF. We could leave it at that: Spec,AGRsP and Spec,AGRoP must be filled at PF; Spec,AGRpP must not. However, one wonders if this variation might be derivable from something else.

There is one other obvious difference between AGRp on the one hand and AGRs and AGRo on the other. The head which supplies AGR with the relevant Case feature is also in a different place at PF. The head P of PP, which is the element providing the Case feature to AGRp, appears in its base position at PF. The head V of VP, which is the element providing the Case feature to AGRo, is overtly in a position higher than AGRoP; and the head T, which is the element providing the Case feature to AGRs, is overtly in a position at least in AGRs. The generalization can be stated as follows:

LF Noun Phrase Positions

76. **Overtly Filled Spec Generalization**:
At PF, Spec,AGR is filled iff the head (or its trace) providing the Case feature to AGR is in AGR.

Another way to look at it is to abstract away from the Case feature question and think of this in terms of the licensing of AGR. AGR phrases are only present in a tree in order to mediate a relation between a head and a phrase. Let us say that each AGR phrase is only licensed in a structure if the appropriate head adjoins to it. Thus, for AGRs to be licensed, T must adjoin to it at some point. For AGRo to be licensed, V must adjoin to it at some point. For AGRp to be licensed, P must adjoin to it at some point. It is in some sense an economy approach: if AGR is not going to be needed in a structure (i.e. used to mediate a relation between a head and a phrase) it is not projected/licensed in that structure. This is a sort of "minimize structure" idea (see also Speas 1994). Seen in this light, the relation between AGR and a head like V, T or P is one of licensing. The generalization can then be restated in slightly broader terms:

77. **Overtly Filled Spec Generalization** (revised):
At PF, Spec,AGR is filled iff the licensor of AGR (or its trace) is in AGR.

To make this statement even a bit more general we might plausibly assume that any specifier that appears must be filled. This seems reasonable and also within the range of "minimize structure". If the specifier is not filled it should not be present. If we can maintain this notion, then the generalization can be simplified to this final form:

78. **Specifier Licensing**:
At PF, AGR licenses its specifier iff AGR is licensed.

Taken literally, this appears to imply that if the licensor of AGR (or its trace) is not in AGR at PF, AGR is not present since it is not licensed. Let us assume this is correct. Then the big difference between AGRs/AGRo and AGRp is that only AGRs and AGRo are licensed at PF. Since they are licensed at PF their specifiers are licensed. Since their specifiers are licensed they must be filled. AGRp is not even licensed at

PF, hence its specifier is not licensed and we never find the NP in Spec,AGRp at PF.

This licensing mechanism captures the generalizations covering the AGR phrases in English. Further research will tell us if it is correct generally. For now I offer it as a possible way to account for the distribution of PF copies of NP.

7.7 CONCLUSION

In this chapter I began by observing that indefinite objects behave like definite ones at S-structure but vary in their behavior at LF. I undertook the task of providing a syntactic account of the distribution of these NPs at LF. The copy and delete strategy for movement was motivated for A-movement, and was shown to provide a neat account of the observed PF/LF mismatches. Along with this theory of movement, however, came several new questions to be dealt with, e.g. what is copying? and what are the constraints on deletion?

I answered the former question with a proposal of Marantz's (1994), which ultimately made several interesting conceptual and empirical predictions which appear to be correct. The answer to the latter question, about constraining deletion, made us look carefully at the various PF and LF NP positions. Ultimately, the claim was defended that deletion is free up to recoverability at each of these levels. However, at PF, independently certain positions must be filled, which ultimately indirectly constrains what can delete at that level.

CHAPTER 8
Extensions and Conclusions

8.1 INTRODUCTION

The copy and delete strategy for movement, combined with the fact that Spec,AGRs must be filled at PF, however that is to be derived, provides a different sort of account for two puzzling constructions in English: existential *there* sentences and the stylistic inversion construction. What the copy and delete account provides us with is the possibility for more than one syntactic element to sit in the same syntactic position at different points in the derivation. In the case of the existential *there* construction we have reasons to want the subject of the sentence to be in Spec,AGRs, its Case checking and agreement triggering position, at some point in the derivation. Yet, what we see at PF is that the subject is not in Spec,AGRs, but that an expletive element, *there*, is. The copy and delete approach allows this state of affairs, as we will see in detail in the next section.

A similar phenomenon is found with stylistic inversion. Again the subject NP does not appear to sit in Spec,AGRs at PF, though we want it to be there at some point in the derivation. At PF we see what, we will argue below following Rochemont & Culicover (1990), is a VP in Spec,AGRs. This would be considered strange were it not for the fact that the subject appearing in Spec,AGRs at an earlier stage in the derivation has deleted, leaving only a lower copy at PF; the "subject" position is empty at PF, in potential violation of the requirement that Spec,AGRs be filled at that level.

Some brief concluding remarks follow.

8.2 *THERE* INSERTION

8.2.1 Expletive Replacement

Chomsky (1986b, 1991, 1993) argues that an expletive element like English *there*, since it receives no interpretation, must be eliminated at LF. He proposed that *there* is an LF affix which requires its "associate" NP to adjoin to it at LF. Thus, a sentence like (1a) has an LF representation like (1b):

1. a. There are many firefighters available
   b. [there-many firefighters$_i$] are t$_i$ available

"Expletive replacement" (ER) can explain three salient properties of the *there* construction. First, the local relation between *there* and its associate follows from the locality of NP movement generally, since ER is simply LF NP movement:

2. * There seems that John saw *a man*

Second, assuming that agreement and Case are checked at LF, it follows that the associate triggers agreement on the verb, since at LF the associate is in subject position (Spec,AGRs):

3. a. There is a firefighter available
   b. There are many firefighters available

Third, the alternate form, in which the associate is actually in subject position, can be assumed to involve something like S-structure, rather than LF NP movement to the position otherwise held by the expletive:

4. a. There are many firefighters available
   b. Many firefighters are available

While ER rightly, I think, establishes an A chain-type relationship between the expletive and its associate, puts the associate in Spec,AGRs

Extensions and Conclusions

at some level, and accounts for alternate forms like those in the previous example, it wrongly assumes this level of representation to be LF.

The main drawback of that proposal is that examples like (4) do not have the same interpretation: if they are identical at LF, which is the level feeding the interpretative component, they must have the same interpretation. This is not the case. The first example is unambiguous; the indefinite receives only an existential reading. The second is ambiguous between having an existential and a proportional reading.

Recall that the LF we want for the existential reading is roughly:

5. [e [are [firefighters available]

The predicate-internal NP is interpreted existentially. The proportional reading we assume to have the following LF (roughly):

6. [many firefighters [are [e available]

ER assigns an LF like (6) to both sentences, predicting them both to have only the proportional interpretation, contrary to fact.

In addition to predicting the wrong reading for the associate in a *there* sentence, ER predicts that the associate should have scope over other elements lower than Spec,AGRs, as pointed out above. Consider these well known contrasts:

7. a. There seem to be many firefighters available
   b. Many firefighters seem to be available
8. a. There aren't many firefighters available
   b. Many firefighters aren't available

The (b) examples are ambiguous; the NP *many firefighters* can be understood to have scope either inside or outside *seem/not*. This is expected if the NP can be interpreted in either its surface or base position at LF. However, the (a) examples are unambiguous; the NP only has the scope of its S-structure position. That strongly suggests it is in that position at LF, as well.

Expletive replacement assigns the (a) sentences LFs in which the NP *many firefighters* is in the position of the expletive. This predicts, again, that a reading in which the NP has scope over *seem/not* should be possible, contrary to fact.

Chomsky (1991) does discuss the question of scope in a footnote. He proposes to account for the narrow scope of the NP in a *there* sentence in the following way. From Chomsky (1991): in (9) *many* has narrow scope only; its LF is in (10):

9. there aren't many linguistics students here
10. [$_{NP}$ [there [$_A$ many linguistics students]] are not t$_A$ here]

"If *many linguistics students* were literally to replace *there*, it would be expected to have scope over *not*, but in (10), no relation is established between the two, and the scope of *many* can be assumed to be narrow, as in *pictures of many students aren't here*." [emphasis added--JTR] (p. 24)

I address a number of points with regards to Chomsky's analysis: (1) If *many linguistics students* has no relation with *not*, how does it have a relation with its trace? Presumably it must bind its trace, implying c-command. If it c-commands its trace, it c-commands *not* and should have scope over it. (2) In fn. 51 the following example is discussed: *there appear (not) to have been many linguistics students here*. In this case, however, the scope of *many* must "fall within that of *appear* and *not*", which implies that the position of the associate's trace must be taken into account. This means that it is not the case that no relation between the two scopal elements is established, contra the comment above. (3) In Diesing-type contrasts, *there are firefighters available* vs. *firefighters are available*, why can only the latter receive a generic interpretation? Even the expletive-adjunction analysis places *firefighters* in the domain of the generic operator at LF. The lack of this reading is completely mysterious on the ER account.

Thus, an adequate account of *there* sentences will capture the local A-type relation between the expletive and the associate, the fact that the associate triggers agreement (and is somehow assigned Case), and the alternate forms derived from the same underlying structure. Most importantly, the correct LF interpretations will be assigned to these sentences. Such an account is available to us based on what has already been established in the preceding chapter.

8.2.2 An Alternative

Consider again the sentences in question:

11. a. There are many firefighters available
    b. Many firefighters are available

As mentioned above, I follow Stowell (1978) and assume that these two sentences have the same underlying structure:

12. [$_{AGRsP}$ e [$_{AGRs}$ be [$_{AP}$ many firefighters available]

The first step for both the *there* sentence and both readings of the other sentence is the same: *many firefighters* moves to Spec,AGRs, leaving a copy in its base position; the NP checks its Φ features (checks NOM Case and triggers Subject-Verb Agreement):

13. [$_{AGRsP}$ many firefighters$_i$ [$_{AGRs}$ are [$_{VP}$ many firefighters$_i$ available]

This step occurs before the split to PF and LF. I assume that all three readings of the above two sentences involve this first step, *before* the split to PF and LF.

As discussed above, deletion is essentially unconstrained, subject to recoverability. While I have spoken of deletion at PF and deletion at LF I assume, as the null hypothesis, that deletion can occur any time, including before the split to PF and LF. The only constraints on deletion are actually constraints on positions or phrases. So, at PF, recall, we found that the constraint was that, since AGR is licensed (because its licensor is adjoined to it at that level), Spec,AGR is licensed. I combined that with the claim that if Spec,AGR is present it must be filled. This requires that at PF something must fill Spec,AGR. At LF the relevant constraints were those imposed by the interpretive component via the mapping hypothesis. Thus, NP is in Spec,AGR iff it receives a nonexistential interpretation. Otherwise NP is predicate-internal receiving an existential reading.

Given these constraints on PF and LF we potentially derive four PF/LF pairs. Let us begin with the two non-*there* sentences:

14. Many firefighters are available [proportional]
    a. [$_{AGRsP}$ many firefighters are [e available]] [PF$_1$]
    b. [$_{AGRsP}$ many firefighters are [e available]] [LF$_1$]

15. Many firefighters are available [existential]
    a. [$_{AGRsP}$ many firefighters are [e available]] [PF$_2$]
    b. [$_{AGRsP}$ [are [many firefighters available]] [LF$_2$]

(14) has the proportional reading of the NP. At PF the subject NP is in Spec,AGRs, satisfying AGR's requirement of being filled. At LF, the NP is in Spec,AGR, and as such is given a nonexistential interpretation. (15) is different in only one way: NP is in VP at LF. This means that NP's interpretation is existential. The PF is the same, NP is in Spec,AGRs.

Let us consider the other two possibilities:

16. There are many firefighters available [*there*-existential]
    a. [$_{AGRsP}$ there [are [many firefighters available]] [PF$_3$]
    b. [$_{AGRsP}$ [are [many firefighters available]] [LF$_3$]

17. * There are many firefighters available [*there*-proportional]
    a. [$_{AGRsP}$ there [are [many firefighters available]] [PF$_4$]
    b. [$_{AGRsP}$ many firefighters are [e available]] [LF$_4$]

The LF of (16) has the NP in VP, so it receives an existential interpretation. The PF has NP in VP. But since Spec,AGRs must be filled, *there* appears. Now let us consider (17). At LF, NP is in Spec,AGR, deriving a proportional reading. At PF, NP is in VP and again *there* appears to satisfy Spec,AGRs's requirement of being filled at PF. However, this is an unattested PF-LF pair. As is well known, the NP in a *there* sentence cannot have a proportional interpretation.

However, as I will outline below, the derivation of the illicit PF-LF pair in (17) is already independently ruled out by the claim, discussed in Chapter 7, that lexical access is denied to PF and LF.

With that in mind, let us reconsider our *there* sentences. *There* clearly is a lexical item. What this means is that "*there* insertion" must happen before the split to PF and LF. Thus, if *there* is to be inserted before the split, then the relevant deletions leading to *there* insertion must occur

Extensions and Conclusions

before the split. If that is the case, then separate deletions at PF and LF will not be possible: all the relevant deletions will have occurred prior to the split. This derives the result that the deletions at PF and LF are identical. Let us work through (16) and (17) again a bit more carefully.

We begin at the pre-SPLIT point in the derivation after which movement and checking has occurred, but no deletion:

18. [$_{AGRsP}$ many firefighters are [many firefighters available]]

Let us follow the correct derivation. The correct derivation of a *there* sentence deletes the top copy of NP prior to the split. This is necessary in order to be able to insert the *there* from the lexicon:

19. [$_{AGRsP}$ [are [many firefighters available]]]   [pre-SPLIT deletion]

In order to get *there* into the representation, before the split it must be inserted into Spec,AGRs:

20. [$_{AGRsP}$ there are [many firefighters available]]   [*there*-insertion]

Now we can move on to PF and LF. Note, that now *there* is in Spec,AGRs and NP is in VP for both PF and LF. This derives us the correct PF-LF pair, (16), repeated here:

21. There are many firefighters available   [*there*-existential]
    a. [$_{AGRsP}$ there [are [many firefighters available]]]   [PF]
    b. [$_{AGRsP}$ [are [many firefighters available]]]   [LF]

Let us consider the derivation of ungrammatical (17). I will start again with the pre-SPLIT representation with both copies present:

22. [$_{AGRsP}$ many firefighters are [many firefighters available]]

If deletion takes place at this pre-SPLIT point, the NP will be present in the same position at both PF and LF, and we will have (21). So, if (17) is to be derived it must involve separate PF and LF deletions:

23. a. [_AGRsP_ [are [many firefighters available]]] [PF]
    b. [_AGRsP_ many firefighters are [e available]] [LF]

At LF the downstairs copy is deleted leaving NP in Spec,AGRs for a proportional interpretation. At PF, however, Spec,AGRs is empty in violation of its PF requirement. *There* insertion cannot apply because access to the lexicon is denied. In this way the unattested PF-LF pair is blocked and we do not have a *there* sentence with a proportional NP.

What about Chomsky's claim that an expletive cannot appear at LF because it is uninterpretable? A couple of possibilities exist. If that claim is taken completely seriously the expletive can simply delete at LF since it does not belong there. A second possibility is that the expletive does have some semantic function and thus is interpretable at LF. Expletive "replacement" however is not possible. This would be LF A movement, an operation I claim is not available to the grammar because it would require access to the lexicon at LF. In fact my view of *there* sentences strongly supports this claim.

8.3 STYLISTIC INVERSION

Rochemont & Culicover (1990) examine sentences like the following:

24. a. Into the room walked John
    b. In front of her sat her mother
25. a. Sitting in front of her was her mother
    b. Happiest to see him was Bill
    c. Under the table was a large box
    d. Found at the scene of the crime was an axe

(24a,b) are examples of directional and locative (D/L) inversion, respectively. Those in (25) are preposing around *be* constructions (Emonds 1976). I will focus on D/L inversion here.

The first point that Rochemont & Culicover (henceforth, R&C) make is that though D/L inversion looks like it could be some form of PP topicalization, such an account would not explain examples like the following:

26. a. Into the room nude walked John
    b. In front of her smiling stood Bill

They argue that these sentences are derivationally related to the following:

27. a. John walked into the room
    b. Bill stood in front of her smiling

R&C suggest that what has happened in (26), in part, is that VP has fronted. This implies, then, that the main verb is not within VP. This accords with the results of this dissertation, and was used as a partial motivation for my claim that V is external to VP at S-structure. Thus, (26a) has fronted a constituent that looks roughly like the following:

28. [$_{VP}$ [$_{V'}$ t$_V$ [$_{PP}$ into the room]] nude]

That the fronting in (26) involves a constituent like a VP and not simply multiple topicalization of VP-internal elements is suggested by the following:

29. a. * Nude, into the room, walked John
    b. * Smiling, in front of her, stood Bill

I will not repeat all the arguments R&C give for this being some form of VP fronting but turn briefly to their analysis and then to the alternative outlined above.

R&C propose that this process is VP-topicalization. This operation adjoins VP to IP. Subsequently, the main verb is also adjoined to IP:

30. [$_{IP}$ [$_{VP}$ into the room nude] [$_{IP}$ walked [$_{IP}$ John t$_V$ t$_{VP}$]]]

This account faces several challenges, conceptual and empirical. First, conceptually, it is at odds with movement theory for a head to adjoin to a maximal projection. The R&C account requires V to adjoin to IP in order to get it in front of the subject, which they assume is in Spec,IP.

Second, empirically this account faces a challenge noted by R&C themselves. It is possible for more than just a single main verb to precede the subject. Sometimes an auxiliary or modal as well as the main verb precedes the subject:

31. a. Into the room (will walk/has walked) John
    b. Across from him should sit Mary
    c. Sitting in front of him will be Mary

The problem here is that the account proposed would require the aux/modal + verb to together adjoin to IP in order to precede the subject. R&C propose, tentatively, a restructuring account which turns aux/modal + verb into a single verbal head.

This proposal faces its own problems, as R&C discuss. For one, an adverb can apparently participate in the restructuring process:

32. Down the stairs into the ballroom slowly walked the Queen

The adverb *slowly* appears between the fronted VP and the fronted verb suggesting that it has also fronted, perhaps as part of the verb. This is their interpretation. However, if an adverb like *slowly* can appear in VP or adjoined to VP on the right, it could be assumed that it fronted with VP, not with V. Therefore this is perhaps not such a damaging counterexample.

R&C end up accepting the restructuring account with hesitation, admitting it has problems. I believe the account we have in place involving copy and delete movement, as outlined above, can work better without requiring the ad hoc rule of restructuring. We need to make one assumption, which I think can be independently justified.

Let us consider the derivation of (a). On the assumptions I have been exploiting throughout this chapter, the first step, before the split to PF and LF, is that NP moves to Spec,AGRs to check its features. It should leave one copy in VP and move one to Spec,AGRs:

33. a. Into the room nude walked John
    b. [$_{AGRsP}$ John walked [$_{VP}$ John into the room nude]]

Deletion at PF can remove the upstairs copy of *John*:

Extensions and Conclusions

34. [$_{\text{AGRsP}}$ [walked [$_{\text{VP}}$ John into the room nude]]]

If it is true that Spec,AGR must be filled at PF, as argued above, then the fronting could satisfy that restriction. However, what should front? If this is the correct structure, then the R&C idea that stylistic fronting is a type of VP fronting cannot be correct. Moving the whole VP would result in: *John into the room nude walked*. We have a couple of options. First, we might claim that *John* is in a higher VP-shell section of VP, while a lower VP-shell is what fronts:

35. [$_{\text{VP}}$ into the room nude] ... walked [$_{\text{VP}}$ John [$_{\text{VP}}$ e]]

This makes a wrong prediction, however. Since *John* is in VP, we predict that VP-adjoined adverbs of the sort that normally come between the verb and PP complements should be able to be left-adjoined to VP between *walked* and *John*. The following illustrates another fact about stylistic inversion (the (b) example is from R&C):

36. a. * Into the room nude walked quietly John
    b. * Down the stairs into the ballroom walked slowly the Queen

For some reason an adverb cannot come before the subject of stylistic inversion. Notice that the sentence is acceptable if the adverb is placed elsewhere:

37. a. Into the room nude quietly walked John
    b. Down the stairs into the ballroom slowly walked the Queen

This adverb restriction recalls a similar restriction we exploited in Chapters 2 and 3: no adverb can adjoin to AGRoP. This restriction ruled out examples like the following:

38. a. * Jan told loudly the story
    b. * Cindy bought quickly the book

I would like to propose that the subject in stylistic inversion in fact does occupy Spec,AGRo. First, one wonders how this is possible. Why would an AGRo projection be present in a structure like this? In talking about AGR licensing above we established that it was licensed if its "licensor" (or trace) was adjoined to it. The licensor of AGRo is V. That minimal requirement seems to be satisfied here. However, all along we have assumed that AGRo is not present when the verb in question is not an accusative Case-assigner. I would like to slightly revise this assumption. Suppose AGRo needs to be licensed by having a verb pass through it. AGRo will be licensed as an accusative Case-assigner only if the verb checks accusative Case there. Otherwise, AGRo will have no obvious function.

What other evidence do we have that this position is AGRo? Another illuminating fact about stylistic inversion is that it is impossible with an object. This is interesting because if the subject is in Spec,AGRo, this could be why such a construction is impossible when an object is actually present:

39. *   Out of the room chased the boys John

There is one other piece of suggestive evidence which I will address only minimally. Itziar Laka (p.c.) pointed out that it is marginally possible to get an echo question with a wh phrase in the position of the subject. However, in such a sentence *whom* is not so bad. The same point can be made about a deictic; in this case *him* seems better:

40. a.   Into the room nude walked ?WHOM/WHO?
    b.   Into the room nude walked HIM/?HE

My own judgment is to prefer *who* but that is consistent with my judgments of *whom* in other uncontroversial domains. If *whom* is acceptable for people, and I think *him* is, I would suggest that, though Spec,AGRo is not a Case position in this construction, some type of analogy is taking place and speakers are assuming it is and are using the accusative form.

Note that agreement is still with the subject, even when the subject is an accusative deictic pronoun. These examples are marginal but the "wrong" agreement is certainly worse:

Extensions and Conclusions 221

41. a. ? Into the room nude walks HIM
    b. * Into the room nude walk HIM
42. a. ? Into the room nude walk THEM
    b. * Into the room nude walks THEM

The (a) examples are not perfect but the (b) examples are really quite bad. I leave these examples aside in what follows.

Let us reconsider the derivation of the grammatical stylistic inversion sentence from above. First the subject moves to Spec,AGRs, apparently stopping in Spec,AGRo and leaving a copy there:

43. [$_{AGRsP}$ John [walked [$_{AGRoP}$ John [$_{VP}$ John into the room nude]]]]

This is followed by deletion of the top and bottom copies:

44. [$_{AGRsP}$ [walked [$_{AGRoP}$ John [$_{VP}$ into the room nude]]]]

The requirement that Spec,AGRs be filled then draws the VP to the front:

45. [$_{AGRsP}$ [$_{VP}$ into the room nude] [walked [$_{AGRoP}$ John [$_{VP}$ e]]]]

The copy and delete account of movement combined with the claim that Spec,AGR must be filled at PF allows an account of stylistic inversion that avoids adjoining a head to a maximal projection and does not require an ad hoc restructuring rule.

8.4 CONCLUSIONS

I began by showing that objects in English move overtly to Spec,AGRo for Case. In this way they turn out to be more analogous to subjects than previously thought. They move from a VP-internal thematic position to a VP-external functional position for Case. We saw that not only simple direct objects in English, but also so-called ECM subjects, as well as both objects of the double object construction, all move overtly to Spec,AGRo.

In studying the LF behavior of objects, as well as subjects, we saw that existential NPs are not in their surface positions at LF. They appear in their base VP-internal positions. Other types of NP appear in their VP-external position at LF. This lead us to examine the question of how the NPs got back into VP. Discarding actual syntactic lowering as a potential account, due in part to the fact that it does not appear to be licit as an overt movement rule, and in part due to theory-internal conceptual concerns, I looked elsewhere for an account.

I developed an account of the observed PF/LF mismatches by exploring the copy and delete approach to movement discussed in Chomsky (1993). This approach nicely allows, in fact predicts, PF/LF mismatches. Once incorporating such a mechanism into the theory, however, we need to deal with the question of what deletes where. The null hypothesis, which I attempted to maintain, is that anything can delete anywhere up to recoverability.

On the LF side the syntactic structures will ultimately be filtered through the semantics via Diesing's (1992) mapping hypothesis, discarding structures in which e.g. a definite NP appears in VP. On the PF side things are trickier. We found that Spec,AGRs and Spec,AGRo appear to require to be filled at PF. We also observed that if it is assumed that PPs are embedded in an AGR phrase, then their specifier position differs from that of AGRs and AGRo. Spec,AGRp must not be filled at PF.

This distinction between types of specifier is correlated, at least in English, with whether or not the licensor of the AGR head (or its trace) overtly appears in AGR. I suggested that if the licensor of AGR is present at a level, then AGR is present at that level. If AGR is present its specifier is present and must be filled. If AGR's licensor is not present at a level, AGR, and therefore its specifier, is not present at that level. Whether this account will ultimately prove correct is a matter for future research; however, it or something like it is going to be needed to replace the feature strength approach. That type of approach simply makes no predictions once the copy and delete strategy for movement is adopted.

Finally, we turned to two intriguing constructions in English which seemed to find a natural account when taking together the copy and delete strategy and the PF specifier filling account, ultimately providing indirect support for that analysis.

An interesting conclusion reached here is that there is no A-movement at LF in English. In fact, if copying is interpreted along the lines of Marantz (1994), there can be no A-movement at LF universally. The

Extensions and Conclusions 223

differences between pre-SPLIT and LF movement, then, follow from the different strategies exploited at these levels: copy and delete in the "overt" syntax, and movement (QR) at LF.

Bibliography

Abbott, B. "Right Node Raising as a Test for Constituenthood." *Linguistic Inquiry* 7 (1976): 639-642.

Abney, S. *The English Noun Phrase in its Sentential Aspect.* Ph.D. thesis, MIT, 1987.

Adger, D. *Functional Heads and Interpretation.* Ph.D. thesis, University of Edinburgh, 1994.

Aissen, J. & J. Runner. "Spanish Left Conjunct Agreement." Paper presented at the 64th Meeting of the Linguistic Society of America, Washington, D.C., 1989.

Baker, M. *Incorporation: a Theory of Grammatical Function Changing.* Chicago: University of Chicago Press, 1988.

Barss, A. & H. Lasnik. "A Note on Anaphora and Double Objects." *Linguistic Inquiry* 17 (1986): 347-354.

Belletti, A. & L. Rizzi. "Psych-Verbs and θ-Theory." *Natural Language and Linguistic Theory* 6 (1988): 291-352.

Berman, S. *On the Semantics and Logical Form of WH-Clauses.* Ph.D. thesis, University of Massachusetts at Amherst, GLSA, 1991.

Bolinger, D. *The Phrasal Verb in English.* Cambridge: Harvard University Press, 1971.

Borer, H. "The Causative Inchoative Alternation: a Case Study in Parallel Morphology." *Linguistic Review* 8 (1991): 119-158.

Bresnan, J. *Theory of Complementation in English Syntax.* Ph.D. thesis, MIT, 1972.

———. "Nonarguments for Raising." *Linguistic Inquiry* 7 (1976): 485-501.

Bibliography

Brugger, G. & C. Poletto. "On Negation in German and Bavarian." *University of Venice Working Papers in Linguistics*, vol. 3, no. 2. Università degli Studi di Venezia, 1993.

Burzio, L. *Italian Syntax.* Dordrecht: Reidel, 1986.

Carlson, G. *Reference to Kinds in English.* Ph.D. thesis, University of Massachusetts at Amherst, GLSA, 1977.

Chomsky, N. "Conditions on Transformations." In *A Festschrift for Morris Halle*, edited by S.R. Anderson & P. Kiparsky. New York: Holt, Rinehart & Winston, 1973.

———. *Lectures on Government and Binding.* Dordrecht: Foris Publications, 1981.

———. *Barriers.* Cambridge: MIT Press, 1986a.

———. *Knowledge of Language: its Nature, Origin and Use.* New York: Praeger, 1986b.

———. "Some Notes on Economy of Derivation and Representation." In *Principles and Parameters in Comparative Grammar*, edited by R. Friedin. Cambridge, MA: MIT Press, 1991.

———. "A Minimalist Program for Linguistic Theory." In *The View from Building 20: Studies in Linguistics in Honor of Sylvain Bromberger*, edited by K. Hale & S. J. Keyser. Cambridge, MA: MIT Press, 1993.

Contreras. H. "A Note on Parasitic Gaps." *Linguistic Inquiry* 15 (1984): 698-701.

Davidson, D. "The Logical Form of Action Sentences." In *The Logic of Decision and Action*, edited by N. Rescher, 81-95. Pittsburgh: University of Pittsburgh Press, 1967.

Diesing, M. *Indefinites.* Cambridge, MA: MIT Press, 1992.

Diesing, M. & E. Jelinek. "Distributing Arguments." *Natural Language Semantics* (1995).

Emonds, J. *A Transformational Approach to English Syntax: Root, Structure-Preserving, and Local Transformations.* New York: Academic Press, 1976.

Emonds, J. "The Verbal Complex V'-V in French." *Linguistic Inquiry* 9 (1978): 151-175.

Green, G. *Semantics and Syntactic Regularity.* Bloomington: Indiana University Press, 1974.

Groat, E. "English Expletives: a Minimalist Approach." *Linguistic Inquiry* 26 (1995): 354-364.

Haiden, M. *On the Semantic Evaluation of NP-Syntax.* M.A. thesis, Universität Wien, 1995.

Heim, I. *The Semantics of Definite and Indefinite Noun Phrases.* Ph.D. thesis, University of Massachusetts at Amherst, GLSA, 1982.

Herslund, M. "The Double Object Construction in Danish." In *Topics in Scandinavian Syntax,* edited by L. Hellan et al. Dordrecht: Reidel, 1986.

Hoop, H. de *Case Configuration and Noun Phrase Interpretation.* Ph.D. thesis, Rijksuniversiteit Groningen,1992.

Hornstein, N. "An Argument for Minimalism: The Case of Antecedent-Contained Deletion." *Linguistic Inquiry* 25 (1994): 455-480.

Jackendoff, R. *Semantic Interpretation in Generative Grammar.* Cambridge: MIT Press, 1972.

———. *X'Syntax.* Cambridge: MIT Press, 1977.

———. "On Larson's Analysis of the Double Object Construction." *Linguistic Inquiry* 21 (1990): 427-456.

Johnson, K. "Object Positions." *Natural Language and Linguistic Theory* 9 (1991): 577-636.

Kamp, H. "A Theory of Truth and Semantic Representation." In *Formal Methods in the Study of Language: Part 1,* edited by J. A. G. Groenendijk, T. M. V. Janssen and M. B. J. Stokhof, 277-322. Amsterdam: Mathematisch Centrum, 1981.

Kayne, R. "Principles of Particle Constructions." In *Grammatical Representation,* edited by J. Guéron et al. Dordrecht: Foris, 1984.

Bibliography

———. "Facets of Romance Past Participle Agreement." In *Dialect Variation and the Theory of Grammar*, edited by P. Beninca. Dordrecht: Foris, 1989.

Kiparsky, P. & C. Kiparsky. "Fact." In *Progress in Linguistics*, edited by M. Bierwisch & K.E. Heidolph. The Hague: Mouton, 1970.

Koopman, H. *The Syntax of Verbs*. Dordrecht: Foris,1984.

Kratzer, A. "Stage-Level and Individual-Level Predicates." In *Papers on Quantification*, NSF Grant Report, University of Massachusetts at Amherst, GLSA, 1989.

Krifka, M. "The Relational Theory of Genericity." In *Genericity in Natural Language: Proceedings of the 1988 Tübingen Conference*, edited by M. Krifka, 285-312. SNS-Bericht 88-42, Seminar für natürlich-sprachliche Systeme, Universität Tübingen, 1988.

Lakoff, R. *Abstract Syntax and Latin Complementation*. Cambridge: MIT Press, 1968.

Larson, R. "On the Double Object Construction in English." *Linguistic Inquiry* 19 (1988): 335-391.

———. "Double Objects Revisited: Reply to Jackendoff." *Linguistic Inquiry* 21 (1990): 589-631.

Lasnik, H. "The Minimalist Theory of Syntax: Motivations and Prospects." Ms., Second Seoul International Conference on Generative Grammar, 1993.

Lasnik, H. & M. Saito. "On the Subject of Infinitives." In *Chicago Linguistics Society 27. Part 1: The General Session*, edited by L.M. Dobrin, et al. Chicago: Chicago Linguistic Society, 1991.

Lewis, D. "Adverbs of Quantification." In *Formal Semantics of Natural Language: Papers from a Colloquium Sponsored by King's College Research Centre, Cambridge*, edited by E. L. Keenan, 3-15. Cambridge: Cambridge University Press, 1975.

Maling, J. "Notes on Quantifier Postposing." *Linguistic Inquiry* 7 (1976): 708-718.

Marantz, A. "A Reader's Guide to 'A Minimalist Program for Linguistic Theory' (Chomsky 1993)." In *The Principles and Parameters Approach to Syntactic Theory: A Synopsis*, edited by G. Webelhuth. Oxford: Basil Blackwell, 1994.

May, R. *The Grammar of Quantification*. Ph.D. thesis, MIT, 1977.

———. *Logical Form*. Cambridge: MIT Press, 1985.

McConnell-Ginet, S. "Adverbs and Logical Form: a Linguistically Realistic Theory." *Language* 58 (1982): 145-184.

Milsark, G. *Existential Sentences in English*. Ph.D. thesis, MIT, 1974.

———. "Toward an Explanation of Certain Peculiarities in the Existential Construction in English." *Linguistic Analysis* 3 (1977): 1-30.

Neijt, A. *Gapping*. Dordrecht: Foris, 1979.

Oehrle, R. *The Grammatical Status of the English Dative Alternation*. Ph.D. thesis, MIT, 1976.

Perlmutter, D. & P. Postal. "Some Proposed Laws of Basic Clause Structure." In *Studies in Relational Grammar 1*, edited by D. Perlmutter. Chicago: University of Chicago Press, 1983.

Pollock, J.-Y. "Verb Movement, Universal Grammar, and the Structure of IP." *Linguistic Inquiry* 20 (1989): 365-424.

Postal, P. *On Raising*. Cambridge: MIT Press, 1974.

Roberts, I. "Excorporation and Minimality." *Linguistic Inquiry* 22 (1991): 209-218.

Rochemont, M. & P. Culicover. *English Focus Constructions and the Theory of Grammar*. Cambridge: Cambridge University Press, 1990.

Rosenbaum, P. *The Grammar of English Predicate Complement Constructions*. Cambridge: MIT Press, 1967.

Rouveret, A. & J.-R. Vergnaud. "Specifying Reference to the Subject: French Causatives and Conditions on Representations." *Linguistic Inquiry* 11 (1980): 97-202.

Bibliography

Runner, J. *Left Conjunct Agreement in Spanish*, B.A. thesis, UC Santa Cruz, 1989.

———. "Expletives, 'Replacement', and Economy." In *Catalan Working Papers in Linguistics*, edited by A. Branchadell et al. Barcelona: Universitat Autònoma de Barcelona, 1992.

———. "Quantificational Objects and Agr-o." In *MIT Working Papers in Linguistics 21: Papers from the Student Conference in Linguistics V*, edited by V. Lindblad & M. Gamon. Cambridge: MITWPL, 1993.

———. "A Specific Role for AGR." In *University of Massachusetts Occasional Papers 17: Functional Projections*, edited by E. Benedicto & J. Runner. Amherst: GLSA, 1994.

———. "Reconstruction and Mapping." In *ConSole 2 Proceedings: Proceedings of the Second Conference of the Student Organization of Linguistics in Europe*, edited by R. Eckardt & V. van Geenhoven. The Hague: Holland Academic Graphics, 1995.

Sabel, J. *Restrukturierung und Lokalitaet. Universelle Beschraenkungen fuer Wortstellungsvarietionen*. Ph.D. thesis, University of Frankfurt/Main, 1994.

Stowell, T. "What Was There Before There Was There?" In *Proceedings of CLS 14*, edited by D. Farkas, et al., 458-471. Chicago: Chicago Linguistic Society, 1978.

Stowell, T. *Origins of Phrase Structure*. Ph. D. thesis, MIT, 1981.

Vikner, S. *Verb Movement and the Licensing of NP-positions in the Germanic Languages*. Ph.D. thesis, Université de Genève, 1990.

Wilkinson, K. "Generic Indefinite NPs." Ms., University of Massachusetts at Amherst, 1986.

Wyngaerd, G.V. & J.-W. Zwart. "Reconstruction and Vehicle Change." In *Linguistics in the Netherlands 1991*, edited by F. Drijkoningen & A. van Kemenade, 1991.

Notes

1. Again, the Kayne (1984) and Johnson (1991) small clause analyses posit different structures which are in fact consistent with the B&L tests. See chapter 6 for details.

2. The notable exceptions, of course, are cognate objects: dance a dance/a jig, jump a jump, etc.

3. In chapter 7 we will return to this structure.

4. Thanks to Phil LeSourd for pointing this out to me.

5. I assume that only the first preposition has the ability to incorporate into V, thus requiring the first NP to move to Spec,AGRo for Case. The second preposition does not incorporate, and its object does not move for Case. Why this should be so is not entirely clear, though it may be some sort of minimality effect.

6. Perhaps surprisingly we found that NP_2 in V (P) NP_1 P NP_2 [$_{ADV}$ ... NP_3 ...] has NP_3 in its domain. Does this fact threaten our claim that "domain" specify asymmetric c-command and not linear precedence? I do not believe so. While linear precedence clearly holds between NP_2 and NP_3, I would also like to claim that in the case in which NP_2 is a quantified NP, it can in fact c-command NP_3. That is, NP_2 undergoes QR to a position which c-commands NP_3 at LF just in case it is a quantified NP:

(i)   ... [NP_2[... [$_{AGRoP}$ NP_1 [$_{VP}$ ... t_2 ... NP_3 ...]]]]]   [LF]

I will remain agnostic as to exactly what position NP_2 QRs to, but from the representation it is clear that it can then bind its own trace in PP as well as c-command NP_3 thus allowing the bound variable anaphora noticed in (97) and (98) in the text.

Independently, an account of scope assignment which relies on hierarchical relations at LF is going to need to assume something like (i) in which NP_2 can have scope over both NP_1 and NP_3. Consider the following examples:
(ii) a.   Sam talked to a good friend about every problem
      b.   Sam talked to every boy about a problem

Example (a) has a reading in which for every problem Sam has he talked to a potentially different good friend about it. Example (b) has a reading in which Sam talked to every boy about the same problem. What these are meant to show is that on standard views of scope interaction NP_2 can get scope over NP_1. On the assumption that this is the result of QR, we have some independent evidence for one claim made by (i): that NP_2 can c-command NP_1 at LF.

Now for the second claim, that NP_2 can c-command NP_3 for scope:

(iii) a. Sam talked to Mary about every problem after a friend left
      b. Sam talked to Mary about two problems after every friend left
Example (a) has a reading in which for every problem Sam has he talked to Mary about it after each potentially different friend left. Example (b) has a reading in which Sam talked to Mary about two particular problems after everyone had left. This means that independently we need to assume that if NP_2 is a quantified NP it can QR to take scope over the adverbial phrase, as indicated in (i).

Thus, the fact that we find quantifier-variable relations between NP_2 and NP_3 in (97) and (98), in the text, does not necessarily mean that NP_2 should be taken always to have NP_3 in its domain. I have independently explained why this is so just in case NP_2 is a quantified NP and thus independently is assumed to QR to a higher position at LF.

7. Thanks to Kyle Johnson for reminding me of this fact.

8. Roger Higgins (p.c.) points out that RNR is most likely not movement of a shared VP, especially if I want my argument to go through. What is different about these examples, on my interpretation of them, is that a single VP is RNR'd, but the verbal trace within it actually corresponds to two separate verbs. Thus, the trace in the following examples must somehow be the trace of *tell* as well as *explain*:
(i) Mary told $[_{AGR_o}$ a story [e]] and Sam explained $[_{AGR_o}$ a problem [e]] $[[_{VP}$ t_V t_{NP} to Bill] after dinner]
More likely, if my interpretation is correct, RNR is a deletion operation deleting the first VP under some sort of structural identity (italicized):
(ii) Mary told $[_{AGR_o}$ a story *$[_{VP}[$ t_V t_{NP} to Bill] after dinner]* and Sam explained $[_{AGR_o}$ a problem $[_{VP}[$ t_V t_{NP} to Bill] after dinner]
This operation needs more careful consideration, which I will leave for further research.

9. I suspect FP might end up being the phrase headed by the verbal material responsible for inflectional (e.g. perfective, imperfective) aspect. In some cases this will not be associated with any overt morphology, but in others it will (*-en* ending in English, for example). The evidence adduced in the text does seem to point to the existence of such a head position, but I prefer to remain agnostic on its exact label and function.

10. The precise positions I have suggested the auxiliaries sit in are not crucial here. All that matters is the point that reference to particular functional positions, whatever they may end up being, seems necessary in order to state the distribution of these adverbs.

11. Recall that though I argued in chapter 2 that the NP in the PP moves to Spec,AGRo for Case, this is not apparent at PF. That is, that movement is "covert", meaning by PF the moved NP has deleted, leaving the PP-internal NP to appear. Thus, according to my account, at PF the NP in PP is in VP, while the object NP is in Spec,AGRo.

12. Bresnan (1972) discusses the *believe* class and the *want* class of predicate that have come to be considered "ECM". This section will study the behavior of the *believe* class, leaving for future research the *want* class, which it is not entirely clear deserve to be treated akin to the other ECM predicates (see Bresnan 1972 for a detailed discussion of the many differences between the classes).

13. The contrasts are weaker in this case. Though unlikely–since QR is thought to be clause-bound–this might due to the possibility of QR in the case of the embedded subject to a position which c-commands the matrix adverbial.

14. To really show that this is asymmetric c-command and not just c-command I would need to go back through all the examples placing the binder in the adverbial and checking for ungrammaticality. I leave this as an exercise for the reader.

15. Perhaps surprisingly for the overt raising account, (a) is not very good, though not bad with intonation breaks. It does however contrast quite dramatically with (b):
(i) a.   I believe Tony ?(,) very strongly ?(,) to be honest
     b.   *   I believe that Tony very strongly is honest
These examples and ones like it will be discussed in §5.3.3.2.

16. A couple of problems remain. First, some speakers do not find the examples involving expletives combined with parentheticals to be so bad. This suggests that there may still be more going on, which I will have to leave for future research.
    Second, Bresnan (1976) does provide one further example which will not so easily be explained as a structural ambiguity:
(i)   I had hoped for the deanship, with my usual false optimism, to be given to Uncle Buddy
A PP/control structure seems unlikely:
(ii) ?   I had hoped for the deanship that it would be given to my Uncle Buddy
    While this sentence is not unacceptable, it is clearly different from (i). Here *for* appears to be thematically selecting *the deanship*, where in (i) the NP appears to be raised there. The expletive-parenthetical combo is bad for me, however:
(iv)   I had hoped for there to be a party for my birthday.

Notes 233

(v) * I had hoped for there, with my usual false optimism, to be a party for my birthday

17. Other examples he considers are: (1) examples like Bresnan's in which the ECM verb is arguably non-manner taking; and (2) double object verbs, which I will set aside until chapter 6.

18. Sportiche's account apparently predicts incorrectly that object NPs, assuming overt movement to Spec,AGRo, should be able to strand a quantifier in VP: *Chris likes the boys all. This question is independent of the question of overt movement of the object since unaccusative and passive subjects also disallow such stranding: *The boys fell all/The boys were arrested all. Though further research is required I will assume that quantifiers like all cannot be stranded VP-internally, only being able to stay in functional specifiers. One reason for this might be Diesing's (1992) mapping hypothesis combined with an economy sort of account. If Diesing is correct (and see more discussion in chapter 7), strong quantifiers cannot appear in VP at LF. To correctly interpret floated quantifier sentences, the NP must be interpreted hierarchically where the quantifier appears, suggesting LF lowering in some cases (see chapter 7): *The contestants all can win (all > can)* vs. *The contestants can all win (can > all)* (Dowty & Brodie 1984). If the quantifier remained in VP, the subject would lower to that position at LF. But then, Diesing's mapping hypothesis would require movement out of VP. Raising and lowering and raising of NP is less economical than just raising and lowering, and thus should be preferred. If this account is on the right track, then the floated quantifier must not remain in VP, thus accounting for the ungrammatical sentences above.

19. Ideally independent justification for the X node would be provided here. As this is not the focus of the dissertation, and what I am doing here is simply providing some background for the argument in favor of raising, to be stated in the following subsection, I will leave such justification for further research. If the positions cannot be independently justified, the argument of course ultimately falls through.

20. The ungrammatical examples in (80) are ungrammatical only for weak pronouns, not focused, stressed, conjoined or deictic ones (Bolinger 1971, p. 39-41).

21. A comment on terminology: under the clausal DP proposal, DP vs. NP becomes a relevant distinction; in what follows I use NP and DP interchangeably, only distinguishing the two where crucial.

22. Larson (1988) assumes the inherent Case approach.

23. Extra machinery might include the perhaps already required minimalist notion of equidistance (Chomsky 1993).

24. Diesing's (1992) approach to NP position and interpretation will be taken up more extensively in chapter 7.

25. This follows technically only if θ government invokes "first branching node" c-command, which I assume.

26. Examples like (b) are cited in Bresnan (1972) as a possible argument against raising to object. The examples she cites (and see also Chomsky 1973) are worse:
(i) a.   You believe a picture of one of us was on the agent's wall
    b. * Which one of us do you believe a picture of to be on the agent's wall?

I have no explanation for why (b) should be so bad. It contrasts dramatically with the related *there* sentence (a), and contrasts somewhat with an embedded passive (as in the text) (b):
(ii) a.   Which one of us do you believe there to be a picture of on the agent's wall
     b. ? Which one of us do you believe a picture of to have been stolen?

Bresnan notes, however, that ungrammaticality like (ib) is true of objects of predicatives as well:
(iii) a.   He regards pictures of actresses as a form of exploitation
      b. * What kind of actresses does he regard pictures of as a form of exploitation?

I have no explanation for the contrasts noted above but hope that Bresnan's observation about predicatives can be exploited somehow.

27. What does my account say about the following ungrammatical examples?
(i) * Who did you see [t's picture]?
(ii) * Whose did you see [t picture]?

If the picture noun phrase is in the V-complement position these should be acceptable. However, to be in that position the whole NP must be interpreted as nonspecific/existential. I would have to say that these are obligatorily specific, like definite or quantificational noun phrases. The examples would be analogous to the following:
(iii) * What did you see [his picture of t]

This is ungrammatical presumably because a possessive NP is specific.

Notes

28. They assume that the object moves to Spec,AGRo at LF, not at S-structure. This does not affect the argument however.

29. Lasnik (1993) points out that ACD with names is not ungrammatical as had previously been assumed. It simply needs a bit of contrastive material in the deleted clause. Hence, the use of *as well* in the text example. *Not* would also work:
(i) Dulles suspected Philby, who Angleton did not.

30. In discussing ACD with Janina Radó (p.c.) we noticed an interesting bifurcation between the types of relative clause heads and the types of relative clauses they accepted in ACD constructions. The examples in (i) are possible only with a restrictive relative; those in (ii) are good only with a nonrestrictive relative.
(i) a. I suspected every man that you did/ *,who you did   [quantifier]
     b. I suspected the man that you did/ *,who you did   [definite]
(ii) a. I suspected John, who you did/ *that you did   [name]
     b. I suspected a guy I met at the LSA, who you did/ *that you did
                                                          [specific ind.]
     c. I suspected all my friends, who you did/ *that you did   [spec. quant.]
     d. I suspected that guy, who you did/ *that you did   [demonstrative]
I do not have an explanation for this, though I suspect it has something to do with "referentiality". The examples in (i) do not necessarily refer to a unique individual or group of individuals. *Every man* can vary depending on context. *The man* could refer to John if I am talking to Sue, but to Bill, if I'm talking to Mary. The examples in (ii) cannot vary in this way. *John, a guy I met at the LSA, all my friends,* and *that guy* are all in some sense rigid designators: they refer to actual individuals or groups of individuals in the real world, which cannot vary.

It is not the case that generally each of those RC heads only allows the above type of RC. The interesting case is the one labeled "specific quantifier". Such an NP can normally head a restrictive RC but for some reason in ACD this is impossible:
(iii) a. All my friends that grew up with me in Chicago turned out to be drug dealers.
      b. * I suspected all my friends that you did.
And interestingly, the head can be rearranged to allow ACD:
(iv) I suspected all the friends of mine that you did
This means something slightly different from the example in (ii). (ii) means that you and I agree that all my friends (not some subset of my friends) are suspect. (iv) means that you and I agree on the subset of my friends who are suspect. I think that in this case the set could vary, as in the examples in (i). I leave this open. Note that this unexpected dichotomy does not affect the claims of this section; it just suggests that while the head NPs in (i) and (ii) have differences between them, they should still be classed together separately from the existential

head NPs, which do not allow ACD at all.

31. This does not automatically exclude the appearance of a definite or strong quantified NP. See the next section where Diesing's (1992) mapping hypothesis is discussed.

32. First, examples like *I believe there to be a riot* might be what we are looking for. Second, the (b) and (c) examples improve greatly if the NP is "heavy", suggesting that yet another account of Heavy NP Shift might be that under certain circumstances VP material can in fact move to Spec,AGRo, satisfying PF condition to be proposed below. If so, then perhaps the strict cycle account to be proposed below in the text is unneeded.

33. I will put aside the question of what happens when examples like (63) are embedded.

Index

A-movement ... xviii, 7, 8, 10, 11, 38, 175, 190, 192-194, 196, 206, 208, 222
Abbott 53, 133
Adger 10, 193
adverb placement ... xvii, 8, 9, 37, 61-65, 85, 86, 90, 126, 134-136, 141-143, 145,176
AGR ... xvi, xxi, 5, 6, 9, 10, 30, 32, 33, 87, 89, 126, 156, 175, 186, 187, 189, 191, 193, 197-199, 201, 203, 204, 206-208, 213, 214, 219-222, 229
AGRo ... xvi, xvii, 3, 4, 6, 8, 9, 11, 13, 14, 19, 20, 25-27, 29, 32-34, 36, 38, 42-45, 47, 49, 51, 53, 64, 66, 85, 87, 89-91, 93, 95-98, 101, 111, 119, 120, 122, 128, 130, 134, 136, 137, 150, 155, 156, 161, 168, 176-181, 190, 191, 197, 203-205, 207, 219, 221, 222
AGRp 5, 32, 33, 206-208, 222
AGRs ... 3-5, 7, 31-33, 55, 56, 63, 91, 92, 96-98, 101, 111-114, 116, 118-120, 123, 135, 156, 193-195, 200-207, 209-211, 213-216, 218, 219, 221, 222
antecedent contained deletion . 9, 180
asymmetric c-command ...13, 14, 17, 21, 23, 37, 39, 41, 46, 47, 93, 95, 139
Baker 28-30, 32, 35, 36
Belletti & Rizzi 144
Berman 189
binding ... 9, 13, 15, 20, 41, 42, 46, 89, 93, 94, 127, 129, 136, 144, 157, 172, 173, 192

Bolinger 121
Borer .... xvi, xix, 37
Bresnan . 88, 91, 101-106, 108, 164
Brugger & Poletto 126
Burzio 25, 26
Carlson .... xx, 183
Chomsky ... xv, xvii, 3-11, 15, 19, 20, 26, 27, 31, 32, 42, 47, 49, 54, 55, 66, 67, 84, 89, 90, 97, 156, 159, 164, 171, 175, 176, 191, 192, 195, 196, 203, 204, 210, 212, 216, 222
clausal DP ... 9, 126, 127, 136, 137, 146, 148-154, 156, 161, 162, 164, 166, 168, 169, 172, 174
connectivity 136, 143-145, 149
Contreras 39, 43, 93
coordination ... 51, 52, 57, 58, 132-134, 178, 179
copy ... xvii, xviii, 10, 11, 38, 160, 171-176, 180, 190, 192-206, 208, 209, 213, 215, 216, 218, 221-223
copy and delete ... xvii, xviii, 10, 11, 38, 160, 171-175, 190, 193, 195-197, 202, 203, 208, 209, 218, 221-223
Danish 147
delete, deletion ... xviii, 9, 10, 38, 53, 64, 89, 160, 171, 173-176, 180, 181, 190, 192-205, 208, 209, 213, 215, 216, 218, 221-223
Diesing ... xv, xvi, xx, 10, 111, 126, 157, 158, 160, 167, 176, 180-189, 198, 212, 222
Diesing & Jelinek 188, 189

237

direct object ... xvii, 3, 25, 39, 40, 42, 50, 51, 59, 60, 84, 87, 96, 109, 122, 166, 176, 178, 180, 186, 221
double object construction ... xvii, 9, 19, 70, 73, 78, 87, 125-128, 130, 131, 134-138, 141, 143, 145-148, 150, 152-157, 161, 162, 164, 166, 172, 174, 196, 221
Dowty & Brodie 111
each ... the other ... 13, 16, 20, 22, 36, 41, 43, 46, 94, 128, 130
ECM ... xvii, 9, 87, 90-98, 100-102, 104, 105, 108-111, 119, 120, 122, 123, 149, 164, 221
ECP ... 101, 102, 110, 149, 150, 155, 156, 158, 165, 167, 168, 170, 172
Emonds 6, 54, 55, 66, 89, 216
English ... xv, xvii, xviii, 3, 6-8, 11, 13, 31, 39, 47, 49, 54-56, 59, 66, 80, 87, 89, 98, 125, 126, 148, 155, 166, 186, 196, 199, 201, 208-210, 221, 222
existential ... xv, 9, 157, 158, 160, 161, 163, 164, 167, 180, 182-190, 193, 194, 197, 199, 202, 209, 211, 213-215, 221
feature strength 8, 10, 176, 203, 222
floating quantifier ... 9, 111, 115, 119, 123, 126, 153, 154, 169, 174
French 6, 9, 49, 54-56, 66
functional projection ... 4, 6, 25, 55, 61-63, 65, 89, 118, 156, 177
gapping 52, 58, 132, 133, 178
Haiden .... xx, 126
Herslund 147, 226
Hornstein 180
Jackendoff ... 14, 17, 21, 23, 24, 35, 37, 39, 42, 43, 52, 62, 67, 68, 75, 99, 100, 103, 105, 107, 108, 134
Johnson ... xix, 9, 20, 40, 51-53, 62, 66-69, 72, 98, 101, 108, 110, 120-123, 126, 136, 145-151, 159, 166, 179
Kayne 4, 20, 146, 150
Kiparsky and Kiparsky 88
Koopman 4
Kratzer ...... xv, xix, 182-186, 189
Krifka 183
Larson ... xvii, 8, 9, 13-20, 39, 42, 47, 49, 50, 52, 53, 59, 61-63, 69-72, 75-80, 83, 85, 86, 125, 126, 128, 136-145, 154, 155, 164-166
Lasnik ... 10, 13-15, 17, 41, 89-91, 93-96, 125, 127, 145, 180, 181, 192, 193
Lasnik & Saito 89-91, 96
LGB 8, 13, 47, 87, 89, 90, 98
Light Predicate Raising ... 62, 69-71, 83, 84, 86, 142
lowering ... xvii, 139, 157, 158, 160, 167, 168, 175, 180, 184, 185, 189-191, 222
Maling 153
mapping hypothesis ... xv, xvi, 10, 111, 157, 158, 161, 167, 180, 186-188, 193, 198, 199, 213, 222
Marantz ... xviii, 7, 11, 175, 195, 196, 206, 208, 222
May 180, 181, 190
Milsark 176, 181, 182, 186, 228
negative polarity ... 13, 17, 41, 43, 46, 95, 128, 130
Neijt 52
Oehrle 20
P-Incorporation ... 28-30, 35, 36, 38
particle verbs 120-122, 179

Index

passive ... 29, 31, 33-35, 37, 88, 89, 96-98, 110, 111, 126, 155, 156, 164, 170, 174
Perlmutter & Postal 155
Pollock 4, 6, 54, 55, 66, 89
Postal ... 9, 88, 97, 99-102, 104-106, 155
QR ... 7, 13, 46, 94, 127, 154, 171-174, 176, 181, 190, 196, 223
quantifier binding ... 13, 16, 20, 127, 129
raising ... 9, 20, 59, 87-93, 95-98, 100, 101, 107, 108, 110, 111, 113, 119, 120, 122, 123, 164, 185
raising to object 87-89, 164
reanalysis 28, 30, 31, 34
reconstruction ... xvi, xviii, 10, 171, 172, 176, 192, 193, 196
Rochemont & Culicover ... 53, 54, 200, 209, 216
Rosenbaum 88
Rouveret & Vergnaud 7
scope freezing .. 126, 154, 172, 174
specificity effect . 161, 166, 167, 174
Sportiche 111
Stowell 65, 98, 193, 213
stylistic inversion ... xviii, 53, 54, 209, 216, 219, 221
superiority ... 13, 16, 20, 22, 36, 40, 128, 129
there sentences ... xv, 7, 10, 186, 204, 209, 212-214, 216
unaccusative ... 26, 28, 31, 33-35, 37, 96-98, 111
Vikner 147
VP-shell 13, 59-61, 63, 64
V' Reanalysis ... 62, 69, 70, 77, 80, 86, 142
weak crossover ... 13, 16, 22, 36, 40, 127, 129

wh-movement 7, 22, 24, 36, 193, 196
Wilkinson 183
Wyngaerd & Zwart 181

For Product Safety Concerns and Information please contact our EU representative GPSR@taylorandfrancis.com
Taylor & Francis Verlag GmbH, Kaufingerstraße 24, 80331 München, Germany

www.ingramcontent.com/pod-product-compliance
Lightning Source LLC
Chambersburg PA
CBHW071349290426
44108CB00014B/1486